About IFPRI

The International Food Policy Research Institute (IFPRI®) was established in 1975 to identify and analyze alternative national and international strategies and policies for meeting food needs of the developing world on a sustainable basis, with particular emphasis on low-income countries and on the poorer groups in those countries. While the research effort is geared to the precise objective of contributing to the reduction of hunger and malnutrition, the factors involved are many and wide-ranging, requiring analysis of underlying processes and extending beyond a narrowly defined food sector. The Institute's research program reflects worldwide collaboration with governments and private and public institutions interested in increasing food production and improving the equity of its distribution. Research results are disseminated to policymakers, opinion formers, administrators, policy analysts, researchers, and others concerned with national and international food and agricultural policy.

About IFPRI Research Monographs

IFPRI Research Monographs are well-focused, policy-relevant monographs based on original and innovative research conducted at IFPRI. All manuscripts submitted for publication as IFPRI Research Monographs undergo extensive external and internal reviews. Prior to submission to the Publications Review Committee, each manuscript is circulated informally among the author's colleagues. Upon submission to the Committee, the manuscript is reviewed by an IFPRI reviewer and presented in a formal seminar. Three additional reviewers—at least two external to IFPRI and one from the Committee—are selected to review the manuscript. Reviewers are chosen for their familiarity with the country setting. The Committee provides the author its reaction to the reviewers' comments. After revising as necessary, the author resubmits the manuscript to the Committee with a written response to the reviewers' and Committee's comments. The Committee then makes its recommendations on publication of the manuscript to the Director General of IFPRI. With the Director General's approval, the manuscript becomes part of the IFPRI Research Monograph series. The publication series, under the original name of IFPRI Research Reports, began in 1977.

Trade Liberalization and Poverty in the Middle East and North Africa

Nicholas Minot, Mohamed Abdelbasset Chemingui,
Marcelle Thomas, Reno Dewina, and David Orden

**RESEARCH
MONOGRAPH**

IFPRI®

INTERNATIONAL FOOD POLICY
RESEARCH INSTITUTE

sustainable solutions for ending hunger and poverty

Supported by the CGIAR

International Food Policy Research Institute
2033 K Street, NW
Washington, D.C. 20006-1002, U.S.A.
Telephone +1-202-862-5600
www.ifpri.org

DOI: 10.2499/9780896291744

Library of Congress Cataloging-in-Publication Data

Trade liberalization and poverty in the Middle East and North Africa / Nicholas Minot . . . [et al.].
p. cm. – (IFPRI research monograph)
Includes bibliographical references and index.
ISBN 978-0-89629-174-4 (alk. paper)
1. Free trade. 2. Agricultural prices—Middle East. 3. Agricultural prices—Africa, North. I. Minot, Nicholas. II. Series: IFPRI research monograph.
HF2296.T73 2009
382′.410956—dc22 2009043356

Contents

Tables

Figures

Foreword

Interest in the effect of trade liberalization on agriculture and poverty in developing countries has increased during the past decade, with the agricultural sector and the effect of trade liberalization on the poor being the focus of numerous debates in the Doha Round of multilateral trade negotiations. The inability to find common ground on these and other issues stalled the negotiations. The global food crisis of 2007–08 further highlighted some of the risks associated with relying on imports for staple foods, as well as the need to strengthen the rules-based agricultural trade system, despite the difficulties involved. The crisis has also led policymakers and researchers to pay greater attention to factors contributing to agricultural growth.

Given that global trade liberalization would (probably) raise agricultural prices, concern has focused on net food-importing regions, including the Middle East and North Africa (MENA). Many of the countries in the MENA region have implemented reforms to lower agricultural tariffs, liberalize domestic markets, and improve targeting in consumer-subsidy programs. Nevertheless, trade restrictions and domestic price supports are still prevalent, particularly for strategic commodities such as wheat. In addition, the countries vary widely in the degree of liberalization.

There is a large volume of research on trade liberalization in the MENA region, but few studies focus on the impact on small farmers and other poor households. This monograph addresses this gap, combining a review of the existing data and literature on the topic with a new analysis of four case studies of Egypt, Tunisia, Syria, and Morocco. The country case studies use household survey data and computable general equilibrium models to estimate the effect of different types of trade reform on small farmers or poor households or both.

The results paint a complex picture, in which the impact depends greatly on the type of liberalization, the initial degree of trade protection in the country, and the structure of the economy. For example, global trade liberalization tends to raise world food prices, which hurts most of the MENA countries on aggregate, but benefits the agricultural sector within these countries. On the other hand, trade liberalization within the MENA countries would lower the price of food, particularly imported staple foodgrains. Finally, the effect of food prices on poverty is somewhat ambiguous because urban households and many rural households benefit from lower prices, while some farm households gain from higher prices. The analysis suggests that the net effect of higher agricultural prices is to lower poverty, but the impact is quite small.

The monograph also discusses the importance of complementary policies to accompany trade liberalization. For example, a favorable investment climate, streamlined customs procedures, lower nontariff barriers, and competitive markets for transportation services may promote trade and growth at least as much as tariff reduction. Similarly, decoupled payments to farmers, labor-intensive public works programs, and conditional cash transfers can be more effective in assisting farmers and poor households than maintaining trade barriers.

We hope that the study will be useful to development practitioners and researchers, and will provide policymakers in the region with the empirically based analysis they need to make informed pro-poor decisions in the area of trade policy.

Shenggen Fan
Director General, International Food Policy Research Institute

Acknowledgments

We gratefully acknowledge the support of the International Fund for Agricultural Development (IFAD), which funded the research leading to this research monograph. The study was commissioned by the Near East and North Africa (NENA) Division of IFAD, under the direction of Mona Beshay. Management and technical guidance were provided by Mylène Kherallah, the project coordinator for IFAD.

The monograph benefited from comments and suggestions by Mylène Kherallah and others in the NENA Division. The monograph draft was further improved in response to comments and suggestions from the participants in a World Bank workshop in October 2008. We also appreciate the detailed comments and suggestions made by three anonymous reviewers as part of the IFPRI peer-review process. We thank John Whitehead for coordinating the production of this monograph. Finally, we are grateful to Maximo Torero, director of IFPRI's Markets, Trade, and Institutions Division, who provided the necessary impetus and resources to complete the revisions.

Acronyms and Abbreviations

AAs	association agreements
AGOA	African Growth and Opportunity Act
AMU	Arab Maghreb Union
AVE	ad valorem equivalent
CAPMAS	Central Agency for Public Mobilization and Statistics
CGE	computable general equilibrium (model)
EBA	Everything But Arms (initiative)
EMAA	European Union-Mediterranean Association Agreement
EMP	Euro-Mediterranean Partnership
E.U.	European Union
EU25	European Union (25 members as of 2004)
FAO	Food and Agriculture Organization of the United Nations
FTA	free trade agreement
GAFTA	Greater Arab Free Trade Area
GATT	General Agreement on Tariffs and Trade
GCC	Gulf Cooperation Council
GDP	gross domestic product
GTAP	Global Trade Analysis Project
IFC	International Finance Corporation of the World Bank
IMF	International Monetary Fund
INS	Institut National de la Statistique
LDC	least developed country
LE	Egyptian pound

MENA	Middle East and North Africa
MFN	most favored nation (status)
NTB	nontariff barrier
OECD	Organisation for Economic Co-operation and Development
SAM	social accounting matrix
SCTs	single commodity transfers
SM	southern Mediterranean
SYP	Syrian pound
TND	Tunisian dinar
UNCTAD	United Nations Conference on Trade and Development
URAA	Uruguay Round Agreement on Agriculture
VAT	value-added tax
WTO	World Trade Organization

Currencies

Djibouti	Djibouti franc (DJF)
Egypt	Egyptian pound (LE)
Jordan	Jordanian dinar (JOD)
Lebanon	Lebanese pound (LBP)
Morocco	Moroccan dirham (DH)
Syria	Syrian pound (SYP)
Tunisia	Tunisian dinar (TND)
West Bank and Gaza	Israeli shekel / Jordanian dinar

Summary

This report examines the impact of trade liberalization on non-oil-exporting countries of the Middle East and North Africa (MENA), with particular emphasis on its impact on the poor. First the report describes the basic characteristics related to agriculture, trade, and poverty for eight MENA countries and reviews previous studies examining the impact of trade liberalization on these countries. The eight are the developing countries in the MENA region that are not major oil exporters: Djibouti, Egypt, Jordan, Lebanon, Morocco, Syria, Tunisia, and the West Bank and Gaza.[1] Second, the report uses household survey data and computable general equilibrium models to simulate the effect of trade liberalization on low-income households in four of these countries: Egypt, Tunisia, Syria, and Morocco.

Background

The MENA region has experienced relatively slow economic growth, with insufficient expansion of formal sector employment and high rates of unemployment. Almost all the MENA countries are net food importers. Wheat is the staple food and a major import in most of the countries under consideration. Many of the MENA countries maintain relatively high levels of agricultural protection, partly to support their farmers, partly to reduce import dependence, and partly to generate revenue. Egypt, Morocco, and Tunisia are among the 15 most protected economies in the world, according to one study. The commodities that are the most protected in the region are wheat, sugar, dairy, and livestock products. The E.U. is the most important trading partner of most of the countries in the region.

The MENA countries have signed a series of multilateral, regional, and bilateral trade agreements. Multilateral agreements are within the framework of the World Trade Organization (WTO), of which, with the exception of Syria and the West Bank and Gaza, all countries in the region are members or have observer status. Within the WTO, the bound rates are often far above the applied tariff rates, particularly for agricultural products. Thus, the WTO

[1] We define major oil exporters as those countries whose exports exceed 80 percent of domestic consumption. Although Egypt and Syria export oil, they are not major exporters under this definition.

commitments to reduce the bound rate have had little effect on the actual level of agricultural protection, which reflects the various regional and bilateral agreements.

Ten MENA countries have signed European Union-Mediterranean Association Agreements (EMAAs) with the E.U. These agreements replace the preferential access to European markets for goods from African, Caribbean, and Pacific countries with a reciprocal reduction in tariffs on many goods. However, these agreements generally exempt agricultural commodities.

Under the U.S.-Middle East Free Trade Initiative, the United States has signed bilateral free trade agreements (FTAs) or entered into trade and investment framework agreements with several MENA countries. The potential effects of these agreements are expected to be small in the case of the U.S.-Jordan FTA because Jordan's level of protection is already low and because the amount of U.S.-Jordan trade is small. The effects of the U.S.-Morocco FTA are expected to be larger because Moroccan trade barriers are higher. Of particular importance, Morocco's wheat tariffs will be phased out over 10 years.

Both the E.U. and the United States have launched initiatives specific to the poorest countries. Under the Everything But Arms (EBA) initiative, the least developed countries have duty-free access to E.U. markets for almost all goods,[2] while the African Growth and Opportunity Act (AGOA) allows duty-free access to U.S. markets for Sub-Saharan African countries that meet certain criteria. Within the MENA region, only Djibouti and Yemen qualify under the EBA, while only Djibouti qualifies for preferences under the AGOA.

A number of bilateral and regional agreements within the MENA region have been signed, but their effectiveness has been limited by the structural similarities of the MENA economies, the prevalence of nontariff barriers, and the granting of exceptions for sensitive products. A number of MENA countries, most notably Egypt and Tunisia, have reduced their tariff barriers unilaterally in recent years. In other words, trade liberalization has occurred outside the context of global, regional, and bilateral trade agreements.

The Impact of Trade Liberalization

The evidence suggests that global trade liberalization will increase world agricultural prices by reducing agricultural support policies in countries of the Organisation for Economic Co-operation and Development (OECD) and by

[2] Duty-free access for bananas, rice, and sugar was phased in under the EBA initiative. Duty-free access for bananas was delayed until January 2006, while sugar and rice were scheduled to be liberalized in the second half of 2009.

reducing protection. The markets for wheat, rice, sugar, cotton, and dairy products are the most distorted, and simulation models suggest that trade liberalization will increase the price of these commodities by 3–20 percent. Almost all the MENA countries are net agricultural importers, so there is clearly some basis for concern that global trade liberalization will worsen the terms of trade for these countries. A simple analysis finds that the terms-of-trade losses associated with a 15 percent increase in world agricultural prices for eight non-oil-exporting MENA countries would be US$922 million, or 0.4 percent of regional gross domestic product (GDP). This estimate is an upper limit because it assumes no response on the part of producers and consumers and because it does not take into account the efficiency gains associated with reducing distortions in domestic agricultural markets. Most studies of trade liberalization suggest that the efficiency benefits are larger than the terms-of-trade losses.

Several dozen studies have been undertaken to examine the macroeconomic impact of various types of trade liberalization in MENA. These studies suggest that multilateral trade liberalization generally results in net gains to countries in the region, with real GDP expanding between 1 and 3 percent. Other studies have illustrated the importance of complementary policies in increasing the benefits of multilateral trade liberalization, including the countries' own domestic liberalization and reforms. Finally, the benefits of multilateral trade liberalization are shown to yield greater gains than the gains associated with bilateral and regional trade agreements. This is because bilateral and regional agreements are more likely to result in trade diversion than is a global agreement.

The Effects of Trade Liberalization on Poverty

Few studies have examined the effects of trade liberalization on the poor in the MENA region. We use household survey data and computable general equilibrium (CGE) models to simulate the impact of trade liberalization on poor households in Egypt, Tunisia, Syria, and Morocco. *Egypt* has undertaken significant trade liberalization, but costly obstacles to doing business and investing remain. The country is a major wheat importer and exports cotton, rice, and horticultural products. We analyze the data from the 1998 Egypt Integrated Household Survey to simulate the distributional effect of hypothetical changes in agricultural prices due to global trade liberalization. According to this analysis, a 40 percent increase in the wheat price would lower the poverty rate among wheat farmers by 3 percentage points. In the case of rice and cotton, the effect would be to reduce the poverty rate among growers of each by 7 percentage points, in the case of fruits and vegetables, by 5 percentage points. And a 40 percent increase in sugar prices would reduce poverty among sugarcane growers by 20 percentage points, largely because they are poor and highly dependent on sugarcane income.

However, the effect of each of these price increases on national poverty would be very small. The higher wheat price would lower national poverty by 1 percentage point, while higher rice and fruit and vegetable prices would raise national poverty by 1 percentage point. The effect of higher prices of cotton and sugarcane on the national poverty rate would be negligible (less than 0.5 percentage points). Finally, a 40 percent increase in all five commodity categories would increase poverty in urban and rural areas, though by just 1-2 percentage points.

Unlike Egypt, *Tunisia* maintains high tariffs on many products, including agricultural commodities. At the same time, Tunisia has a relatively good investment climate, which contributed to significant inflows of foreign direct investment and a healthy growth rate through the 1990s. Tunisia's main exports are olives and dates, while its principal imports are wheat and maize. In order to study the distributional impact of trade liberalization in Tunisia, we use a CGE model linked to survey data for 397 representative households. The model is used to simulate the elimination of industrial tariffs on goods from the E.U., the removal of *all* tariffs on imports from the E.U., the elimination of all tariffs from all countries, and the elimination of all tariffs combined with global liberalization, which it is assumed would raise world agricultural prices by 15 percent. Domestic trade liberalization would have the largest positive effect on GDP, but the fourth scenario (global trade liberalization) would have the most positive effect on agriculture and poverty. In this scenario, poverty would decline to its lowest level among the four scenarios.

Syria has one of the most highly regulated economies in the region. Reforms in recent years have only begun to dismantle some of these restrictions. Although Syria has been successful in achieving wheat self-sufficiency and promoting cotton exports, these accomplishments have come at a high cost in terms of inefficiency and an unsustainable fiscal burden. The likely depletion of oil reserves is forcing the government to reduce costs and find new sources of revenue. We use a CGE model to simulate the effect of liberalizing wheat markets on households in 10 income categories. The macroeconomic effects would be relatively modest, although government savings would increase by almost 3 percent of GDP. Complete liberalization would reduce the producer price of wheat by about 17 percent and production by about 2 percent. The effects of subsidy removal on Syrian households would be regressive in the sense that high-income households would gain, while lower-income households would lose. The size of the effects, however, would be less than 1 percent of the base income of all but the richest income group.

Since the mid-1980s, *Morocco* has carried out a series of economic reforms to allow the market to play a larger role in the economy, including price liberalization, reduction of the role of state enterprises, and the promotion of private investment. Morocco has signed an EMAA with the E.U. and an FTA with the United States. The level of agricultural protection remains quite high but will be reduced under the U.S.-Morocco FTA. One study combined household survey data and a CGE model to simulate the impact of liberalization of cereal imports. Our analysis uses two versions of a global CGE model. The static version of the model is used to simulate the impact of alternative types of trade liberalization. An FTA with the other North African countries appears likely to have little impact on the Moroccan economy because of the similarities in the economies in the region. A bilateral FTA with the E.U. would stimulate exports significantly but would have a small negative effect on national income and returns to unskilled agricultural labor. Global trade liberalization would combine a strong positive effect on exports and a small positive effect on national income but would have a large negative effect on unskilled agricultural labor. Simulations with the dynamic version of the model show that liberalization in services, trade facilitation, and increased investment would have a positive effect on exports and income but would not fully offset the negative effect of trade liberalization on the returns to unskilled agricultural labor.

Implications for Trade Policy

Global trade liberalization will likely increase world agricultural prices by 3–20 percent, imposing a terms-of-trade loss on all the MENA countries under consideration. The net food-importing countries have used the expected terms-of-trade loss associated with global trade liberalization to request special concessions in the form of reduced commitments to opening their own borders. This mercantilist logic is flawed in that it takes into account only the gains and losses of producers, ignoring the effects of trade policy on consumers. Studies of trade liberalization suggest that most of the benefits to a given country from trade liberalization are the result of reforms within the country. Thus, the net food-importing countries appear to be demanding the right to forgo the efficiency gains associated with domestic trade liberalization as "compensation" for the terms-of-trade losses associated with reforms in other countries.

The effect of agricultural trade liberalization on poverty varies widely across countries, in part because the effect of liberalization on agricultural prices is ambiguous. Global agricultural trade reform is likely to increase world agricultural prices, but domestic trade liberalization will reduce domestic agricultural prices relative to the world price. The net effect of liberalization on domestic agricultural prices will depend partly on each country's trade patterns, the original level of protection, and the details of the liberalization. If the initial level of domestic agricultural protection is high, as in Morocco and Tunisia, full trade liberalization is likely to reduce domestic agricultural prices. If, on the other hand, initial agricultural protection is modest, as in Egypt and Lebanon, full trade liberalization should have no effect or slightly increase domestic agricultural prices.

Furthermore, the impact of changes in agricultural prices on poverty is ambiguous. Higher agricultural prices benefit farmers who can produce a marketed surplus, but they hurt the urban poor and rural net buyers. The analysis presented in this report suggests that higher agricultural prices generally benefit the poor on balance, but the effect is quite small.[3] Thus, the link between trade liberalization and agricultural price changes is ambiguous, and the effect of agricultural price changes on poverty is weak. This suggests that trade policy is a poor instrument for addressing overall poverty in the MENA region.

The economic benefits of *regional integration* (such as that achieved through the agreement to create the Greater Arab Free Trade Area) have been limited to date. One reason is that these agreements tend to be fairly flexible, allowing numerous exceptions for "sensitive goods." A relatively small number of exceptions can largely negate the gains from trade liberalization. To generate significant gains for member countries, the Greater Arab Free Trade Area and other regional trade zones will have to achieve a greater level of discipline over tariff and nontariff barriers. The second reason for the modest benefits associated with these trade agreements is that regional trade is hampered by a variety of factors in addition to trade policy. The transportation infrastructure linking MENA countries is generally poor, transportation services in the region are characterized by a lack of competition and high costs, and many of the countries in the region suffer from cumbersome customs procedures that raise the cost of trade. Measures to streamline customs procedures and introduce greater competition in regional transportation services would enhance the benefits of regional trade agreements. The third reason for the modest gains associated with regional trade agreements is the similarity of the economic structures in the member countries. If all member countries import wheat and maize, export fruits and vegetables, and have similar wage rates, the gains from agricultural trade are likely to be limited.

Regarding *bilateral agreements*, the EMAAs generally exclude agriculture. Simulation studies confirm the economic intuition that the gains from these

---

[3] In Egypt this is true for wheat but not for agricultural prices in general.

agreements would be much larger if they included liberalization in the agricultural sector. The five countries with EMAAs should begin to explore the feasibility of a second round of negotiations that would include agriculture. While recognizing the political sensitivity of agricultural prices, MENA countries should keep in mind that most of the benefits of an expanded association agreement will be related to the degree of domestic liberalization in their own countries. At the same time, the liberalization of E.U. tariff and nontariff barriers on fruits, vegetables, olive oil, and sugar would be particularly beneficial to the MENA countries.

Regarding the U.S. FTAs, the United States is a relatively minor trading partner with all of these countries, so, the MENA countries should not expect large impacts, positive or negative, as a result of these agreements. On the other hand, these agreements may facilitate investment (local and foreign) in the MENA countries, partly because they include measures to create a more favorable climate for private investment and partly because they signal a commitment to greater integration in the global economy.

Regarding *unilateral liberalization,* economic analysis suggests that, in general, unilaterally reducing import protection and domestic support of agriculture will increase aggregate income. Indeed, it is easy to demonstrate that, in most cases, the benefits of lower domestic prices to consumers are greater than the losses to producers. Yet policymakers, trade negotiators, and many noneconomists see reducing domestic protection as the "price" a country must pay to gain access to markets in other countries. One argument is that poor farmers in developing countries cannot compete with large-scale technologically advanced farmers in developed countries, particularly if the latter receive production subsidies. Certainly commercial farmers in developing countries are hurt by the subsidies given to farmers in the countries of the OECD. However, in spite of these subsidies, Egypt is a competitive exporter of cotton and rice, Morocco is able to export tomatoes to Europe, and Tunisia is a major exporter of olive oil. These examples suggest that the MENA countries can compete in markets where they have a comparative advantage.

According to another argument, domestic import barriers to agricultural products help poor farmers by raising domestic agricultural prices. The analysis presented in this report suggests that higher agricultural prices have mixed effects on poor households. This is because (1) higher agricultural prices benefit some poor households (farmers with net sales) but hurt other poor households (the urban poor and net buyers in rural areas); (2) the percentage of households that are net sellers of agricultural goods is relatively small; (3) farmers who are net sellers tend to be richer than the average farmer, so higher farm income does not always translate into lower poverty; and (4) even those farmers who are both poor and net sellers rely on nonagricultural activities for a significant share of their incomes. In other words, agricultural protection is a costly and imprecise tool with which to address the problem of rural poverty.

Complementary Policies

The impact of trade liberalization on small farmers and other poor households in the MENA region partly depends on nontrade policies. Several studies have indicated that the size of the gains from trade liberalization will be greater when there are *flexible factor markets* that allow land, labor, and capital to be reallocated from formerly protected sectors to newly profitable sectors. Regulations that constrain the response of these factor markets reduce the positive impact of liberalization. In agriculture, flexibility is likely to be enhanced by effective agricultural services such as extension and market information systems that can provide farmers with useful information about the agronomic and economic aspects of shifting into new commodities.

Another type of policy that enhances the economic effect of trade liberalization is *trade facilitation*. This refers to measures that reduce the transaction costs related to trade, including the costs of excessive documentation requirements, the need to obtain authorizations from multiple agencies, unclear or subjective criteria for applications of duties, and delays and uncertainties related to customs clearance. One study found that the gains from trade liberalization are twice as large if combined with trade facilitation measures.

Under WTO rules, the agricultural sector can be directly supported through a variety of *green box expenditures*, such as investments in agricultural research and extension, pest and disease control, inspection services, marketing infrastructure, market information services, environmental protection programs, and regional assistance programs. Most of these investments involve the provision of public goods, implying that they may be justified in terms of economic efficiency as well as in terms of supporting poor farmers.

One type of green box support does not involve the provision of public goods: *decoupled payments* to farmers. Payments are decoupled when they are based not on current production but rather on some fixed measure such as production or area planted in a base year. Over the past 15 years, economists and policymakers have become increasingly interested in agricultural reform that shifts from producer subsidies and import protection toward decoupled payments to farmers. This type of reform has been tried in the E.U., Mexico, Turkey, and the United States with some success. At the same time, it should be recognized that switching from import protection to a program of decoupled payments implies both a loss in tariff revenue and significant new expenditure.

If the objective is to assist poor and vulnerable households regardless of their occupation, a different type of measure should be considered. A wide variety of *safety net programs* have been established in developing countries with the goal of reducing poverty. Targeted food subsidies make subsidized food available to selected households either geographically, through low-priced shops located in poor neighborhoods, or through some form of ration card that entitles the bearer to purchase food at subsidized prices. Egypt, Jordan, and Tunisia have attempted to introduce targeting into food subsidy programs. Labor-intensive public works programs usually combine infrastructure development (such as road building) with hiring policies to maximize their pro-poor impact. If designed well, they can improve community infrastructure and provide assistance to the poorest households with able-bodied members. Conditional cash transfer programs have generated considerable interest in the past 10–15 years. These programs provide cash grants to households that comply with certain requirements, usually keeping children in school, attending health clinics, or receiving pre- and postnatal care. Conditional cash transfers serve a dual purpose: providing assistance to poor households and encouraging investments in human capital that reduce the chance that poverty will be transmitted to the next generation.

CHAPTER 1

Introduction

Agriculture and Trade Liberalization

Agriculture is one of the most problematic areas in international trade negotiations. Although significant progress has been achieved in reducing trade barriers and other policy distortions in manufacturing through various multilateral agreements, in regional and bilateral arrangements and under unilateral trade reforms, agricultural markets remain highly distorted. Both industrial and developing countries still provide relatively high levels of protection to agricultural sectors. In addition, many countries, particularly the industrialized countries, provide various forms of support for agriculture. Agricultural trade liberalization is a politically sensitive topic in developing countries because policymakers are concerned about the potential impact on small-scale farmers, who typically account for a large share of the poor. The issue is politically sensitive in industrialized countries as well, at least partly because of the disproportionate political power of farm groups.

In spite of this sensitivity, there is a widespread belief that reducing the trade barriers and policy distortions affecting agriculture will increase economic efficiency and aggregate income. The theory of comparative advantage suggests that aggregate income is higher when trade barriers are lower. Empirical studies of trade liberalization generally show that the aggregate benefits of trade liberalization outweigh the costs. Studies also show that more outward-oriented countries tend to grow more rapidly over time, suggesting that trade liberalization generates dynamic gains through the free flow of investment and technology. By this logic, even unilateral trade liberalization should usually benefit a country. In the political arena, however, there is strong resistance to unilateral liberalization. In the view of many policymakers, reducing domestic protection is a necessary cost used as a bargaining chip to gain access to markets in other countries. In addition, there is concern that even if liberalization brings benefits in the aggregate, it may adversely affect the poor or exacerbate income inequality.

Economic theory and empirical studies suggest that current agricultural policies suppress the world price of many agricultural commodities below what they would be under liberalized trade. This is because import restrictions reduce world demand and agricultural producer support tends to stimulate supply. The effect on domestic agricultural prices in countries that protect their agriculture is ambiguous, however, because multilateral trade liberalization would probably increase world agricultural prices, but tariff reduction within a country will reduce domestic prices relative to world prices. In addition to trade barriers, imperfect transmission of world prices resulting from transaction costs may mute the signals from changes in world prices.

The impact of trade policy reforms varies substantially across commodities, countries, and households within a country. Some commodity markets, such as those for sugar and rice, are more distorted than others, so trade liberalization will likely have a larger effect on the prices of these commodities. Some countries are net exporters of agricultural commodities, so they would gain from the higher agricultural prices associated with multilateral liberalization. Net importers of agricultural commodities could lose from multilateral trade liberalization, though this will depend on the degree of reform they carry out in their domestic policies.

The issues of trade liberalization and agriculture are of particular importance to the non-oil-exporting countries of the Middle East and North Africa (MENA) for several reasons:

- The growth of per capita gross domestic product (GDP) in the MENA region stagnated at around 2 percent between the periods 1990–99 and 2000–06 and in the more recent period lagged behind the average of most of the developing country groups (Table 1.1). The slow economic growth has led to various social problems, including high levels of unemployment.
- The countries of the region generally have levels of trade protection that are higher than in most of the developing world (see "Structure of Protection" in Chapter 2). This is particularly true in agricultural protection among the non-oil-exporting MENA countries.
- High rates of agricultural protection in countries like Morocco and Tunisia imply that domestic trade liberalization will have significant adverse effects on farmers, and thus on the rural poor.
- Almost all the MENA countries are net food importers, so they are vulnerable to fluctuations in food prices, such as the dramatic rise in commodity prices in 2007–08. The non-oil-exporting MENA countries are more vulnerable to commodity price shocks because they do not have increased oil revenue to offset the higher cost of imported food.

Table 1.1 Summary statistics for selected MENA economies, 2006

Region/country	Real GDP per capita (2000 US$)	Annual growth in GDP per capita (%) 1990-2000	2000-06	Unemployment rate (%)[a]	Share of urban population (%)	Population below poverty line (%) Less than US$2 per day	Less than US$1 per day
MENA							
Djibouti	817	-4.3	0.8	62.0	87.0	87.0	56.0
Egypt	1,724	2.5	2.5	11.0	43.0	43.9	3.1
Jordan	2,173	0.7	3.3	12.0	83.0	6.9	2.0
Lebanon	5,059	6.9	1.9	9.0	87.0	18.0	6.3
Morocco	1,667	1.0	3.7	10.0	59.0	14.3	2.0
Syria	1,287	2.6	1.4	12.0	51.0	–	–
Tunisia	2,513	3.3	3.6	14.0	66.0	6.6	2.0
West Bank and Gaza	1,014	1.8	-5.4	27.0	72.0	36.0	24.0
MENA average	1,862	1.9	2.2	14.0	57.0	19.7	1.5
East Asia and the Pacific	1,475	6.8	7.4	4.9	42.0	40.7	14.9
South Asia	604	3.2	4.7	5.3	29.0	77.8	31.3
Latin America and the Caribbean	4,329	1.3	1.8	8.9	78.0	22.6	9.5
Sub-Saharan Africa	578	-0.5	2.0	–	36.0	74.9	46.4

Sources: Laithy, Abu-Ismail, and Hamdan (2008); World Bank (2008a, 2008b); CIA (2009).

Notes: –, data not available. The poverty rates for Lebanon are based on estimations by Laithy, Abu-Ismail, and Hamdan (2008) relative to two poverty lines of US$4.00 and US$2.40 per day instead of the World Bank's lines of US$2.00 and US$1.00 per day, respectively.

[a]Latest year available: 2007 for Djibouti; 2004 for Egypt, the West Bank and Gaza, Jordan, MENA (Middle East and North Africa), South Asia, and Latin America and the Caribbean; 2006 for Morocco; 2003 for Syria; and 2005 for Tunisia and East Asia and the Pacific.

- The proximity of the MENA region to the high-income markets in Europe creates significant opportunities for international trade, yet the importance of trade in the economy is no greater than in Sub-Saharan Africa or in developing countries in general.[1]

[1] A common measure of the importance of trade in the economy is the sum of the value of exports and imports as a ratio of GDP. The ratio is 65-70 percent for the MENA countries and for developing countries in general (World Bank 2008b).

These patterns raise the question of whether there is a connection between the relatively high rates of protection among the non-oil-exporting MENA countries and the relatively low rates of economic growth in the region. The distributional impact of trade liberalization is important because it has implications for the desirability of trade liberalization, its political acceptability, and the need for complementary policies to ameliorate the adverse effects.

Objectives

In light of the previous discussion, this report has four objectives:

- to describe the current agricultural and trade policies of the non-oil-exporting MENA countries and their impact on the agricultural economy of the region;
- to describe the current status of agricultural trade liberalization in the region and the extent of additional agricultural trade liberalization that will result from the Euro-Mediterranean Partnership (EMP) agreements, bilateral free trade agreements (FTAs), and World Trade Organization (WTO) multilateral trade negotiations;
- to analyze the potential impact of unilateral, bilateral, and multilateral trade liberalization efforts (including the reduction of domestic support) on the agricultural economy in the MENA region, with particular emphasis on their distributional impact; and
- to explore the types of measures that could be used to mitigate the potential negative impact of trade liberalization on the poor, particularly the rural poor, in the MENA region.

This study adopts two levels of geographic focus. First, we provide a descriptive analysis of trade patterns and levels of trade protection and a review of previous research on the impact of trade liberalization for eight MENA countries: Djibouti, Egypt, Jordan, Lebanon, Morocco, Syria, Tunisia, and the West Bank and Gaza. This list was derived using two criteria:

- Among the 21 MENA countries, we exclude major oil exporters, defined as those whose oil exports are more than 80 percent of their domestic consumption, that is, Algeria, Bahrain, Iran, Iraq, Kuwait, Libya, Oman, Qatar, Saudi Arabia, the United Arab Emirates, and Yemen.[2]
- We also exclude the two high-income countries in the region, Israel and Malta, for which poverty is not a major issue.

---

[2] The MENA region, as defined by the World Bank, includes Algeria, Bahrain, Djibouti, Egypt, Iran, Iraq, Israel, Jordan, Kuwait, Lebanon, Libya, Malta, Morocco, Oman, Qatar, Saudi Arabia, Syria, Tunisia, the United Arab Emirates, the West Bank and Gaza, and Yemen.

Second, we use household survey data and computable general equilibrium (CGE) models to simulate the effects of trade liberalization on the poor in four of them: Egypt, Morocco, Syria, and Tunisia. Although we do not claim that these countries are representative of the region, we hope that the study contributes further to the empirical evidence on the distributional effects of agricultural trade liberalization in a region that has received limited attention.

Organization of the Report

Chapter 2 of the report provides a regional overview on agriculture, trade, and poverty in the non-oil-exporting MENA countries. MENA is an economically diverse region that comprises 21 countries. The region's economic development over the past 25 years has been influenced by both the price of oil and the dominance of the role of the state in economic policies and structures (World Bank 2009). The MENA region has experienced slow economic growth in recent years, leading to various social problems, including high levels of unemployment. The growth of per capita GDP in the region has generally lagged behind the average of developing countries (World Bank 2008b). Agriculture contributes modestly to GDP but employs a sizable share of the labor force.

This chapter also explores the global and regional trade environment by analyzing the structure of protection that the countries in the region apply and face and examines the trade integration options in the region. These countries share levels of trade protection that are higher than the levels in many other regions of the world, especially in agriculture. But the countries enjoy good market access to developed economies due to the multiple trade preferences granted by their two main trading partners, the E.U. and the United States. In spite of high applied tariffs, nontariff barriers constitute even a higher trade impediment in the region. For these countries, complementary policies aimed at reducing the transport costs and improving the quality standards of traded goods must accompany a more outward-oriented trade policy in order to stimulate more rapid growth in the region and contribute positively to reducing poverty.

Chapter 3 reviews the evidence on the impact of trade liberalization in the selected MENA countries, with emphasis on studies that examine its impact on poor households. The relationship between trade liberalization and poverty alleviation is a complex one because although the relationship can be positive, it must take into account several key factors in addition to prices (Winters, McCulloch, and McKay 2004). The traditional argument focuses on prices of goods and factors. Given that the majority of poor people live in rural areas and work in the agricultural sector, where trade distortion is usually higher, global trade liberalization could imply higher world agricultural prices and increased activity and returns to the sector in developing countries (Bouët 2008).

Chapters 4–7 address the potential distributional impact from trade liberalization in four MENA countries. As described in Chapter 4, Egypt represents an early reformer with relatively low levels of agricultural protection, though it maintains a large system of consumer food subsidies. We simulate the impact of trade liberalization on different types of households using a partial equilibrium analysis that combines household survey data and hypothetical changes in the price of individual agricultural commodities. This analysis allows us to estimate the change in poverty overall, in urban and rural areas, and for specific types of households.

Chapter 5 examines Tunisia, a country that has made significant progress in recent years by opening its borders to trade and foreign investment, though the overall level of agricultural protection remains high. A CGE model of the Tunisian economy is linked to data from 397 representative households, allowing estimation of the impact of three variants of domestic trade liberalization and one scenario combining domestic and multilateral trade liberalization.

In Chapter 6 we focus on Syria, which has retained many of the policies that characterized the region 20 years ago: fixed producer prices, large-scale public procurement of major crops, and high levels of agricultural protection. The Syrian CGE model incorporates 10 household groups represented by income deciles of the population. Because wheat is the most distorted agricultural market and the most sensitive crop politically, the model is used to simulate a reduction in producer wheat subsidies and consumer bread subsidies of 20 percent, 50 percent, and 100 percent.

Chapter 7 describes the case of Morocco. Although Morocco has negotiated a number of trade agreements with the E.U., the United States, and its neighbors in the region, it maintains relatively high levels of protection, particularly on wheat. We use a global trade model to examine the impact of different types of trade liberalization on the returns to different categories of labor, including unskilled agricultural labor.

In the final chapter of the report we summarize the main findings and discuss the implications for policy. In particular, we explore alternative policies and programs that might enhance the positive impact of trade liberalization and alleviate some of its negative effects, with attention to its impact on the poor, particularly the rural poor.

CHAPTER 2

Overview of Selected MENA Economies

The MENA countries form a heterogeneous group of countries with respect to income, food security, and their integration in the global economy. As discussed in Chapter 1, we focus our overview on the lower- and middle-income non-oil-exporting countries of MENA: Djibouti, Egypt, Jordan, Lebanon, Morocco, Syria, Tunisia, and the West Bank and Gaza. These countries fall under the categories of low-income food-deficit countries or net-food-importing developing countries. This second category is a WTO classification that has implications for the negotiations in agriculture. WTO recognizes that this last group of countries (together with the group of least developing countries, or LDCs) is vulnerable to the possible negative effects of implementing agreements for free trade in agriculture and experiences difficulties in financing food imports (WTO 2006).[1]

Economic Performance and the Role of Agriculture

Among the selected MENA countries, the per capita GDP ranges from US$817 in Djibouti to US$5,069 in Lebanon, though most fall in the range of US$1,000–2,500 and the average for all MENA countries is US$1,862 (see Table 1.1).[2] The average growth in per capita GDP for the region as a whole was around 2 percent over the periods 1990–99 and 2000–06, but growth was uneven among countries. Lebanon, the West Bank and Gaza, and Tunisia experienced

[1] The net food-importing developing countries are a WTO-defined group that is subject to differential treatment under a special ministerial decision agreed during the Uruguay Round WTO negotiations. The decision recognizes that trade reforms in agriculture could have negative effects on these groups "in terms of the availability of adequate supplies of basic foodstuffs from external sources on reasonable terms and conditions, including short-term difficulties in financing normal levels of commercial imports of basic foodstuffs." The ministerial decision recommends such measures as food aid and aid for agricultural development. It also refers to the possibility of assistance from the International Monetary Fund and the World Bank to finance commercial food imports (WTO 2006). The definition of low-income food-deficit countries provided by the Food and Agriculture Organization of the United Nations may overlap with the classification of net food-importing developing countries.

[2] These figures are expressed in constant 2000 U.S. dollars.

solid economic growth (above 3 percent in per capita GDP) during the 1990s. While Tunisia continued to enjoy solid growth in 2000–06, joined by Jordan and Morocco, Lebanon and the West Bank and Gaza experienced a sharp slowing of their economies due to conflict. Most regions experienced higher growth over 2000–06 than in the 1990s, but growth in the MENA region barely increased. During 2000–06, growth in the MENA region was comparable to that in Sub-Saharan Africa and lagged behind growth in South Asia and in East Asia and the Pacific (see Table 1.1).

Various hypotheses have been advanced for the relatively weak growth rates among the MENA countries:

- *Conflict:* While some of our selected countries have known relative stability, many have been affected by the Israeli-Palestinian conflict, the Iraq war, and the 2006 conflict between Hezbollah and Israel in Lebanon. For example, Lebanon's economy went from a strong growth rate (6 percent) in 2004 to negative growth (-1 percent) in 2006 (World Bank 2008b). Conflicts have direct costs in terms of lives and property, but they also destroy social capital (Collier 1999). Moreover, conflicts create a climate of uncertainty and discourage investment.
- *The policy and regulatory environment:* In 2005, the International Finance Corporation (IFC) of the World Bank started ranking countries annually on the ease of doing business within them based on 39 indicators grouped into 10 categories. The categories include starting a business, dealing with construction permits, employing workers, registering property, obtaining credit, protecting investors, paying taxes, trading across borders, enforcing contracts, and closing a business. While on average the MENA region is on an upward trend with regard to the ease of doing business, only one country, Tunisia, is ranked in the top half. On the other hand, Syria ranks in the bottom 25 percent of all countries (IFC 2009).
- *Trade barriers:* High import barriers in the region distort economic incentives and impede the flow of new technology, thus reducing productivity growth. As discussed later, import protection is higher on average in the MENA region than in other developing countries. In Morocco and Tunisia, agricultural import tariffs are 30 percentage points higher than the average for other developing countries.

A serious economic problem facing many of the MENA countries is unemployment. Reflecting the low rates of economic growth combined with the rapid population growth in some countries, the unemployment rate averaged 14 percent for the MENA region, higher than in other developing regions. A recent report summarized the situation as follows:

> Average unemployment rates are highest among both youth and adults in MENA, when compared to all other developing regions. The share of young people among the region's unemployed is higher than 50 percent in most countries. In Egypt and Syria, youth make up more than 60 percent of the unemployed. In Tunisia, the unemployment rate for 20–24 year olds is more than three times higher than that for people above 40. And low labor force participation rate among females persists, even among younger cohorts with higher educational attainment. (World Bank 2007)

The MENA region is relatively urbanized, with 57 percent of the population in urban areas. Djibouti, Jordan, and Lebanon are the most urbanized, with urbanization rates of more than 80 percent (see Table 1.1). According to Fedjari (2000, cited in Radwan and Reiffers 2003), there are 180,000 rural migrants per year in Morocco, and 60,000 of these head for Casablanca. The high proportion of the population in urban area contributes to the dependence on food imports to satisfy domestic demand.

The incidence of poverty using the poverty line of US$2 per day is on average 20 percent for the MENA region, but the incidence varies greatly across the countries (see Table 1.1). Using the poverty line of US$1 per day, Djibouti has the highest poverty incidence (56 percent), followed by the West Bank and Gaza (24 percent). The subnational indicators (not shown here) reveal unambiguously that poverty in the MENA region, as in many developing countries, is more prevalent in rural areas than in urban ones (World Bank 2008b).

The GDP structure of the MENA countries indicates the dominant role of services and industry in these economies. On average, in the region the service sector contributes nearly half of GDP and industry more than a third. But countries differ widely around these averages. Services account for two-thirds or more of GDP in Djibouti, Jordan, and Lebanon (Table 2.1). In Djibouti, port and transport services are an important part of the economy because the country serves as the main trans-shipment route for Ethiopian trade.

The contribution of industry to GDP averages 40 percent for the MENA region, but it is less than this in all eight of the non-oil-exporting countries under consideration. For most of these countries, manufacturing dominates the contribution of the industrial sector to GDP. Egypt, Jordan, and Syria are the most industrialized, with this sector accounting for 30 percent or more of their GDP (see Table 2.1).

The agricultural sector accounts for 12 percent of GDP on average for the MENA region. Among the eight countries under consideration, the contribu-

Table 2.1 Structure of the economies and the agricultural sectors of selected MENA countries, 2006

	Structure of production (% share in GDP)				Trade (% share in GDP)		Agriculture			
		Industry					Annual growth (%)			
Region/country	Agriculture	Total industry	Percent of which manufacturing	Services	Exports	Imports	1990-2000	2000-06	Share (%) in total employment[b]	Share (%) in total exports[c]
MENA										
Djibouti	4	16	3	80	40	57	-0	3	2	<1
Egypt	14	38	17	48	30	32	3	3	30	3
Jordan	3	30	19	67	55	92	3	8	4	9
Lebanon	7	24	11	70	24	40	3	1	3	5
Morocco	16	28	16	57	33	38	4	7	45	6
Syria	18	32	7	49	39	36	8	6	27	15
Tunisia	11	28	17	60	54	54	6	2	23	8
West Bank and Gaza	–	–	–	–	14	70	–	–	16	<1
MENA average[a]	12	40	13	48	38	35	3	4	–	7
East Asia and the Pacific	12	47	32	41	47	40	3	4	44	2
South Asia	18	28	17	54	22	26	3	3	65	2
Latin America and the Caribbean	6	31	18	62	26	23	2	3	17	2
Sub-Saharan Africa	15	30	14	55	35	36	3	3	–	6

Sources: World Bank (2008b); WTO (2008); FAO (2009a,b).

Note: –, data not available.

[a]1991 for Djibouti; 1995 for South Asia; 2002 for East Asia and the Pacific; 2003 for Egypt and Jordan; 2004 for the West Bank and Gaza, Syria, and Latin America and the Caribbean; 2006 for Morocco.

[b]2003 for Sub-Saharan Africa; 2006 for all other countries and regions.

[c]The MENA (Middle East and North Africa) average is for 2005.

tion is less than 10 percent in Djibouti, Jordan, and Lebanon. On the other hand, it is more than 15 percent in just two countries: Morocco and Syria.

Although the agricultural sector in most MENA countries is relatively small, this does not imply that it is a stagnant sector. As shown in Table 2.1, the agricultural sector grew at 4 percent per year on average over 2000-06 and at more than 5 percent per year in Jordan, Morocco, and Syria.

Furthermore, the agricultural sector accounts for an important share in national employment. As in most developing countries, its share of employment is significantly larger than its share in GDP. This pattern reflects the low productivity in agriculture in these countries and, consequently, the relatively large share of poverty in rural areas (IFAD 2003). In the MENA region, Morocco has the highest share of employment in agriculture, 45 percent, followed by Egypt and Syria, with 30 and 27 percent, respectively (see Table 2.1).

Another measure of the importance of the agricultural sector is the share of agricultural exports in total exports. The contribution of agriculture to exports is below 10 percent in the region as a whole and for most selected countries with the exception of Syria (see Table 2.1). However, the impact of agricultural trade liberalization on households may be large even if only a small share of exports is from the agricultural sector because agriculture trade affects food prices, and thus food security, especially among poor households.

The Structure of Agricultural Production and Trade in MENA

Trade liberalization is expected to result in relative price changes that will affect each country at the national level according to its pattern of production and trade. MENA countries are characterized by a high dependence on food imports, a situation that may threaten their food security when international food prices rise significantly, as they did in 2007-08 (Benson et al. 2008; Von Braun 2008). This section examines the patterns of agricultural production and trade in the eight countries under consideration.

Production

The MENA region faces adverse climatic conditions, including low and highly variable annual rainfall patterns and poor soils for the most part. According to the Food and Agriculture Organization of the United Nations (FAO 2004), 62 percent of the region is hyperarid, 17 percent arid, 11 percent semiarid, and 4.4 percent subhumid. Agriculture in the region operates under severe limitations in water resources. Irrigation plays an essential role in the agricultural sector of Egypt, where all cropland is irrigated, and an important supporting role in Jordan, Lebanon, and Syria, where 24-31 percent of the cropland is irrigated (Table 2.2). Agriculture in the other MENA countries relies largely on rainfall (FAO 2003).

Table 2.2 Average agricultural production of selected MENA economies, 2005-07

Country	Share of irrigated land in cropland (%)	Total production (1,000 tons)								
		Meat and dairy products	Total cereals	Wheat	Milled rice	Fruits and vegetables	Sugar		Cotton lint	Olive oil
							Beets	Cane		
Djibouti	–	25	0	–	–	28	–	0	–	–
Egypt	100	5,988	22,682	7,931	4,385	24,190	4,777	16,172	199	8
Jordan	29	441	82	31	–	1,620	0	0	–	26
Lebanon	31	449	173	140	–	1,617	53	0	–	6
Morocco	15	2,275	5,354	3,651	20	7,847	2,951	893	–	73
Syria	24	2,408	5,636	4,690	–	4,624	1,129	0	292	150
Tunisia	7	1,220	1,934	1,440	–	3,413	0	0	–	192
West Bank and Gaza	7	280	62	41	–	830	–	–	–	21

Sources: World Bank (2008b); FAO (2009a); USDA (2009).
Note: –, data not available.

Yet irrigated agriculture often plays a critical role in agricultural exports. For example, in Morocco products from irrigated land account for 75 percent of the total primary and processed agricultural exports (Roe et al. 2005). In the countries where irrigated agriculture is important, water for expansion will have to come mainly from efficiency savings on existing schemes (FAO 2004).

In Egypt, agricultural production is highly concentrated along the Nile River and in the Nile Delta. About 97 percent of the area of Egypt is uncultivated due to the extremely limited rainfall. Virtually all agricultural land is allocated to crop production, and all crop production is irrigated (World Bank 2008b and Table 2.2). Although the amount of arable land per person is quite small (0.04 hectares), this is offset by multiple cropping and intensive production.

For the other countries, fruits and vegetables and meat products constitute an important share of agricultural production. Cereal production is substantial in Egypt, Morocco, Syria, and Tunisia. Wheat is the dominant cereal in all eight countries, though rice is also important in Egypt.

Sugar crop production is concentrated in Egypt, Morocco, and Syria. In Egypt it is mainly in the form of sugarcane, while in the other two countries sugar beets are dominant. Egypt and Syria are the only cotton producers in the region. Egyptian cotton commands a premium in world markets because of the length of its fibers. Almost all the countries under consideration grow olives and produce olive oil, but production is concentrated in Tunisia, Syria, and, to a lesser degree, Morocco (see Table 2.2).

Trade

The MENA region is a net importer of many agricultural commodities, including cereals, sugar, and cotton. Among the eight MENA countries under consideration, all but Syria are net importers of wheat, and all but Egypt are net importers of rice. On the other hand, all the countries under consideration are net exporters of olive oil except Djibouti. Tunisia is by far the most important olive oil exporter among the eight (Table 2.3).

Agricultural imports are dominated by food and animal products, which represent about three quarters of the total value for the MENA region. Cereals represent 25–40 percent of the value of agricultural imports in all the countries except Djibouti and Lebanon, where the share is less than 15 percent. Within cereal imports, wheat accounts for almost half of the total for the MENA region. Egypt is one of the largest wheat importers in the world, in part due to its policy of subsidizing some types of bread. Morocco and Tunisia are also major importers of wheat. Fruit and vegetable imports are a particularly large share of agricultural imports in the West Bank and Gaza and in

Table 2.3 Average net exports of selected commodities, 2004-06 (thousand metric tons)

Country	Total cereals	Wheat	Rice (milled)	Sugar (raw equivalent)	Cotton lint	Olive oil
Djibouti	-149	-102	-19	-34	0	-0
Egypt	-8,099	-5,290	911	-336	64	1
Jordan	-1,967	-671	-134	-243	0	3
Lebanon	-802	-401	-45	-146	0	1
Morocco	-4,110	-2,368	-1	-63	-33	21
Syria	-1,383	683	-177	-574	135	41
Tunisia	-2,337	-1,145	-19	-372	-18	197
West Bank and Gaza	-626	-126	-19	-78	—	1
Total MENA	-54,108	-26,962	-3,067	-7,703	-393	328

Source: FAO (2009a).
Note: MENA, Middle East and North Africa; —, data not available.

Lebanon. Other significant components of agricultural imports include dairy and eggs (particularly in Lebanon), meat and meat products (most notably in Egypt), and sugar (particularly in Syria) (Table 2.4).

Fruits and vegetables make up the main export sector in the MENA region as a whole and in most of the selected countries. Fruits and vegetables account for nearly two-thirds of agricultural exports in Morocco and over half in the West Bank and Gaza. Tunisia is an exception; there olive oil represents 60 percent of total agricultural export revenue. Egypt and Syria display a more diverse export structure, with an important role played by cereal exports, rice in Egypt and wheat in Syria (Table 2.5).

Cotton is the most important nonfood agricultural export of Egypt, contributing 22 percent of its total agriculture export revenue. It should be noted, however, that the cotton export revenue in Egypt has been quite volatile due to fluctuations in the world price and in domestic production. Over the period 2004-06 (the latest years available from the FAO database), the annual cotton export revenue was US$265 million, a third below the 2002-04 average of US$393 million, after reaching a record high of close to US$500 million in 2004. Higher world prices were recorded between 2006 and 2008, which may spur export revenues, especially if production follows the same trend. Cotton is also used in Egypt's textile sector, which produces cloth and garments for domestic use and for export. The Multi-Fiber Arrangement, which established quotas to regulate trade in textiles and apparel, expired in January 2005, exposing textile and apparel exporters in the MENA region to greater competition, particularly from China, India, and Pakistan.

Table 2.4 Average structure of agricultural imports, 2004-06

Country	Total agriculture imports (thousands of US$)[a]	Share in agricultural imports (%) Food and animals	Meat and meat products	Dairy and eggs	Cereals	Wheat	Rice	Fruits and vegetables	Sugar (raw equivalent)	Cotton lint	Olive oil
Djibouti	196,817	57.7	6.0	8.2	14.9	8.2	3.6	7.5	7.6	0.0	0.1
Egypt	3,617,136	74.1	9.4	3.8	39.2	24.1	0.1	7.8	3.3	2.0	0.0
Jordan	1,430,454	78.1	7.0	8.0	25.3	8.1	4.4	10.0	5.9	0.0	0.0
Lebanon	1,393,300	77.6	6.6	12.7	10.4	5.0	1.5	12.8	3.2	0.0	0.2
Morocco	2,213,534	69.2	0.3	5.6	33.7	20.7	0.1	4.6	8.1	2.0	0.2
Syria	1,387,528	79.3	0.1	5.7	25.1	1.7	6.5	9.0	18.0	0.0	0.0
Tunisia	1,200,446	69.0	2.2	3.2	32.0	16.3	0.5	5.1	8.8	2.0	0.3
West Bank and Gaza	537,128	88.4	4.6	6.3	27.1	5.2	4.8	16.2	5.8	–	0.1
Total MENA	48,448,982	75.2	6.3	8.4	23.1	10.2	3.9	10.5	5.7	2.2	0.1

Source: Based on trade values from FAO (2009a).
Note: MENA, Middle East and North Africa; –, data not available.
[a]FAO defines imports as including food aid.

Table 2.5 Average structure of agricultural exports, 2004-06

Country	Total agriculture imports (thousands of US$)[a]	Share in agricultural imports (%)									
		Food and animals	Meat and meat products	Dairy and eggs	Cereals	Wheat	Rice	Fruits and vegetables	Sugar (raw equivalent)	Cotton lint	Olive oil
Djibouti	28,084	75.4	0.0	1.7	5.1	0.0	5.0	7.9	24.3	–	–
Egypt	1,190,216	69.0	0.1	2.9	24.2	0.0	23.7	30.9	2.1	22.3	0.2
Jordan	636,523	66.8	3.3	8.7	0.3	0.0	0.1	39.0	0.3	0.0	1.3
Lebanon	281,325	70.3	2.5	1.6	1.3	0.2	0.4	39.6	0.1	0.0	2.0
Morocco	1,213,075	79.4	0.1	6.1	1.6	0.0	0.0	65.5	0.0	0.0	6.6
Syria	1,367,990	73.7	0.0	3.3	10.2	9.2	0.0	23.3	4.2	12.1	7.5
Tunisia	1,063,060	27.8	0.0	1.0	1.4	0.0	0.0	14.2	0.0	0.0	59.8
West Bank and Gaza	52,623	85.1	1.5	3.8	5.6	1.3	0.4	53.1	1.2	–	3.5
Total MENA	19,120,630	71.9	1.4	4.7	5.7	1.1	1.9	39.8	2.5	3.5	5.6

Source: Based on trade values from FAO (2009a).

Note: MENA, Middle East and North Africa; –, data not available.

The high dependence on food imports of the MENA region as a whole and of individual MENA countries in particular challenges the countries' efforts to improve their food security. In the study by Diaz-Bonilla et al. (2000), the authors generated indicators of the food security status of countries. They used cluster analysis to classify 163 developed and developing countries based on five measures of food security: food production per capita (measuring the ability of a country to feed itself), the ratio of food imports to total exports (an indication of a country's ability to finance its food imports), calories per capita and protein per capita (measuring the level of nutrition), and the nonagricultural population share (an indication of how vulnerable the population is to changes in trade and agricultural policies). Results from the cluster analysis classify the six middle-income MENA countries, Egypt, Jordan, Lebanon, Morocco, Syria, and Tunisia, as "food neutral" but suggest that these countries are nonetheless trade stressed due to a high ratio of food imports to total exports. Figure 2.1 shows that these ratios have been on a declining trend for some of the countries under consideration in this study, but the ratio is still above 15 percent in Egypt and Jordan and reached an average of 42 percent in Lebanon for the period 2000–06. This trend in

Figure 2.1 Ratio of food imports to total exports for selected MENA countries

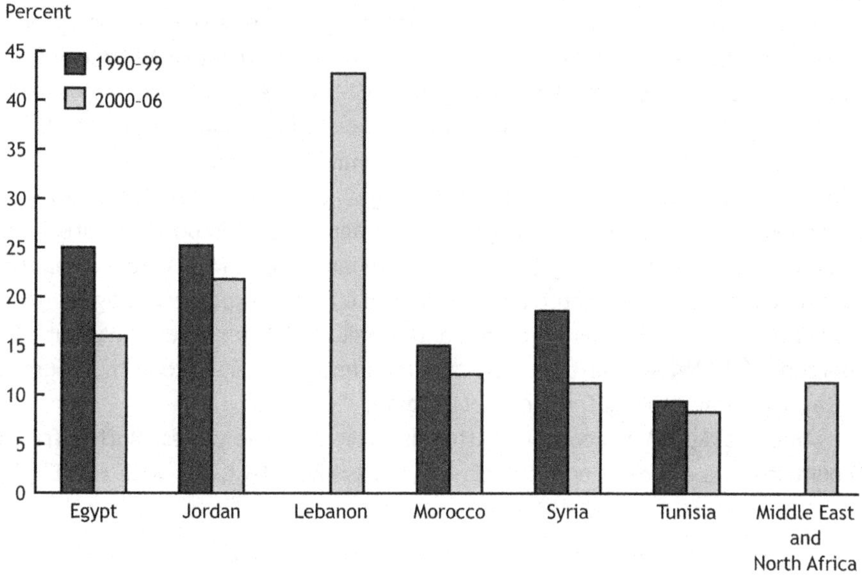

Source: World Bank (2008b).
Note: Data not available for Djibouti or for the West Bank and Gaza.

some of the MENA countries may have reversed during the recent spike in food prices, which worsened the terms of trade of non-oil-exporting MENA countries (World Bank 2009).

The Pattern of Trade and Protection of MENA Countries

The potential effects of trade liberalization on the MENA countries are dependent on the patterns of trade flows of the countries and the original level of protection they apply and face with respect to their trade partners. This section uses the MAcMap-HS6 database developed by CEPII (2008) to illustrate the patterns of agricultural trade in the region and compute average levels of protection among the selected MENA countries and their trading partners. The MAcMap-HS6 database provides a set of consistent and exhaustive ad valorem equivalents (AVEs) of applied border protection for 165 reporting countries, 5,111 commodities, and 208 trading partners. The tariff equivalents reflect tariffs (ad valorem, specific, mixed, compound, and antidumping duties), and tariff quotas, taking into account all regional agreements and trade preferences. The trade data in MAcMap-HS6 are sourced from Base pour l'Analyse du Commerce International (BACI) (CEPII 2008).

Patterns of Agricultural Trade Flows

Intraregional trade in MENA with respect to agriculture is dominant in exports, representing 41 percent of the region's total agricultural exports. Outside the region, the EU25 and the group of developing countries absorb 29 and 20 percent of MENA agricultural exports, respectively.[3] Among single-country destinations, the United States is the destination of 2 percent of MENA exports. Imports present a different structure in which intraregional trade represents only 13 percent of agricultural imports and developing countries and the EU25 are the main sources of MENA imports, 42 and 26 percent, respectively. The United States plays a larger role in the region's imports than in its exports, contributing 9 percent of the region's total agricultural imports (Figure 2.2). Developing countries as a group play a dominant role in MENA trade: imports are much more concentrated and dominated by large exporters of agriculture in Latin America, such as Argentina and Brazil, which together contribute 15 percent of MENA agricultural imports. China and India are also active sources of agricultural imports for the MENA region.

Among single MENA countries, the direction of trade varies: North African countries like Morocco and Tunisia are more likely to trade with the EU25,

[3] EU25 refers to the membership of the European Union as of 2004. In 2007 two more countries joined the E.U.: Bulgaria and Romania.

Figure 2.2 Composition of trading partners in agricultural trade for the MENA region, 2004

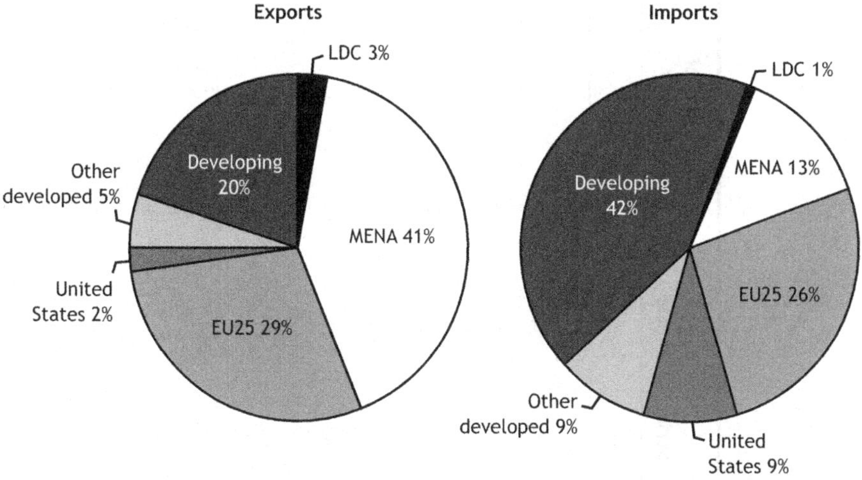

Source: Authors' calculations based on the MAcMap-HS6 database, 2004.
Notes: Developing, developing countries not including LDC; EU25, European Union (25 members as of 2004); LDC, least developed countries; MENA, Middle East and North Africa; Other developed, other developed countries.

while Middle Eastern countries favor South-South trade within the MENA region, with shares of exports ranging between 39 percent for Egypt and 82 percent for Jordan. In terms of imports, all countries mostly import from the EU25, with the exception of Syria, which seems to favor imports from developing countries (see Table 2.6).

The Structure of Protection

Table 2.7 indicates that although overall protection continues to be higher in developing countries and in the MENA region than in developed countries, agricultural protection is very similar across various groups of countries. MENA protection in agriculture is slightly higher on average than the level in developed countries and lower than the average protection in developing countries and the LDCs. Among the MENA countries, overall protection is highest in Tunisia followed by Morocco, Syria, and Egypt. Bouët (2006) ranks Egypt, Morocco, and Tunisia among the 11 most protectionist countries among countries in the MAcMap-HS6 database for 2001. For these countries, the results are consistent with earlier tariff rankings generated between 1988 and 1998 by various international organizations, including the United Nations Conference on Trade and Development (UNCTAD), the Organisation for Economic

Table 2.6 Agricultural trade flows in MENA, 2004 (percent)

Region/country	Djibouti	Egypt	Jordan	Lebanon	Morocco	Syria	Tunisia	West Bank and Gaza	Rest of MENA	Total MENA
	Export shares									
MENA										
Djibouti	0	0	0	0	0	0	0	0	0	0
Egypt	0	0	2	4	1	8	0	0	0	1
Jordan	0	4		7	1	12	0	36	2	3
Lebanon	0	5	8	0	1	10	0	0	1	2
Morocco	0	1	0	0	0	1	2	0	0	0
Syria	0	5	10	8	1	0	0	0	2	2
Tunisia	0	2	0	0	0	1	0	0	0	1
West Bank and Gaza	n.a.	n.a.	n.a.	n.a.	n.a.	n.a.	n.a.	n.a.	n.a.	n.a.
Rest of MENA	8	21	62	44	3	37	20	16	45	32
Total MENA	**8**	**39**	**82**	**63**	**7**	**68**	**22**	**52**	**52**	**41**
OECD										
EU25	4	33	6	15	68	15	67	44	10	29
United States	1	2	2	7	4	1	3	0	1	2
Japan	0	1	0	0	7	0	1	0	1	2
Total developed countries	**8**	**41**	**12**	**26**	**83**	**21**	**73**	**47**	**15**	**36**
Other										
Argentina	2	0	0	0	0	0	0	0	0	0
Brazil	0	0	0	0	0	1	0	0	0	0
China	4	2	0	1	0	0	0	0	3	2
India	1	0	0	0	0	0	0	0	2	1
Total developing countries	**10**	**17**	**5**	**10**	**9**	**10**	**3**	**2**	**30**	**20**
Total LDCs	**74**	**3**	**2**	**1**	**2**	**1**	**2**	**0**	**3**	**3**

	Import shares									
MENA										
Djibouti	0	0	0	0	0	0	0	n.a.	0	0
Egypt	0		3	4	1	4	2	n.a.	1	1
Jordan	0	0		2	0	2	0	n.a.	1	1
Lebanon	0	0	2	0	0	2	0	n.a.	1	1
Morocco	0	0	1	1	0	1	1	n.a.	0	0
Syria	0	2	6	7	0	0	1	n.a.	1	2
Tunisia	0	0	0	0	1	0	0	n.a.	1	0
West Bank and Gaza	0	0	0	0	0	0	0	0	0	0
Rest of MENA	7	0	9	6	1	10	2	n.a.	11	8
Total MENA	**7**	**3**	**22**	**20**	**3**	**19**	**5**	**n.a.**	**15**	**13**
OECD										
EU25	24	19	17	36	37	17	39	n.a.	26	26
United States	24	27	11	9	10	10	11	n.a.	6	9
Japan	0	0	0	0	0	0	0	n.a.	0	0
Total developed countries	**55**	**50**	**35**	**49**	**55**	**29**	**57**	**n.a.**	**42**	**44**
Other										
Argentina	0	13	9	4	9	11	10	n.a.	5	6
Brazil	3	8	2	4	12	7	6	n.a.	10	9
China	0	2	2	2	5	1	1	n.a.	3	3
India	5	1	5	2	0	1	1	n.a.	6	5
Total developing countries	**21**	**45**	**42**	**29**	**41**	**51**	**37**	**n.a.**	**42**	**42**
Total LDCs	**17**	**2**	**1**	**2**	**1**	**1**	**1**	**n.a.**	**1**	**1**

Source: Authors' calculations based on MAcMap-HS6 database for 2004.

Notes: EU25, European Union (25 members as of 2004); LDCs, least developed countries; MENA, Middle East and North Africa; OECD, Organisation for Economic Co-operation and Development; n.a., not applicable.

Co-operation and Development (OECD), the World Bank, and the International Monetary Fund (IMF), summarized in Oliva (2000). These organizations rank Egypt, Morocco, and Tunisia as more often restrictive than not, but the rankings differ among the studies.[4] There is less consistency on Jordan and Syria, which appear restrictive in some studies (such as that of the IMF and Oliva's own index in the case of Syria) and open in others (that of UNCTAD). Zarrouk and Zallio (2000) argue that industrial strategies founded on import substitution and a large public sector have led to high protection in MENA countries and that governments have ended up relying on import duties as a main source of revenues. By contrast, Egypt, Jordan, and Lebanon are more open, with levels of protection in agriculture that are comparable to the average in developed countries.[5]

Table 2.7 identifies countries as protectors of agriculture if the ratio of the level of agricultural protection to industrial protection is at least 1.4. On average, countries protect agriculture more than industry, and this is particularly notable for developed countries, which have low levels of industrial protection combined with high rates of protection of agriculture (Japan and Switzerland are the most illustrative). The MENA countries are protectors of agriculture on average: the level of their protection in agriculture is more than twice the industrial rate. Since the advent of structural adjustment programs and accession to the WTO, which curtailed industrial protection, the average global tariff has decreased (WTO 2002), but agriculture protection has been reduced at a much slower pace. The exceptions are Djibouti, Egypt, and Syria, which have higher rates of protection in industry than in agriculture. Morocco and Tunisia have very high levels of agricultural protection, matched only by Switzerland among the OECD countries and India among the developing countries and more than double the average for the MENA region.

These results testify to the shift in protection by developing countries since the findings in Schiff and Valdes (1992), which illustrate the bias against agriculture emanating from agricultural sector policies (direct effects) and from industrial protection and macroeconomic policies (indirect effects) in 18 developing countries. Considering only the direct effects, the study estimated that taxation on agriculture was 25 percent in Egypt over the period 1964–84 and 15 percent in Morocco over the same period.[6]

---

[4] These assessments do not take into account the substantial liberalization of trade policy in Egypt in 2004, as discussed later.

[5] In this aggregation, the beverages and tobacco sector is not included in agriculture. This classification matters in the case of Egypt, which has an AVE of 818 percent for beverages and tobacco.

[6] To maintain consistency in comparing the results of Schiff and Valdes (1992) and the MAcMap-HS6 database, we do not include the indirect effect of the tax on agriculture from the former study.

Table 2.7 Applied levels of protection by region, 2004

Region/country	Level of protection (%) Overall (1)	Agriculture (2)	Industry (3)	Ratio (2)/(3)	Is agriculture more protected? (ratio > 1.4)
MENA	30	14	32	0.4	No
Djibouti					
Egypt	15	8	15	0.5	No
Jordan	8	11	8	1.3	No
Lebanon	4	9	3	2.7	Yes
Morocco	19	44	17	2.6	Yes
Syria	16	13	16	0.8	No
Tunisia	20	50	17	2.9	Yes
West Bank and Gaza	n.a.	n.a.	n.a.	n.a.	n.a.
Rest of MENA	8	14	8	1.7	Yes
MENA average	**11**	**14**	**10**	**2.5**	**Yes**
OECD	4	23	4	0.6	No
Australia					
Canada	3	16	3	6.2	Yes
EU25	2	11	1	8.0	Yes
Japan	3	27	1	18.5	Yes
Switzerland	5	51	1	44.7	Yes
United States	2	8	2	4.0	Yes
Developed-country average	**2**	**13**	**2**	**6.5**	**Yes**
Other					
Argentina	11	11	11	1.0	No
Brazil	11	10	11	0.9	No
China	5	6	5	1.3	No
India	19	61	15	4.0	Yes
Developing-country average	**8**	**18**	**7**	**2.4**	**Yes**
LDCs average	**12**	**15**	**11**	**1.4**	**No**

Source: Authors' calculations based on MAcMap-HS6 database for 2004.
Notes: EU25, European Union (25 members as of 2004); LDCs, least developed countries; MENA, Middle East and North Africa; OECD, Organisation for Economic Co-operation and Development; n.a., not applicable.

Agricultural protection in the MENA countries also varies relative to their trading partners. Table 2.8 shows applied protection by importers along the rows and the protection faced by exporters along the columns. MENA countries apply, on average, slightly higher rates on agricultural imports from the rest of the world than on those from other MENA countries. In particular, Morocco and Tunisia are more protectionist with respect to the rest of the world than to other MENA countries, applying rates of 45 and 50 percent, respectively. The protection faced by MENA countries varies across countries. Djibouti and the West Bank and Gaza face higher protection in MENA than in developed countries, as is the case for Jordan, Lebanon, and Morocco. But

Table 2.8 Applied bilateral protection on agriculture, 2004 (percent)

Importers	Exporters									
Region/country	Djibouti	Egypt	Jordan	Lebanon	Morocco	Syria	Tunisia	West Bank and Gaza	Rest of MENA	Rest of world
MENA										
Djibouti	0	0	16	22	18	9	17	0	14	14
Egypt	0	0	4	7	4	4	6	10	7	8
Jordan	10	5	0	6	5	4	7	11	9	11
Lebanon	6	7	20	0	4	2	7	6	8	9
Morocco	63	28	19	13	0	18	18	18	23	45
Syria	16	19	19	17	14	0	22	23	19	12
Tunisia	35	26	46	26	32	42		68	41	50
West Bank and Gaza	n.a.	n.a.	n.a.	n.a.	n.a.	n.a.	n.a.	n.a.	n.a.	n.a.
Rest of MENA	9	11	12	14	5	11	17	20	11	10
MENA average	**9**	**13**	**14**	**14**	**6**	**12**	**15**	**21**	**13**	**14**
OECD										
Australia	0	1	1	2	1	1	1	0	2	2
Canada	1	5	12	8	3	6	1	6	27	16
EU25	0	12	9	1	4	19	32	11	25	10
Japan	11	44	8	26	8	25	3	3	43	27
Switzerland	7	55	24	49	10	51	16	148	93	51
United States	0	7	1	12	2	5	2	4	14	8
Developed-country average	**1**	**14**	**9**	**8**	**4**	**16**	**20**	**12**	**25**	**13**
Other										
Argentina	13	12	14	14	13	12	14	13	14	11
Brazil	12	13	13	9	15	9	14	14	13	10
China	4	7	11	15	5	32	10	15	11	6
India	50	68	45	48	40	59	33	0	41	62
Developing-country average	**25**	**23**	**21**	**21**	**21**	**22**	**16**	**20**	**21**	**18**
LDCs average	**8**	**10**	**13**	**16**	**20**	**11**	**17**	**15**	**15**	**15**

Source: Authors' calculations based on MAcMap-HS6 database for 2004.

Notes: EU25, European Union (25 members as of 2004); LDCs, least developed countries; MENA, Middle East and North Africa; OECD, Organisation for Economic Co-operation and Development; n.a., not applicable.

countries such as Egypt, Syria, and Tunisia face higher tariffs among developed countries, especially with respect to the EU25 in the case of Tunisia and Switzerland in the case of Syria.

The regional average translates to a wide range of equivalent tariffs among MENA countries. The highest AVEs are applied by Tunisia and Morocco, ranging from 26 to 68 percent in the former and from 13 to 63 percent in the latter. Egypt, Jordan, and Lebanon apply some of the lowest rates to most other MENA countries (see Table 2.8).

Among developed countries, Japan and Switzerland apply the highest protection to imports from MENA countries, especially with regard to Egypt, Lebanon, and Syria. Among developing countries, protection is higher, in India ranging from 41 to 68 percent. MENA countries face lower tariffs with respect to the United States than the EU25, but Lebanon is an exception. The rates are particularly low for Jordan, Morocco, and Tunisia in the case of the United States, which has signed FTAs with the three countries, and for Lebanon and Morocco in the case of the EU25 (see Table 2.8).

The MENA countries with the highest average tariff rates also have very high tariffs on selected commodities: Morocco has a 172 percent equivalent tariff on livestock, 71 percent on meat, and 140 percent on milled rice. Tunisia protects fruits and vegetables at an average tariff of 137 percent and olive oil at 152 percent. Both countries apply high protection to wheat, 58 and 50 percent, respectively. Fruits and vegetables, olive oil, meat, and cotton are consistently protected across the region (Table 2.9).

Egypt has a more evenly distributed protection pattern and lower rates on agricultural imports. Since the swearing in of a new cabinet in July 2004, Egypt has reduced its tariff bands, annulled import fees and surcharges incompatible with the old General Agreement on Tariffs and Trade (GATT), and made drastic cuts in tariff rates on most imports. These reforms are reflected in Table 2.7, which shows that the AVE in agriculture is less than half the one computed from the 2001 version of the MAcMAP database (IFAD/IFPRI 2007). Egypt also exhibits the highest reform progress ranking, 100, in the World Bank's structural reform indicators, which rank countries with respect to the restrictiveness of their current trade policies and the progress they made in trade reforms over 2000–04 (World Bank 2005).[7] According to these indicators, Lebanon also ranks high, 87, implying that it has made more progress than 87 percent of the world's countries. On the other hand, Morocco and Tunisia are among the 5 percent of countries with the most restrictive

---

[7] The trade reform index measures the change in country rank in a worldwide ranking of simple average tariffs in 2000 and 2004 (World Bank 2005).

Table 2.9 Applied protection rates for selected agricultural sectors, 2004

	Agricultural sectors												
Country	Total agriculture	Livestock	Meat	Dairy	Wheat	Milled rice	Other cereals	Fruits and vegetables	Sugar (raw equivalent)	Sugar (semiprocessed)	Cotton	Olive oil	Fisheries
Djibouti	14	6	23	14	5	5	5	2	33	9	33	10	21
Egypt	8	5	13	6	2	2	3	16	2	4	22	12	5
Jordan	11	6	17	9	0	5	4	29	30	10	10	29	23
Lebanon	9	0	16	11	0	5	1	37	5	5	0	68	5
Morocco	44	172	71	79	58	140	73	43	32	35	29	50	46
Syria	13	2	15	12	1	7	1	26	3	12	30	12	11
Tunisia	50	111	83	53	50	24	9	137	110	18	33	152	40
West Bank and Gaza	n.a.	n.a.	n.a.	n.a.	n.a.	n.a.	n.a.	n.a.	n.a.	n.a.	n.a.	n.a.	n.a.
Rest of MENA	14	8	11	11	5	12	3	7	13	23	29	8	5
EU25	11	6	15	11	15	90	22	9	4	92	1	9	4
United States	8	0	4	37	2	4	1	2	0	54	0	1	0
Rest of world	42	14	27	36	17	51	19	17	11	35	12	6	9

Source: Authors' calculations based on MAcMap-HS6 database for 2004.
Note: EU25, European Union (25 members as of 2004); MENA, Middle East and North Africa; n.a., not applicable.

trade policies, and both rank 49, indicating some progress in trade reforms (World Bank 2005).

Among the protection instruments used by MENA countries, in addition to standard tariffs there are paratariff measures (customs surcharges, additional taxes and surcharges, stamp taxes, statistics taxes, and sales taxes levied on imports) and nontariff barriers (quantitative restrictions and technical requirements). A recent study by Kee, Nicita, and Olarreaga (2006) provides indicators of trade restrictiveness that include measures of both tariff and nontariff barriers for 91 developing and developed countries. One of these authors' main observations is the contribution to the level of trade restrictiveness by nontariff barriers (NTBs): on average, 70 percent in addition to tariffs. In Egypt and Tunisia, NTBs add an additional 50 percent to tariff restrictiveness. In Jordan and Morocco, measures with NTBs are twice the equivalent tariffs indexes, and in Lebanon the contribution of NTBs is higher than that of tariffs (Kee, Nicita, and Olarreaga 2006).

NTBs are usually not addressed by trade liberalization policies, but they represent institutional constraints that would lower the ability of MENA countries to benefit fully from trade liberalization. For example, the elimination of tariffs among the partners in the Greater Arab Free Trade Area (GAFTA) by 2005 has not led to free intraregional trade in practice because of the requirement of import permits for exporting countries to benefit from the trade preferences. These permits are often not granted if it is felt that import-competing industries can be harmed by imports (World Bank 2009).

Trade Agreements

Trade reform in the MENA countries has been motivated in part by the region's participation in multilateral negotiations in the context of the WTO framework and in North-South regional agreements with the E.U. and the United States. Most countries in the region also participate in South-South regional and bilateral integration.

In most cases, regional and bilateral trade accords are driven by political interests. For example, the creation of associations agreements (AAs) within the EMP is seen as a key element in support of peace and stability in the region because these agreements both promote the security of the E.U. and reduce the problem of illegal immigration (McQueen 2002). These agreements are usually limited by lack of coverage (agriculture and services are effectively excluded), lack of depth (technical barriers to trade remain because of differences in regulatory requirements and the need to duplicate testing), and restrictive rules of origin that limit the degree of effective market access (Zarrouk and Zallio 2000; World Bank 2005). Next we briefly cover the main trade agreements pertinent to the region.

The World Trade Organization

In 1947, the GATT was signed with the goal of reducing protectionism and discrimination in international trade. The agreement was followed by a series of rounds of international negotiations to reduce protectionism and other distortions in trade. These agreements have been successful in dramatically reducing the protection on manufactured goods; the average tariff fell from 38 to 4 percent between 1947 and 1994. Because of a reluctance to extend trade liberalization to agriculture, however, the average agricultural tariff remained high, 60 percent in 1994 (Ingco and Nash 2004). The Uruguay Round, signed in 1994, established the WTO to monitor and enforce the trade agreements; it also included the Uruguay Round Agreement on Agriculture (URAA), which attempts to reduce agricultural protection, limit agricultural subsidies, and make trade policy more transparent.

The URAA reduces agricultural protection through the following commitments:

- Quantitative restrictions (such as import quotas) and other NTBs (such as variable levies) were to be converted to tariffs or tariff rate quotas. An exception is import requirements related to sanitary and phytosanitary products; these are regulated by the Agreement on the Application of Sanitary and Phytosanitary Measures, which also came out of the Uruguay Round.
- Each country sets a maximum (bound) tariff rate for each product. In industrialized countries, the bound tariff is the tariff equivalent of the earlier quantitative restrictions.
- Countries agree to reduce the bound tariff rate for each product according to a specific schedule.
- Developing countries are given special and differential treatment. They are allowed to set bound tariffs above the tariff equivalent of the earlier quantitative restrictions. They have a longer schedule (10 years instead of 6 years) to implement the changes, and their tariff reductions are generally two-thirds those required of industrialized countries. The LDCs are exempt from commitments.

In order to reduce farm subsidies, the URAA defines different types of government spending on agriculture, as follows:

- Green box expenditures include those on agricultural research and extension, infrastructure, animal and plant health programs, food safety programs, disaster relief, anti-poverty feeding programs, and farm credit. These are not subject to limits by the URAA.
- Blue box expenditures include payments to farmers, which are combined with supply controls and are based on production or planted area in a base period. These are not subject to limits by the URAA.

- Amber box expenditures include those for subsidies on agricultural inputs such as fertilizers and irrigation, as well as price supports for agricultural production. Under *de minimis* exemptions, product-specific subsidies are permitted if they are less than 5 percent of the value of the output of the commodity, and non-product-specific subsidies are permitted if they are less than 5 percent of the value of all agricultural output. The value of nonexempt amber box expenditures is called the aggregate measurement of support. Some 30 countries declared this support spending and made commitments to reduce it over 1995–2001.

Developing countries are given “special and differential treatment” in that their *de minimis* exemption is 10 percent rather than 5 percent and they had ten years (1995–2005) to reduce their aggregate measurement of support spending. In addition, the LDCs are not required to cap or reduce such support spending.

With the exception of Syria and the West Bank and Gaza, all MENA countries are members of or in the process of accession to the WTO (Table 2.10). As developing countries, the MENA countries that are WTO members have been given greater flexibility under the URAA with regard to cutting their subsidies and lowering their tariffs: the average cuts for all agricultural products are two-thirds the rates of developed countries. The MENA countries in the WTO were also given more time to meet their commit-

Table 2.10 MENA countries’ trade agreements outside the MENA region, 2009

Country	WTO status	European Union	United States	Other
Djibouti	Member (1995)	EBA	AGOA	
Egypt	Member (1995)	EMAA (2004) + ENP	MEFTA TIFA	EFTA (2007)
Jordan	Member (2000)	EMAA (2002) + ENP	MEFTA FTA	EFTA (2002)
Lebanon	Observer	Interim AA (2003) + ENP		EFTA (2007)
Morocco	Member (1995)	EMAA (2000) + ENP	MEFTA FTA	EFTA (2004)
Syria	Nonmember	Initialized		
Tunisia	Member (1995)	EMAA (1998) + ENP	MEFTA TIFA	EFTA (2005/6)
West Bank and Gaza	Nonmember	Interim AA (1997) + ENP		

Sources: WTO website; USTR (2006); European Commission (2009).

Notes: AGOA, African Growth and Opportunity Act; EBA, Everything But Arms initiative; EFTA, European Free Trade Association (Iceland, Lichtenstein, Norway, and Switzerland); EMAA, Euro-Med Association Agreement; ENP, European Neighborhood Policy; MEFTA, Middle East Free Trade Area (includes other members such as Bahrain, Israel, and Oman); TIFA, Trade and Investment Framework Agreement (within MEFTA); WTO, World Trade Organization.

ments: 10 years from 1995 instead of 6. Djibouti, a LDC, is exempt from all URAA commitments.

The Doha Round, launched in 2001, was supposed to reflect both the increased prominence of development concerns in WTO negotiations and the increased participation by developing countries in the trading system (Hoekman, Mattoo, and English 2002). Specifically, the new round was to incorporate the negotiations on agriculture and services that started in 2000. But this new round, originally targeted to conclude by January 2005, has been marked by missed deadlines, failed discussions, and inconclusive conferences (Pal and Prakash 2005). Ministerial meetings in Cancun (2003) and Hong Kong (2005) saw few results in terms of achieving better market access for developing countries. Developing countries continue to complain that they still face exceptionally high tariffs, "tariff peaks," on selected products that are important for their exports (textiles, clothing, fish, and fish products). They are also subject to tariff escalation whereby an importing country protects its processing or manufacturing industries by setting lower duties on imports of raw materials and components and higher duties on finished products (WTO 2005c). This is especially important for MENA countries, which experience high levels of unemployment and would benefit from better market access for their processed products.

According to Hanrahan and Schnepf (2005), in the Doha Round negotiations the U.S. made proposals to do the following:

- eliminate agricultural export subsidies,
- cut amber box ceilings by at least 60 percent,
- limit blue box expenditures to 2.5 percent of the value of production,
- reduce *de minimis* exemptions to 2.5 percent of the value of production,
- cut tariffs by 55-90 percent,
- set maximum agricultural tariffs at 75 percent (100 percent for developing countries), and
- limit "sensitive products" to 1 percent of tariff lines.

In contrast, the E.U. made proposals to do the following:

- eliminate agricultural export subsidies,
- reduce amber box ceilings by 60-70 percent,
- reduce *de minimis* exemptions to 1 percent of the value of production,
- tighten the limits on blue box programs,
- reduce tariffs 35-60 percent,
- limit sensitive products to 8 percent of tariff lines,
- establish new provisions to protect geographic indication labeling,
- implement smaller tariff cuts for developing countries, and
- eliminate tariff cuts for LDCs.

Multilateral trade liberalization as it is negotiated under the WTO can lead to the erosion of trade preferences for developing countries. The negotiated tariff cuts are applied to bound tariffs, which can result in rates that are higher or equal to most favored nation (MFN) applied tariffs, which are greater or equal to preferential tariffs. The difference between the MFN rate and the preferential tariff rates is the preferential margin enjoyed by countries benefiting from trade preferences, and they can vary greatly across countries. This variation in preferential margins across countries combines two effects: a composition effect, which reflects the variation in product specialization and the geographic destination of exports, and a true preferential effect, which reflects on average the preferences from which the countries benefit (Bouët, Fontagné, and Jean 2006).

Decomposing preferential margins for the MENA countries shows that, overall, these countries have positive but modest true preferential margins, meaning that they benefit on average from preferential treatment. On the other hand, they all have negative composition effects, meaning that the countries concentrate on exports on which import tariffs are high globally. This means that for middle-income MENA countries, multilateral trade liberalization is more likely to improve market access than to result in erosion of trade preferences.

These indicators computed for agriculture show a much more diverse situation. Half of the middle-income countries in MENA, Egypt, Jordan, and Lebanon, have a negative apparent margin in agriculture, meaning that they face on average higher tariffs than the world average, but the contribution to this margin is different across these countries. Egypt and Jordan have negative composition effects, meaning that they export agricultural products that are highly protected globally or to countries that are protectors of agriculture. So for these countries global trade liberalization is expected to improve their market access; only in the case of Egypt, which has a positive true preferential margin, could trade liberalization also result in erosion of preferences. All the other countries have negative true preferential margins in agriculture. This is not surprising because agriculture has been left out of most regional agreements, so the countries do not benefit from preferences in agriculture. Morocco and Syria both have enjoyed positive composition effects, meaning that they already export goods on which import duties are low. For these countries, erosion of preferences may not be an issue and market access may not improve much as a result of trade liberalization in agriculture (Bouët 2006).

Increasingly, WTO member countries are forming groups and alliances within the WTO to increase their bargaining power in negotiations. The G20, a group of developing countries that became active at the WTO meeting in

Cancun, favors substantial reforms of developed country agricultural subsidies and protection. Other alliances, such as the G10 and the G33, have made separate proposals (Hanrahan and Schnepf 2005). Djibouti, Egypt, Morocco, and Tunisia belong to the African group and the G90. Egypt and Morocco have submitted their own proposals arguing for the substantial and rapid dismantling of tariffs and the elimination of domestic support on the part of developed countries, more flexibility for developing countries that is consistent with their development needs, and an increased level of technical and financial assistance to net food-importing developing countries and LDCs (WTO 2001a, 2001b).

The Euro-Mediterranean Partnership

The EMP, or Barcelona Process, was signed on November 28, 1995, by the E.U. and 12 Mediterranean partner countries to create a framework for political, economic, cultural, and social ties among the partners.[8] The main instruments of the EMP, European Union–Mediterranean Association Agreements (EMAAs), have replaced the cooperation agreements of the 1970s, which were characterized by nonreciprocal preferences accorded by the E.U. to developing countries (McQueen 2002).

EMAAs are based on reciprocal liberalization for industrial trade and eventual liberalization for agricultural and fisheries products. The measures to liberalize trade in manufactured products are well defined and adhere to fixed timetables. However, with regard to agriculture and services, the measures are less clear and involve no specific schedule (McQueen 2002). Under the EMAAs, at the end of a fixed schedule for phasing out the tariffs on manufactured products the E.U. will benefit from duty-free access to its partners' markets. By contrast, the E.U. has not offered significant new concessions to Mediterranean partner countries in terms of market access for their agricultural exports (Garcia-Alvarez-Coque 2002).

The agreements largely eliminated the tariffs on industrial goods exported from MENA to the E.U., but the benefits were expected to be modest because the E.U. industrial tariffs were already low and because the manufacturing sector in the MENA countries faced difficulties competing in European markets. Furthermore, the agreements opened MENA markets to imports of manufactured goods from the E.U. This may have had negative effects on the Mediterranean countries' terms of trade and on employment in local

---

[8] The E.U. Member States (then 15, today 27) and Mediterranean countries (12 then, 10 after Cyprus and Malta joined the E.U.) agreed on the Barcelona Declaration, which laid the foundations of a new regional relationship. See <http://www.euromedinfo.eu/site.151.content.en.html>. This section is based on Beuchelt (2005), unless otherwise indicated.

industries that are unable to compete with E.U. imports. Finally, reducing import tariffs in the MENA region meant the loss of tariff revenue from the E.U., which during 1994–96 was, as a share of fiscal revenue, 19.2 percent in Algeria, 8 percent in Egypt, 12 percent in Jordan, 29 percent in Lebanon, 10 percent in Morocco, and nearly 16 percent in Tunisia (Garcia-Alvarez-Coque 2002; McQueen 2002). The expected benefits were more likely to come from efficiency gains resulting from eliminating the distortions caused by import barriers. In other words, the countries will gain if the losses to producers and the government are outweighed by the gains to consumers, who face lower prices. Most observers agree, however, that the EMP would be even more beneficial to partner countries if it included agricultural trade liberalization.

One way to overcome the slow progress in agricultural trade liberalization (in part due to the influence of southern European producers who benefit from tariff protection) is to take advantage of seasonal market opportunities for Mediterranean partner countries that do not compete with E.U. production. In a study for the Forum Euro-Méditerranéen des Instituts Economiques Research, Muaz (2004) identified five horticultural crops (green beans, grapes, melons, strawberries, and dates) that could be produced and exported by the Mediterranean partners without competing with E.U. production seasons and could enjoy a comparative advantage. The author predicted that the partner countries could fulfill unsatisfied E.U. demand for these crops during the winter months. The study estimated that the gains to the five countries from expanded grape exports could reach US$227 million, while expanded strawberry exports could generate benefits of US$167 million. The export of dates would have the most positive impact on employment, generating 98,000 jobs in five countries: Egypt, Jordan, Lebanon, Syria, and the West Bank and Gaza.

In the long run, benefits from the EMAAs may also come from the domestic economic reforms they encouraged. Free trade areas have the potential to stimulate modernization and efficiency in the region. With services accounting for around 60 percent of GDP, the MENA countries in the EMP stand to make substantial gains from the gradual opening of the services sector and by attracting new investments. These predictions are tested empirically in a study by Thomas et al. (2008) that estimates the contribution of liberalization of services, trade facilitation, and domestic increased investments on gains from FTAs for the E.U., the United States, and the Maghreb region. The results from a CGE analysis show that when these complementary policies are included, efficiency gains offset terms-of-trade loses in all cases: in particular, Morocco and Tunisia show real income gains of 2 and 5 percent, respectively.

In an effort to revitalize the EMP, the E.U. has extended the relationships existing under the AAs. In particular, ministers have agreed on a Trade

Roadmap to guide their countries until 2010 and beyond. Among other things, the roadmap for agriculture trade, launched in 2005, provided for an increase in the liberalization of agricultural trade, including processed agricultural products and fishery products. The five year program retains the possibility of excluding a limited number of sensitive products given the possible negative impact on countries and sectors. It provides for progressive implementation and asymmetrical liberalization, recognizing the specific characteristics of each partner and development gap between the partner countries on the two sides of the Mediterranean. Finally, the liberalization process must also deal with NTBs to trade (European Commission 2006).

The U.S.-Middle East Free Trade Initiative

The U.S.-Middle East Free Trade Initiative was proposed in May 2003 by the United States to increase trade and investment between Middle Eastern nations and the United States and others in the world economy. For some countries, Algeria, Lebanon, and Yemen, the U.S. efforts have been a first step in expediting their accession to the WTO. As a second step, the United States may enter into Trade and Investment Framework Agreements, as have Algeria, Egypt, Tunisia, and Yemen. Finally, the process may result in FTAs. To date, FTAs are in force with only Bahrain, Jordan, Morocco, and Oman. But these countries represent marginal U.S. trade partners. U.S. exports to the MENA region amount to less than 3 percent of total U.S. exports. Exports to the United States account for 12 percent of total exports for Egypt, 28 percent for Jordan, and 10 percent for Morocco but only 2 percent for Tunisia (MAcMapHS4 database 2004). These agreements are too recent to assess their impact, but the results of Thomas et al. (2008) suggest that Maghreb countries, for example, are not expected to benefit as much from FTAs with the United States as from those with the E.U. because they face initially lower tariffs in the United States than in the E.U.

Both the E.U. and the United States have launched initiatives specific to the poorest countries. Under the Everything But Arms (EBA) initiative, the LDCs have duty-free access to E.U. markets for almost all goods, with three important exceptions: bananas, rice, and sugar.[9] The African Growth and Oppor-

[9] The European Commission committed to end the tariff quota regime for bananas by January 1, 2006. All nonpreferential suppliers would be subject to a MFN tariff, whereas bananas from the African, Caribbean, and Pacific Group of States (as well as bananas originating in the LDCs under the Everything But Arms Initiative) would continue to enter duty free. On January 1, 2006, with the change of the import regime, a reform of the banana Common Market Organization was launched. Honoring the agreement concluded in 2001 with the United States and taking into account the results of arbitrations within the WTO, the E.U. substituted a tariff-only regime for the previous system of import quotas by region of origin. A customs duty of €176 per metric ton

tunity Act (AGOA) allows duty-free access to U.S. markets for countries of Sub-Saharan Africa that meet certain criteria. Within the MENA region, only Djibouti and Yemen qualify under the EBA, while only Djibouti qualifies for preferences under the AGOA.

The Greater Arab Free Trade Area

Intraregional integration in MENA is very limited in spite of several attempts toward that end in the past 50 years (Zarrouk 1998; Khasawneh 2000). Some of the more active regional agreements involving MENA countries are shown in Figure 2.3. Among the various attempts at regional integration, the revived GAFTA (1997) seemed to offer some hope of success where others have failed.[10] The program has more specific commitments and schedules than its earlier version and can be summarized in terms of the following main provisions (Lebanon 2009):

- gradual reduction in tariff rates, fees, and taxes with similar implications at an annual rate of 10 percent;
- exemption of products that are forbidden to be traded for religious, environmental, security, and health reasons from the Execution Program of GAFTA;
- removal of all NTBs;
- application of the "Agricultural Calendar" and agricultural exemptions (each state was allowed to use protectionist measures for at most 10 agricultural products from the agreement during the harvest season, at most 7 months per year, with a maximum of 45 months in total for all listed products); and
- the possibility of exempting a number of industrial products from the Execution Program of GAFTA, subject to certain rules and conditions and based on a decision of the Social and Economic Council of the Arab League.

The full implementation of the free trade area, originally set for January 1, 2007, was fully completed in 2005, at least on paper.

GAFTA is the most comprehensive trade agreement in MENA with respect to markets and products: most Arab countries are either members or potential

now applies uniformly to banana imports, except for a volume of 0.77 million metric tons from the African, Caribbean, and Pacific Group of States that can enter the E.U. duty free (Europa 2006).

[10] At present, 14 members of the Arab League are effective members of the free trade area and comply with total procedures of adhesion. These are Bahrain, Egypt, Iraq, Jordan, Kuwait, Lebanon, Libya, Morocco, Oman, Qatar, Saudi Arabia, Syria, Tunisia, and the United Arab Emirates. The other three include two LDCs, Sudan and Yemen, which have a transitional period for achieving 0 percent customs tariffs by 2010, and the West Bank and Gaza, which is exempt from tariff reductions (Lebanon 2009).

Figure 2.3 Regional agreement for MENA countries

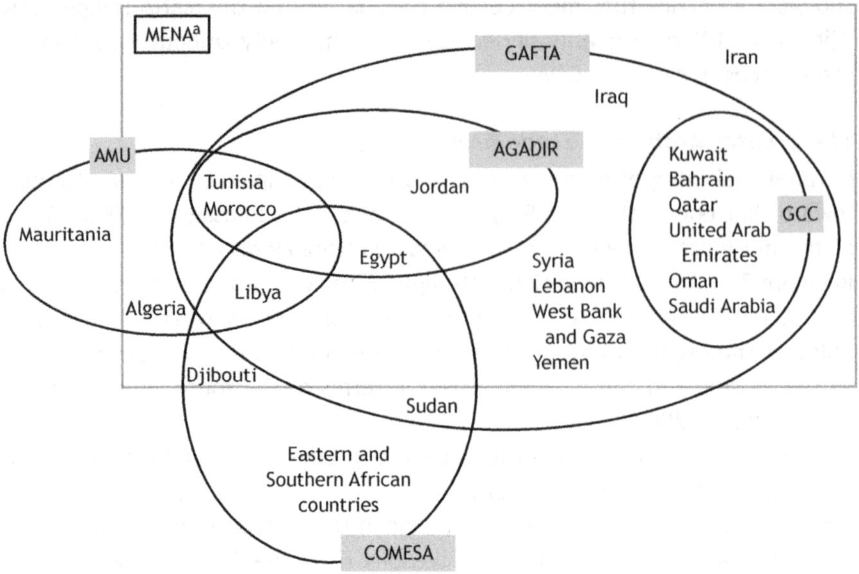

Source: Devised by the authors.
Notes: AGADIR, Agadir Agreement (2004); AMU, Arab Maghreb Union (1989); COMESA, Common Market for Eastern and Southern Africa; GAFTA, Greater Arab Free Trade Area; GCC, Gulf Cooperation Council; MENA, Middle East and North Africa.
[a]Israel is omitted from the MENA region.

future members, and the agreement includes the removal of tariffs and NTBs as well as provisions to liberalize agriculture, a step up from the EMAAs. Still, the agreement suffers from impediments that limit the expected economic benefits. The agreement does not cover service trade and investment or sanitary and phytosanitary standards and technical barriers to trade. Strict rules regarding origins require that over 40 percent of the value added to products be contributed by a GAFTA country, and countries must undergo a cumbersome approval process to qualify. Finally, GAFTA does not seem to have a regulatory body that will enforce the commitments made by its members or settle disputes: countries may change (unilaterally or within the context of bilateral agreements) their agricultural calendars without notification, leaving other members to face the amended schedules at customs (Brunel 2008).

The Agadir Agreement

At the end of the 1990s, four Mediterranean Arab countries—Jordan, Egypt, Morocco, and Tunisia—concluded bilateral FTAs with each other. By 2004 these four countries had signed the Agadir Agreement, and implementation began in March 2007. This agreement is seen as a first step toward the implementation of a larger Pan-Arab FTA and is open to other countries in the region that are in the EMP or have implemented GAFTA.

Provisions of the agreement are as follows:

- full exemption from the custom fees, charges, and other taxes of similar effect on the exchange of agricultural goods, processed agricultural goods, and industrial goods;
- adoption of the Euro-Mediterranean rules of origin, which authorize the cumulation of origins and the free circulation of goods within the Euro-Mediterranean area through the adoption of a circulation certificate;
- commitment to national treatment for the exchanged goods; and
- treatment of the services trade in accordance with the obligations of the WTO member countries.

So, in addition to the liberalization of goods along the lines followed in GAFTA, the agreement makes provisions for the trade liberalization of services within the framework of the General Agreement on Trade in Services. Much as in GAFTA, NTBs are to be completely eliminated as soon as the agreement comes into effect, and exemptions are permitted to protect local production from substantial damage, infant industries, or sectors under reorganization. These exemptions are to be applied restrictively and for a limited period. On issues such as subsidies and antidumping measures, disequilibria in balances of payment, intellectual property rights, and sanitary and phytosanitary measures, the agreement explicitly refers to the WTO regulations. It also calls for the coordination of global and sectoral economic policies and a certain harmonization of the economic legislation and standards of the respective partners (Wippel 2005). The Agadir Agreement is expected to have limited trade effects given the lack of complementarity between the few current members, but it seems to build on provisions that are more compatible with the global environment than is GAFTA, and it may hold more promise once it is extended to the rest of the Arab countries.

Other Regional Agreements

Other regional agreements include those that led to the creation of the Arab Maghreb Union (AMU) and the Gulf Cooperation Council (GCC). The AMU was established in 1989 among all five Maghreb countries: Algeria, Libya, Mauritania, Morocco, and Tunisia. The aim was to establish a customs union by 1995 and an economic common market in 2000. Neither objective was achieved because the AMU was faced with two major obstacles: the requirement of unanimity for all decisions to be implemented and the eruption of political tensions between Algeria and Morocco over the western Sahara, which led to the closing of the border between the two countries in 1994. The agreement generates only limited benefits to its members, and intraregional trade as a share of total trade has remained at its 1989 level, 1.3 percent (Brunel 2008).

The GCC includes six oil-exporting Gulf countries: Bahrain, Kuwait, Oman, Qatar, Saudi Arabia, and the United Arab Emirates. It was created in 1981 and over the next two decades adopted several resolutions relating to the GCC customs union, the common market, development integration, and the economic and monetary union. The common market was launched in 2008, and the establishment of a common currency is planned for 2010. All the GCC members are also members of GAFTA, but their agenda in GCC is much more ambitious, including the implementation of a Common Agricultural Policy of the GCC member states (GCC 2001). These countries are also in the high-income range of the MENA countries, with per capita GDPs greater than US$10,000 in constant 2000 dollars.

Summary

The eight non-oil-exporting MENA countries under consideration in this study share a number of challenges with respect to economic performance in general and agriculture in particular.

Seven of the eight countries are lower-middle-income countries according to the World Bank (Lebanon is classified as a middle-income country). The economic performance of many of the MENA countries has been relatively weak, with growth in real per capita GDP during the 1990s of 2.0 percent per year. Their performance was barely better during 2000–06 (2.2 percent) in spite of the global economic recovery during those years. The economies of these countries have been adversely affected by various conflicts, including the Israeli-Palestinian conflict, the Iraq War, and more recently the Hezbollah-Israeli conflict in Lebanon. Other possible explanations for their slow economic growth include the business climates and relatively high trade barriers in many MENA countries. This slow economic growth means there has been little expansion in formal sector employment, resulting in persistent problems of unemployment, particularly among youth. Nonetheless, strong economic performance in Lebanon (until 2006) and Tunisia suggest that these problems are not insurmountable.

The incidence of poverty is lower on average than in other developing regional groups but varies across countries: Djibouti and the West Bank and Gaza register the highest rates with respect to the US$1-per-day poverty line. The region is also more urbanized than the average developing country. In describing the agricultural trade patterns of the MENA countries, one notices some common patterns. Most of the MENA countries are semiarid, with limited water and arable land per capita, making agricultural production highly dependent on rainfall. Exceptions are Djibouti and Egypt, where virtually all crop production is irrigated. Agricultural exports represent a relatively small share of total exports, exceeding 10 percent only in Syria. All the MENA countries are net food importers. Wheat is a staple food and an important import for many of the MENA countries. It represents more than 15 percent of the agricultural imports of Egypt, Morocco, and Tunisia. Some countries in the region, Morocco and Tunisia, continue to apply relatively high levels of protection for farmers, while the region's average level of protection in agriculture is comparable to that of other groups, including developed countries. The commodities that are the most protected in the region are wheat, sugar, dairy, and livestock products. Finally, the E.U. is the most important trading partner of most of the countries in the region.

The MENA countries have signed a series of multilateral, regional, and bilateral trade agreements. The URAA imposes some commitments on member countries, including the conversion of quantitative restrictions into tariffs or tariff rate quotas, the binding of tariff rates, the reduction of bound tariff rates by an average of 36 percent, and the reduction of trade-distorting measures of support to agriculture by 20 percent, on average. Developing countries have been given more modest targets for tariff rate reductions and more time to comply, while the LDCs are effectively exempted from most commitments under the URAA. The direct impact of these commitments on the MENA countries has been modest. Syria and the West Bank and Gaza are not WTO members, while Djibouti, a LDC, is exempt from most URAA commitments. For the remaining MENA countries, the bound rates are often far above the applied tariff rates, particularly for agricultural products. Thus, commitments to reduce the bound rate have had little effect on the actual level of agricultural protection.

The E.U. has signed EMAAs with five MENA countries as part of the EMP, and three others are in the process of ratification. These EMAAs commit both parties to phase out almost all tariffs on manufactured goods, though the MENA countries have a longer period during which to comply. Until recently, plans to incorporate agriculture had not been supported by firm targets or schedules for agricultural liberalization, but the agricultural roadmap initiated in 2005 can be seen as providing renewed incentives from all concerned to accelerate and intensify the EMAA agenda.

As part of the U.S.-Middle East Free Trade Initiative, the United States has signed bilateral FTAs with Bahrain, Jordan, and Morocco and intermediate agreements with four other MENA countries. The effect of the U.S.-Jordan FTA will be small because Jordan's level of protection is already low and because the amount of U.S.-Jordan trade is small. The effect of the U.S.-Morocco FTA will be larger because Moroccan trade barriers are higher. Of particular importance, Morocco's wheat tariffs will be phased out over 10 years.

Djibouti is the only country in the region that qualifies for preferences under both the EBA and the AGOA.

Among regional agreements, GAFTA and the Agadir Agreement seem to be the most promising. The former has a more extended coverage across markets and products, with special provisions to include agriculture in the liberalization process, but it needs to address such impediments to trade as sanitary and phytosanitary standards, technical barriers to trade, and strict rules of origin. The latter includes provisions that are more compatible with the global environment but would gain from extending its four-country membership to the rest of the Arab countries.

Under the U.S. AGOA, Sub-Saharan African countries that meet certain criteria in terms of human rights, reducing corruption, and combating terrorism will have free access to U.S. markets. Djibouti qualifies, but its exports to the United States are negligible.

A number of bilateral and regional agreements within the MENA region have been signed, but their effectiveness has been limited by the structural similarities of the MENA economies and the granting of exceptions for sensitive products. Nonetheless, a number of MENA countries, most notably Egypt and Tunisia, have reduced their tariff barriers unilaterally in recent years. In other words, trade liberalization does occur outside the context of global, regional, and bilateral trade agreements.

CHAPTER 3

The Impact of Trade Liberalization

The effect of changes in trade policy on a given country can be divided into two components. First, the "terms-of-trade effect" refers to the gains or losses associated with changes in world prices as a result of the policy. Most countries are too small for their trade policy to have a noticeable effect on world prices, but global trade agreements can significantly influence world prices. To the extent that most interventions in agriculture contribute to higher world production and lower imports, they depress world prices of agricultural commodities relative to a world without distortions. Eliminating the distortions could have adverse terms-of-trade effects for net-food-importing countries, including most of the MENA countries, while benefiting net exporters of agriculture. Second, the "efficiency effect" refers to gains or losses associated with removing distortions in the country's own market. Unless there are significant externalities, a reduction in market distortions is generally expected to have positive efficiency effects. In other words, domestic market liberalization, to the extent that it reduces distortions in the economy, will generate more benefits than costs on balance, regardless of what trade partners do (Bouët 2008).

This view of trade liberalization differs considerably from the perspective of trade negotiators, for whom the goal is often to maximize trade liberalization in other countries while minimizing trade liberalization in their own countries. From this view, tariff reductions in one's own country are unfortunate concessions that must be made to achieve tariff reduction in export markets. Because it attempts to maximize exports and minimize imports, this approach is essentially mercantilist. This perspective is often attributed to the greater political influence of producers, who compete with imports, as opposed to consumers, who would gain from lower prices. It also reflects concerns by governments regarding the uncertainty of the benefits and costs associated with trade liberalization and how they are distributed among the various economic actors in the economy. In particular, there is concern that the poorest may bear the cost of adjustment or not benefit as much from the new opportunities.

In this chapter we briefly examine the literature that has addressed these issues in the context of the liberalization options for MENA countries, with a focus on poverty. The chapter is divided into two sections. Reflecting the study's concentration on agriculture, the first section describes the global markets for five agricultural commodities (wheat, rice, sugar, cotton, and dairy products) that are more distorted by import barriers and production subsidies and that are important for MENA countries. This information is important in understanding the direction and size of the terms-of-trade effect associated with trade liberalization. The second section provides a selective review of studies that evaluate the impact of trade liberalization on the MENA countries. These studies consider the impact of multilateral, regional, and bilateral trade liberalization as well as trade reform undertaken within the context of countries' domestic policy agendas.

Global Agricultural Markets

In this section we review policies that distort the global markets for five agricultural commodities (wheat, rice, sugar, cotton, and dairy products), as well as estimates of the impact that global trade liberalization would have on the related prices. As mentioned earlier, this information sheds light on the direction and size of the terms-of-trade effects that global trade liberalization would have on the MENA countries.[1]

Wheat

Wheat provides nearly one-fifth of the world's calorie supply. More than 18 percent of the global demand for wheat is met through international trade, mostly as exports from the OECD countries to developing countries. Although nearly 30 percent of wheat production was stored as a buffer against production shortages in the early 2000s (Mitchell and Mielke 2004), more recent events stemming from the food crisis have brought the global stock level to its lowest in 25 years, 18 percent of wheat production.

The major single-country exporters in descending order of importance are the United States, Canada, Argentina, Australia, and Russia. These five countries account for nearly 60 percent of world wheat exports. The EU25 is a net exporter, accounting for 26 percent of world wheat exports and 22 percent of world wheat imports. Among net importing regions, MENA accounts for 22 percent of world wheat imports. Algeria and Egypt are the world's fourth

[1] Trade flows and AVE rate calculations for the five commodities presented in this section are based on the MAcMap-HS6 database for 2004 unless otherwise indicated (CEPII 2008; Boumellassa, Laborde, and Mitaritonna 2009).

and eighth largest importers, and although Syria contributes only 1 percent of world wheat exports, it is among the 10 largest suppliers.

Since 2000, wheat exporters such as the E.U. and the United States have largely eliminated export subsidies under the URAA, but they continue to provide support to domestic production through programs that include marketing assistance loan payments, direct and countercyclical payments, crop insurance, and surplus disposal programs for export assistance (Vocke, Allen, and Ali 2005). Still, the OECD countries' support for wheat, as measured through single commodity transfers (SCTs), has dropped dramatically, from 45 percent of gross farm receipts for wheat in 1986–88 to under 10 percent in 2004–06 (OECD 2007).

World protection for wheat is high on balance, with AVE rates for MFNs of 34 and 15 percent, respectively.[2] Japan has the highest AVE rate, 96 percent, among the OECD countries, and Morocco and Tunisia have the highest AVE rates, 58 and 50 percent, respectively, among the MENA countries. Among importing countries, bound tariffs can be even higher, especially when these result from tariff rate quotas: for example, in Morocco bound tariffs are 198 percent out-of-quota and 144 percent in-quota. Several kinds of NTBs have also been imposed by governments, such as import licenses, quantity and quality restrictions, state trading requirements, and the imposition of bureaucratic red tape, to control wheat imports (Mitchell and Mielke 2004).

Rice

Rice is one of the most important foodgrains, accounting for 20 percent of caloric intake overall and 29 percent among low-income countries. However, only a small share of rice production (less than 7 percent) is traded internationally (Wailes 2004).

The leading rice exporters in descending order of importance are Thailand, India, the U.S., Pakistan, and Vietnam. Together they account for 76 percent of world rice exports. Nigeria, Iran, Japan, Indonesia, the Philippines, and Senegal are the largest importers among net importing countries. Together they account for 23 percent of world rice imports. Imports to the MENA region are mostly directed to Middle Eastern countries, Saudi Arabia, Iran, and Iraq, which together account for 20 percent of world rice import. Egypt is the 10th-largest exporter of rice, contributing 2 percent of world exports.

Unlike wheat and other commodities, for which most of the distortion in world markets is attributed to the policies of high-income countries, rice is

[2] See details on the definition and computation of AVEs in Chapter 2.

subjected to government support in both developed and developing countries. Among developing-country exporters, Thailand has a loan program that provided a 10 percent support price in 2002. India, the second-largest producer and consumer of rice in the world, has a large government procurement and distribution system, as well as price supports and export subsidies. Vietnam has a largely market-driven rice sector, although state enterprises play an important role in processing and exporting rice. China has a government procurement system that strongly supported the price of rice in the 1990s. After accumulating large stocks in the late 1990s, China has reduced the level of its support and disposed of its stocks. The SCT for rice in OECD countries has come down only marginally, from 80 percent in 1986–88 to 70 percent in 2004–06 (OECD 2007).

Rice is one of the most protected agricultural commodities at the border, with average global AVE and MFN rates of 53 and 76 percent, respectively. Most of the major rice importers use various measures to limit rice imports. Indonesia, the largest rice importer, uses a state trading enterprise, Badan Urusan Logistik, to support the domestic price, assisted by import tariffs of around 17 percent. To comply with the URAA, Japan and the Republic of Korea no longer ban the importation of rice, but they maintain with Taiwan AVEs of 450, 436, and 391 percent, respectively. The E.U. recently switched from a variable levy to an import tariff, resulting in an AVE of 90 percent on average.

Sugar

The market for sugar is also one of the most distorted in the world. The average level of protection for sugar is over 50 percent, the second-highest level after rice.

Brazil is by far the largest sugar exporter, supplying 20 percent of world exports. Russia and the United States are the main importers. The EU25 contributes 27 percent of world export but is a net importer. Among the MENA countries, Algeria, Egypt, and Morocco are the largest importers, and the region as a whole accounts for 10 percent of world imports.

The OECD countries provide transfers to sugar farmers amounting to 45 percent of the commodity gross farm receipts in 2004–06, only 5 percent less than in 1986–88 (OECD 2007). Much of this support was provided by the E.U., Japan, and the United States.

The annual support for sugar producers (largely sugar beet growers) in the E.U. was estimated at US$2.4 billion in 2002. The E.U. also subsidized sugar exports, and the AVE tariff averaged 92 percent in 2004 (see Table 2.8). In 2006 the E.U. reformed its sugar policy, reducing the difference between the in-quota tariffs and the out-of-quota tariffs, a policy that is expected to reduce the preferences of preferential exporters (the African, Caribbean, and

Pacific group of states). The reforms also included reducing the intervention price by 36 percent, introduction of a voluntary buyout scheme for production quotas, and a disallowance of exports of nonquota sugar in order to reduce domestic production and bring export subsidies within the WTO limits (Elbehri, Umstaetter, and Kelch 2008).

Japan uses a specific tariff to limit sugar imports and protect its farmers. The support given to Japanese farmers is roughly US$400 million, and Japan maintains one of the highest AVEs, 190 percent.

As of 2008, the United States continued to maintain a tariff rate quota of 1.3 million tons, restricting imports enough to make domestic prices twice as high as the international price. Forty-two countries are given quotas to export sugar to the United States, but U.S. imports are only a fraction of what the United States would import without import restrictions. The AVE tariff for the United States averaged 54 percent in 2004 (see Table 2.8).

Many developing countries also have high levels of protection for local farmers. China, India, Mexico, the Philippines, Thailand, and Turkey all have high tariff barriers that protect domestic farmers from import competition. A few countries also maintain production quotas or consumer subsidies, but these measures are less common. Egypt and Morocco are two of the few countries that have programs to subsidize sugar for consumers. The MENA countries' AVE tariffs range between 4 and 46 percent for semiprocessed sugar, below the global average. On the other hand, nonprocessed sugar is protected at a much higher rate, especially in Tunisia (see Table 2.8).

Cotton

Cotton prices slid from a peak in 2003 until 2005, but they have steadily rebounded since then, in spite of continued government support for cotton growers that has been estimated at around US$5 billion worldwide by the International Cotton Advisory Committee (ICAC 2006). The long-term trend is affected by competition with synthetic fibers, which increased their share of the textile fiber market from 48 percent in 1995 to 55 percent in 1999. In addition, the global recession of 2001–02 depressed cotton prices further, because textile demand is more income elastic than is the demand for grains (Minot and Daniels 2005).

Of the five largest exporters of cotton, two are net importers, China and Korea. The EU25 supplies 60 percent of world exports, followed by Japan and the United States, which contribute 11 and 4 percent of cotton exports, respectively. In the MENA region, Egypt is the largest producer and consumer but a net exporter.

Eight countries offered direct income and price support to cotton growers. Between 2004/05 and 2005/06, assistance to production decreased in the

United States and the E.U. (Greece and Spain are the only beneficiaries) by 19 and 13 percent, respectively. On the other hand, it doubled in China, which became the largest provider of subsidies to local cotton growers in 2005/06 (ICAC 2006).

Compared to a global average of 8 percent, border protection measured by the AVE is highest in the MENA countries with the exception of Lebanon, ranging from 10 percent in Jordan to 33 percent in Tunisia.

Dairy Products

Dairy products are not, in general, widely traded: only 7 percent of global demand is met through international trade. Virtually all the trade in dairy products involves butter, cheese, and dried milk. Australia, the E.U., and New Zealand are the dominant exporters of dairy products, while Canada, Japan, and the United States are net importers of dairy products.

Dairy markets are highly protected through a combination of import restrictions (such as tariff and tariff rate quotas), consumer subsidies, and, in the case of a few developed countries, income and price supports, export subsidies, and milk production quotas to limit supply. The SCT for milk in 2004–06 is estimated as 28 percent of gross farm receipts for milk, less than half its 1986–88 level (OECD 2007).

The average bound tariffs for dairy remain among the highest for all agricultural commodities (Blayney and Gehlhar 2005). The protection rates presented in Table 2.8 show AVEs of 11 percent for the E.U. and 37 percent for the United States relative to a global rate of 27 percent. Support for dairy producers makes up a large share of the aggregate domestic support in some countries: 84 percent in Canada, 55 percent in the United States, and 12 percent in the E.U. Although export subsidies were reduced under the Agreement on Agriculture, a third to a half of cheese, butter, and dry milk exports continue to be subsidized (Langley, Somwaru, and Normile 2006).

The E.U. dairy program consists of a production quota for milk, import protection, an intervention program that supports the price of skim milk powder and butter, and export refunds that are used to market surplus dairy products. In addition, the E.U. subsidizes the consumption of the butter used in pastries and ice cream and that of skim milk for calf feed (Bailey 2005). The combination of border and domestic policies has resulted in a producer support estimate of 51 percent (Turner 2005).

Japan maintains a complex network of policies that provide high protection for domestic milk production, including supply quotas, environmental subsidies, and a variety of programs that support farm and market infrastructure, extension services, and milk consumption and benefit producers of drinking milk as well as manufacturing milk. The producer support estimate in 2003 for milk represented 77 percent of the value of production, an indication that more than two-thirds of the value of Japanese milk production relies on government interventions either through barriers to imports or through subsidies to farmers (Obara, Dyck, and Stout 2005).

The United States created the Milk Income Loss Contract Program to provide targeted countercyclical payments to small dairy farms. In addition, the United States uses foreign donation programs and casein production subsidies to reduce excessive stocks of surplus skim milk powder (Bailey 2005). The producer support estimate for the U.S. dairy sector is 45 percent, significantly lower than the estimate for Japan and somewhat lower than that for the E.U. (Turner 2005).

Canada's dairy policy is a complex web of interrelated policies, programs, and people nested in a number of private and public institutions under the federal-provincial supply management marketing scheme; it results in a producer support estimate of around 60 percent (Stanbury 2002).

Expected Effects of Trade Liberalization on World Prices

Although studies on the effects of trade liberalization on commodity prices are abundant, they present a broad range of results that have to do with the types of models used, the level of liberalization simulated, and the sectoral and geographical aggregation of the studies. We first present the results from Bouët (2008), which estimates changes in world prices for agricultural commodities using MIRAGE, a multisector, multiregion CGE model. The inclusion of all five commodities in the model provides a consistent base to which we can compare other findings.

The study reports price changes from a stylized full trade liberalization simulation that consists of eliminating import tariffs as well as production and export subsidies.[3] Although the model uses earlier versions of the Global Trade Analysis Project (GTAP) and MAcMap-HS6 databases for 2001, a preliminary experiment was conducted to bring the equivalent tariffs to 2005, the base year for the study.[4] The results represent percentage changes from a baseline without liberalization in 2015. It is estimated that world prices

[3] For a summary of the basic technical specifications of the Modeling International Relationships in Applied General Equilibrium model, see Chapter 7.

[4] In particular, tariffs are adjusted to take into account such changes as the last implementation of the Uruguay Round, the elimination of the Multi-Fibre Arrangement, enlargement of the E.U., implementation of the EBA initiative and the AGOA, and, finally, the accession of China to the WTO (Bouët 2008).

would increase by over 2 percent for sugar, 3 percent for rice, and nearly 5 percent for dairy products.[5] Plant-based fibers (including cotton) and wheat would experience the largest increases, 7 and 11 percent, respectively. Smaller increases are expected if more recent versions of the databases are used, reflecting a more open world in 2004 than in 2001.

Other studies have also shown that the removal of all distortions (full liberalization) would lead to increases in wheat prices ranging from 4.8 percent (FAPRI 2002) to 18.1 percent (USDA 2001). The contribution of domestic support to changes in world prices from trade liberalization is illustrated in FAPRI (2002), which shows that the increase in wheat prices would be 7.6 percent higher under a tariff-removal-only scenario than under a full liberalization scenario, implying that the removal of domestic support policies such as set-aside programs in the E.U. and the United States would result in a substantial increase in production and exports (7.9 percent compared to 5 percent under the tariff-removal-only scenario), dampening the price effect. But USDA (2001) shows that the increase in wheat prices of 12 percent resulting from the elimination of OECD domestic policies, mostly reflecting market price support, would be larger than the price increase of 3.4 percent resulting from the elimination of tariffs.

The results of small increase in rice prices seen in Bouët (2008) are similar to the results found in Tokarick (2005) but much smaller than the USDA (2001) estimates of 10 percent. Wailes (2004), using a partial equilibrium model on a highly disaggregated sector by type of rice, estimates that full trade liberalization would increase the price of long-grain rice by 2 percent, on average, and that of medium- and short-grain rice by a full 90 percent.

Much as in the case of wheat, removal of domestic support policies for sugar and cotton would have a greater impact on price increases than just the removal of border restrictions. The removal of trade restrictions alone for sugar would result in a smaller price increase, 27 percent, than if liberalization included the removal of all production support: the world price would then rise to 48 percent compared to the base scenario (El-Obeid and Beghin 2005). Removing import restrictions on textiles and clothing would independently raise cotton prices by 2 percent (CIE 2001), while removing U.S. cotton subsidies was estimated to have resulted in increasing the world price by 20 percent in 2001/02, and removing all cotton subsidies worldwide would have raised the world price by over 50 percent (ICAC 2002).

---

[5] It should be noted that the price of a commodity in MIRAGE reflects a weighted average of export prices across countries and therefore is highly dependent on the geographic decomposition selected for a particular study. In the case of rice, the inclusion of high-tariff countries, such as Japan and Korea, as single countries instead of as part of a larger region may reverse the direction of world price changes in rice.

Estimates of the price changes in dairy products are larger in Langley, Somwaru, and Normile (2006) than those reported in Bouët (2008). The authors use a partial equilibrium, multiple-commodity, multiple-region model of agricultural trade to simulate the elimination of four policy instruments: (1) production quotas, tariffs, and tariff rate quotas; (2) domestic price supports and producer payments; (3) export subsidies; and (4) subsidies for consumers. According to this model, full trade liberalization in the dairy sector would result in a lower volume of dairy products but higher world prices. The price increases would range from 13 percent for nonfat dry milk to 66 percent for butter.

The Effect of Higher Agricultural Prices on the MENA Countries

The description of the effects of global trade liberalization on agricultural prices in the previous sections indicates that the agricultural prices of the most distorted commodities will rise between 2 percent and 20 percent, with a fair amount of variation across estimates depending on the commodity, the type of model used (general equilibrium versus partial equilibrium), the type of liberalization simulated, and the assumptions built into the model. In this section we examine the potential effect of higher agricultural prices on the eight selected MENA countries and the region as a whole. More specifically, we calculate the welfare cost of a 15 percent increase in agricultural prices by multiplying the value of the net agricultural imports of each country (or the region) by 0.15. The results are expressed in terms of both absolute value and a percentage of GDP. This calculation yields the additional cost to the country to maintain its current pattern of production and consumption. These estimates should be considered an upper limit of the impact of higher agricultural prices for the following reasons:

- The analysis does not take into consideration the fact that farmers and consumers would respond to the higher price by producing more and consuming less of these products, thus reducing the negative welfare impact (or increasing the positive welfare impact) of the higher price.
- The analysis assumes a 15 percent increase in agricultural prices, but most studies show smaller increases in the prices of the main commodities, such as wheat, rice, cotton, sugar, and dairy.
- The markets for the main agricultural commodities are more heavily protected that those for minor crops, so the weighted average of the change in all agricultural prices as a result of trade liberalization is likely to be even lower.
- The analysis does not take into account issues of transmission of price shocks to local producers.

- Furthermore, the analysis examines the terms-of-trade costs associated with trade liberalization outside the MENA region without taking into account the efficiency gains that may result from domestic trade liberalization.

The analysis, shown in Table 3.1, indicates that some MENA countries and the region as a whole were clearly net importers of agricultural commodities over the period 2004–06, with net imports ranging from less than 1 percent of GDP in the case of Syria and Tunisia to nearly 24 percent in the case of Djibouti.

The last two columns of Table 3.1 show the cost of a uniform 15 percent increase in agricultural prices. Not surprisingly, all the countries would have experienced terms-of-trade losses, although the losses would have been under 1 percent of GDP for most countries and the region. The largest losses would have been borne by the poorest countries: Djibouti, more than 3 percent, and the West Bank and Gaza, almost 2 percent. The dollar cost would have ranged from US$3 million in Syria to US$364 million in Egypt. The total loss across all eight countries would have been US$922 million, or 0.4 percent of GDP. The losses for the MENA region as a whole would have been much larger, both in absolute terms (US$4.4 billion) and relative to the size of the regional GDP (0.7 percent). This is because the other MENA countries, most of which are oil exporters, rely to an even greater degree on agricultural

Table 3.1 Impact of higher agricultural prices on MENA countries, 2004-06

Country	GDP	Agricultural imports (millions of US$)	Agricultural exports (millions of US$)	Net agricultural imports (millions of US$)	Net agricultural imports (% of GDP)	Cost of a 15% increase in agricultural prices (millions of US$)	Cost of a 15% increase in agricultural prices (% of GDP)
Djibouti	715	197	28	169	23.6	25	3.5
Egypt	92,005	3,617	1,190	2,427	2.6	364	0.4
Jordan	12,708	1,430	637	794	6.2	119	0.9
Lebanon	21,903	1,393	281	1,112	5.1	167	0.8
Morocco	60,250	2,214	1,213	1,000	1.7	150	0.2
Syria	28,695	1,388	1,368	20	0.1	3	0.0
Tunisia	29,037	1,200	1,063	137	0.5	21	0.1
West Bank and Gaza	3,894	537	53	485	12.4	73	1.9
Eight countries	249,207	11,976	5,833	6,144	2.5	922	0.4
All MENA	645,103	48,449	19,121	29,328	4.5	4,399	0.7

Sources: Authors' calculation based on data from World Bank (2008b) for GDP, FAO (2009a) for agricultural imports and exports.

Notes: GDP, gross domestic product; MENA, Middle East and North Africa.

imports. On the other hand, because oil and food prices often move together (as they did during the 2007-08 commodity boom), the major oil exporters are generally less vulnerable to food price shocks than the eight MENA countries under consideration.

The Effects of Trade Liberalization on the MENA Countries: A Review of the Literature

Numerous studies have tried to quantify the expected benefits of trade liberalization on poverty using such empirical models as spatial and nonspatial partial equilibrium models, gravity equations, and single- and multicountry CGE models (Bouët 2008). In particular, CGE models have become a standard tool of empirical economic analysis, especially when measuring the economywide effects of policy changes and identifying the gainers and losers from trade liberalization (Devarajan and Robinson 2002). Although most CGE analyses show aggregate benefits from trade liberalization, the size and sectoral details of these results vary widely. Bouët (2008) identifies the factors behind these differences:

- *The geographic scope of the liberalization.* The liberalization may be multilateral (global reforms in the context of WTO negotiations), regional, bilateral (between two countries), or unilateral (reforms carried out by a single country in isolation).
- *The sectoral scope of the liberalization.* The liberalization may be limited to the agricultural or industrial sector, or it may encompass all sectors.
- *The type of liberalization.* The study may simulate reductions in tariffs, cuts in export subsidies, lower domestic price supports, reduced input subsidies, or other reforms.
- *The base year.* Generally, the earlier the base year, the higher the base level of protection and domestic support, implying that the effects of full liberalization will be larger.
- *The extent of reform.* Some studies simulate partial liberalization that corresponds to the possible outcomes of trade negotiations, while others simulate full trade liberalization.
- *Whether or not the model includes dynamic effects.* Some models only count the one-time static impact of trade liberalization, while other models attempt to capture its dynamic effects on investment and economic growth. Models that include dynamic gains usually show much larger effects.
- *The assumptions in the model.* All trade models are based on a large number of assumptions about the economy, including the operation of labor markets, investment, the trade balance, and the degree of factor mobility, all of which may affect the results.

As discussed earlier, global trade liberalization generally results in higher international prices for goods subjected to protectionist policies and subsidies. This is because the elimination of import tariffs increases import demand, while the elimination of domestic subsidies reduces supply. Because agricultural products are subject to higher rates of protection and (in developed countries) large domestic support programs, trade liberalization is expected to increase world agricultural prices. This is particularly true for the products for which the markets are more distorted, such as wheat, rice, sugar, cotton, and dairy products. Higher agricultural prices may worsen the terms of trade of net importers of agricultural products (most MENA countries) while benefiting net exporters of agricultural products (for example, Syria in its export of wheat).

The effect of trade liberalization on domestic producer prices depends on changes in international prices as well as changes in the level of agricultural protection within a country. As countries dismantle agricultural trade barriers, imports of formerly protected commodities will expand, pushing down domestic agricultural prices. Thus, multilateral and unilateral trade liberalization generally have opposite effects on domestic agricultural prices.

How will changes in agricultural prices affect household income and poverty? The short-run effect on households will largely depend on the direction of change in agricultural prices and wages, on the structure of household incomes, and on the composition of household spending. In the long run, factors of production are mobile, so the effect on households will depend on changes in factor prices (such as wages and returns on land) and household factor endowments. Economic theory suggests that removing large distortions in the economy will increase aggregate output, but it does not tell us how farm income or poverty will be affected. The relationship between trade liberalization and poverty alleviation is complex and can be addressed only through empirical research, as evidenced in Winters, McCulloch, and McKay (2004), which identifies four paths between trade liberalization and poverty: economic growth and stability, the behavior of households and markets, wages and employment, and the government. In spite of their limitations, we find that CGE models dominate in studies that have attempted to capture some of these links to poverty, in particular through economic growth, the behavior of agricultural markets, and returns to productive factors. When available, household surveys have complemented macroeconomic effects to trace their impact on household welfare and poverty indicators. In the following subsections we provide a selective review of such studies insofar as they address trade liberalization in the MENA countries.

Global Trade Liberalization

Bouët (2008) reviews the findings of 18 studies of global trade liberalization, including studies produced by the U.S. Department of Agriculture, the World

Bank, and individual researchers. All studies show positive estimates of the aggregate benefits of full trade liberalization represented by an increase in world welfare, but the magnitude varies from US$31 billion, or 0.13 percent (Diao, Somwaru, and Roe 2001), to US$1.2 trillion, or 3 percent (Dessus, Fukasaku, and Safadi 1999). All five studies that estimate the impact of liberalization on poverty show that the poverty headcount would decrease, but the findings range from 72 million (Anderson, Martin, and Van der Mensbrugghe 2005) to 440 million (Cline 2004). Only one study shows the impact on world agricultural prices, estimating an increase of 12 percent (Diao, Somwaru, and Roe 2001). So in spite of the large differences in magnitude, there are some common findings across these studies:

- Full trade liberalization would be beneficial in terms of global income as well as reducing global poverty, but some countries, such as Mexico and Malaysia, may be potential losers.
- Most of the benefits of full trade liberalization would come from liberalizing the agricultural sector, precisely because it tends to be the most protected: liberalizing the agricultural sector would contribute between 57 and 69 percent of the total income or welfare gains from trade liberalization (Hoekman, Mattoo, and English 2002; Beghin and Van der Mensbrugghe 2003; Cline 2004; World Bank 2004).
- A large majority of the global benefits of trade liberalization would come from reducing tariffs and other import barriers rather than from reducing producer subsidies. This is not surprising given that import barriers are almost universal across countries, while producer subsidies are concentrated in a few (albeit large) economies: the E.U., Japan, and the United States. Results from five studies estimate that tariff cuts would contribute between 91 and 99 percent of the welfare gains.
- The benefits to developing countries would be larger as a percentage of the incomes of these countries than would be the corresponding benefits to developed countries. All studies show that there would be positive gains to developing countries, but they would range from 8 percent of global welfare gains (Diao, Somwaru, and Roe 2001) to 67 percent (World Bank 2004).
- The benefits to each country or region would derive largely from liberalization carried out within the country or region rather than from opening up the borders of trading partners. In other words, "What you get is what you do."

Most of these studies are based on models that include from 12 to 40 countries and regions, so there are usually results for a region that corresponds roughly to the MENA region. Among the 17 studies reviewed, only one shows that there would be losses from global trade liberalization for the MENA countries on balance, but the magnitude would not exceed 0.1 percent (Anderson, Martin, and Van der Mensbrugghe 2005). This is in spite of the terms-of-trade losses associated with their status as net food importers.

Estimations of global trade liberalization on the welfare of MENA countries are found in Bouët, Mevel, and Orden (2006). The authors use the global CGE model MIRAGE to compare different partial liberalization scenarios of the Doha Round to a full trade liberalization scenario.[6] The study covers 41 regions (including Morocco, Tunisia, and the rest of the MENA region) and 18 sectors, including agricultural sectors (including wheat, rice, sugar, meat, dairy products, and cotton) and manufacturing (textiles and wearing apparel). These sectors are of particular importance to the MENA countries and also represent highly protected commodities (see Chapter 2). Among middle-income countries, Tunisia would gain the most from the partial liberalization scenario, and the gains would be larger the more ambitious the scenario resulting from strong efficiency gains that offset the negative terms-of-trade effect. Full trade liberalization would be better for Tunisia than the less ambitious scenario but not as good as the most ambitious. Morocco would benefit more from partial trade liberalization, where the terms-of-trade losses are offset by efficiency gains, than from full trade liberalization, where they are not.

Full trade liberalization implies larger increases in world agricultural prices, and of course the complete erosion of preferences, than in the ambitious partial liberalization scenario. Current beneficiaries of trade preferences, such as the North African countries in MENA, and agricultural net importers may incur less gain in efficiency but also smaller losses in the terms of trade under partial liberalization than under full trade liberalization. For a net agricultural exporter like Turkey, better market access will unambiguously generate more gains.

Tokarick (2005) uses a partial equilibrium model of 10 agricultural commodities to simulate the effect of trade liberalization. In this model, full trade liberalization would raise world agricultural prices by 2–23 percent. By applying these price increases to agricultural trade patterns, Tokarick estimates the increase in agricultural import costs for each developing country. The cost of agricultural imports would increase US$4 million–US$10 million for most MENA countries. The exception is Djibouti, for which agricultural import costs would decline because of higher prices for its exports.

[6] The Doha Round scenarios are partial liberalization scenarios and call for the elimination of export subsidies; in addition, the more ambitious scenario includes a 20 percent cut in domestic supports, sharper reductions in agricultural tariffs, caps on agricultural tariffs, and fewer exemptions (for sensitive and special products). The study uses the dynamic version of the MIRAGE model and runs the experiment over a 15-year period, from 2005 to 2020. A detailed presentation of the model and the corresponding assumptions is included in Bouët, Mevel, and Orden (2006).

In a separate analysis, Tokarick (2005) compares the effects of trade liberalization in developed countries only, in developing countries only, and in all countries using an 18-region global CGE model. The MENA region would gain more from a *developing-country-only* scenario—US$10.4 billion, or 1.4 percent of GDP—than from a global trade liberalization scenario (US$9 billion, or 1.2 percent of GDP), largely because of eliminating internal distortions. The region would lose US$1.9 billion (0.3 percent of GDP) from a *developed-country-only* trade liberalization scenario. In this last case, the higher agricultural prices would hurt the region because it is a net importer of agricultural goods, and there would be no offsetting efficiency gains from domestic trade liberalization.

A study by Anderson (2003) found similar results. Using a CGE model with 18 regions, the author found that liberalizing agriculture would contribute the larger share (65 percent) of the global benefits from trade liberalization. The author also showed that developing countries would capture, on balance, a larger share of the gains from trade liberalization in developing countries than from liberalization in developed countries. These results confirm that a country or region is more likely to benefit from trade liberalization the stronger its participation in the trade liberalization. Results for MENA show that the region would lose from all trade liberalization scenarios, but the losses would be larger in a developed-countries-only trade liberalization scenario than in a developing-countries-only scenario. In the developed-countries scenarios, the terms-of-trade losses due to agriculture liberalization would be large and would be only partially offset by terms-of-trade gains from the liberalization of manufacturing.

What would be the impact of trade liberalization on the poor, particularly the rural poor? Trade theory suggests that, under certain conditions, trade liberalization should equalize the return to labor across countries because exports of labor-intensive goods from low-wage economies to high-wage economies increase wages in the former and reduce wages in the latter. In practice, the impact of liberalization is more complicated because of variations in protection across sectors, preferential agreements, and the imperfect mobility of factors. In particular, if trade liberalization reduces protection on a labor-intensive sector such as agriculture, agricultural labor demand could decline.

Few of the global trade models are designed to simulate the impact of liberalization on different types of households, but some of them disaggregate the labor market into skilled and unskilled categories, the latter of which contributes wage income to the poor.

Anderson, Martin, and Van der Mensbrugghe (2005) showed that unskilled wages would increase by 4.1 percent for the MENA region, and Bayar et al. (2000) found that trade liberalization in manufactured goods would induce a 1.3 percent increase in wages for unskilled labor in MENA, while broader all-sector trade liberalization would increase unskilled wage rates by 1.4 percent. When unskilled labor is further differentiated between agricultural and nonagricultural labor, it was found that liberalization would lead to different impacts: Bouët (2008) showed that full trade liberalization would increase real income in the MENA region as a whole by 0.9 percent but would have negative effects of -2.3 percent on agriculture unskilled real wages, while unskilled real nonagricultural wages would increase by 1 percent and skilled real wages would increase by 1.3 percent. Bouët, Mevel, and Orden (2006) showed that partial trade liberalization scenarios would be more beneficial to unskilled agricultural labor in Morocco and the MENA region on balance than would full trade liberalization.

These findings suggest that although there is some variation in the estimates, most studies suggest that global trade liberalization would increase unskilled wage rates in MENA, but the gains may not be distributed equally between rural and urban areas.

Regional Trade Liberalization

With the multilateral trade negotiations at a standstill, regional trade agreements have proliferated, leading to a debate over whether they act as a "stumbling block" or a "building block" to multilateral integration. The preferential nature of regional trade agreements implies that such agreements may lead to trade diversion from nonpreferential partners to preferential ones and consequently lead to welfare loss. Another debate has been whether developing countries would benefit more from integration with developed countries (North-South trade) or from regional integration with "similar" countries (South-South trade). These issues are relevant to the MENA countries, which have entered into various trade agreements with the E.U., the United States, and other countries within the region.

Bouët (2006) investigates the consequences of trade strategies for southern Mediterranean (SM) countries (illustrated by a geographical decomposition that includes Morocco, Tunisia, the rest of the Middle East, and the rest of North Africa). The macroeconomic impacts of a South-South regional agreement that eliminates all tariff barriers among these four regions and Turkey are compared with the impacts of a North-South agreement whereby SM countries negotiate separately a free trade agreement with the E.U. in a "hub-and-spokes" structure.

The main beneficiaries from a South-South liberalization scenario would be Turkey and Tunisia, where welfare would increase by 0.8 and 0.7 percent, respectively. The rest of North Africa, excluding Morocco and Tunisia, would gain, on average, by nearly 2 percent. Morocco and the rest of the Middle

East would not register noticeable changes. The sectoral results suggest that the production of dairy and other food products in Morocco and Tunisia would increase slightly and Tunisia would increase its production of rice and other grains, but wheat production would suffer in both Morocco and Tunisia. A South-South agreement would increase Moroccan exports by 2.5 percent, but in Tunisia exports would increase by 8 percent. The agreement implies that there would be trade diversion for Morocco: imports of rice, wheat, fruits and vegetables, and meat from Europe would be partially replaced by imports from countries in the region.

A North-South agreement would have a larger impact on exports, which would increase by more than 40 percent in Morocco and Tunisia. The welfare effects would also be larger, but although they would lead to gains of 1.3 percent in Tunisia, Morocco and the rest of North Africa would show a small decline in welfare of less than 1 percent. When these regional agreements are compared to multilateral full trade liberalization, the results indicate that the latter strategy would provide a more efficient outcome for south Mediterranean countries. All four regions would experience welfare gains, ranging from 0.4 percent in the rest of the Middle East to 2.3 percent in Tunisia. This would allow for a large reduction in domestic distortions and stimulate GDP growth, especially in Morocco, Tunisia, and the other countries of the southern Mediterranean zone. The efficiency gains would offset the deterioration in the terms of trade linked to an augmentation of world agricultural prices, which would be detrimental to most of these countries.

To test whether regional trade agreements represent desirable steps toward multilateral liberalization, Bouët (2006) built an index of structural congruence that measures the similarity of sectoral changes between two alternative scenarios. His results show that a South-South agreement would not move the economies toward a multilateral trade liberalization structure. For some sectors, it would direct the economies in the opposite direction. On the other hand, integration with the E.U. would be a better "first step" toward integration into the global economy.

The superiority of the North-South trade alternative finds evidence in Dennis (2006a) in the context of GAFTA.[7] The author compared the benefits from two integration scenarios: GAFTA and a combination of GAFTA-E.U. The MENA region includes Morocco, Tunisia, the rest of North Africa, and the rest of the Middle East. In the GAFTA simulation, all tariffs between the four MENA zones were set to zero. In the GAFTA-E.U. simulation, all tariffs between MENA zones were set to zero, all industrial tariffs between MENA zones and

[7] For details of the GAFTA agreement, see Chapter 2.

the E.U. were set to zero, and all agricultural tariffs between MENA zones and the E.U. were reduced by 50 percent. The MENA region would benefit twice as much from the GAFTA-E.U. than from GAFTA alone, but the gains would be small, 0.2 and 0.1 percent of GDP, respectively. Dennis (2006a) argued that intra-MENA trade is hampered by burdensome customs procedures, poor infrastructure, and regulations that impede efficient transportation services. Examples include regulations favoring national airlines, restrictions on private transportation companies, restrictions on foreign truck drivers, regulations prohibiting backhaul freight, and various fees and taxes. For example, Hoekman and Konan (2005) estimated that the removal of NTBs would lead to an increase in welfare more than twice as large as that resulting from tariff liberalization. In an earlier study on Egypt, Konan and Maskus (1997) found that the elimination of regulatory barriers and red-tape measures would result in larger welfare gains from an FTA. Dennis (2006a) simulated the role of trade facilitation in the context of GAFTA and E.U.-GAFTA trade agreements, finding that the welfare benefits would increase four- or fivefold if trade facilitation were included.

The studies just summarized point to the negative impact of these trade agreements on unskilled wage rates. Bouët (2006) found that the South-South scenario would lead to negative but small changes in unskilled wage rates in agriculture in Morocco and Tunisia, but the rest of North Africa would see an increase of nearly 2 percent. The North-South scenario would benefit unskilled wage rates only in Tunisia but would lead to negative changes in Morocco and the rest of the MENA region. In another study, Hoekman and Konan (2005) found that GAFTA would increase wage rates in Egypt by 0.7 percent, considerably less than the wage rate increase associated with an E.U. partnership agreement (1.3 percent) and from global liberalization (1.98 percent).

Bilateral Trade Liberalization

The impact of the bilateral trade liberalization of MENA countries with the E.U. has been extensively researched in the context of the EMAAs. As in the global context, the variety of studies has led to results that have been dependent on the specificities of the models, the agreements, and the countries beneficiary to these agreements. These features are summarized in a comprehensive and critical survey of the literature, Kuiper (2004), which examines the ways in which 11 selected studies have modeled the EMAAs. The survey points to some of the limitations of the CGE models used in addressing the issues pertinent to the MENA region, among others—for example, the issues of unemployment, reliance on remittances, and the role of the state in production. Realizing these limitations, we review the evidence on selected outcomes of the bilateral agreements and attempt to draw some conclusions on the potential impact of such agreements on welfare and trade.

We summarize the findings of a few studies reviewed in Augier and Gasiorek (2001) in the context of the EMAAs. The results for Egypt obtained by Konan and Maskus (1997, 2000) are interesting because they highlight the role of agriculture and complementary policies in the effects of trade liberalization. For example, Cockburn, Decaluwé, and Costi (1998) generated welfare gains for Egypt ranging from 0.2 and 0.89 percent of GDP from trade liberalization with the E.U., but when tariff reductions were extended to agriculture and services and accompanied by changes such as market access and improved harmonization of standards, the welfare gains increased to 13–21 percent of GDP (Hoekman and Konan 1998). These large effects are also attributed to the inclusion in the latter model of dynamic effects that account for increases in investment and productivity growth.

From their review Augier and Gasiorek (2001) concluded that in most of these studies, the static welfare gains that would result from FTAs between southern Mediterranean countries and the E.U. are usually found to be very small. One reason is that these agreements would result in a large asymmetric reduction in tariffs on the part of the southern Mediterranean countries that grant the E.U. better access to their markets, while the southern Mediterranean countries already have access to the E.U. The study of Augier and Gasiorek (2001) generated much larger results using a CGE model to simulate a full elimination of tariffs by southern Mediterranean economies on imports from the E.U. (leaving external tariffs on imports from the rest of the world unchanged, with the exception of Turkey, which would adopt the E.U.'s common external tariffs). They found that Egypt, Morocco, and Tunisia would experience welfare gains of 6 percent, 13 percent, and 18 percent, respectively. In all three countries, the trade creation effects would be much larger than the trade diversion effects. The cheaper and more abundant imports would generate these gains, though all sectors in these economies would experience a decline in production.

There was also evidence that Egypt, Morocco, and Tunisia would experience augmented gains if other changes were realized, such as improved productivity through the pro-competitive effect of trade and greater integration with the E.U. markets resulting from a harmonization of standards and regulations. Under these conditions, the welfare effects would reach 18 percent, 24 percent, and 33 percent for Egypt, Morocco, and Tunisia, respectively. It seems that allowing changes in the exchange rate would reduce the welfare gains for Morocco and Tunisia but improve the gains for Egypt. Finally, in agreement with Bouët (2006), Augier and Gasiorek (2001) found that multilateral trade liberalization would generate the largest results, while regional (intra-southern Mediterranean) trade liberalization would generate positive but small welfare gains.

FTAs with the E.U. were also analyzed within the context of a single country model by Chemingui and Dessus (2001), who examined the impact of various options of trade liberalization for Tunisia. The model of the Tunisian economy includes 57 sectors and five types of labor. The model is dynamic and tests five liberalization scenarios, two that eliminate unitarily barriers to trade by Tunisia, one that reduces E.U. preferential and maximum tariffs with regard to Tunisia exports, and one that combines all three scenarios. The authors found that unilateral liberalization of the agricultural sector would not necessarily improve the income of rural households (they actually showed decreases in welfare of 1.1 and 3.2 percent), results that the authors attribute to the limited capacity of the Tunisian agriculture for reallocation and adjustment due to its dependence on tree crops. On the other hand, access to E.U. markets without any reduction in Tunisian import barriers (the third scenario) would result in higher returns to farm families (2.7 percent) and agricultural workers.

Chaherli (2002) conducted an extensive review of 17 studies of trade liberalization in the MENA region that were carried out between 1997 and 2001. The level of the impact (measured by welfare gains as a share of GDP) tends to be higher from multilateral trade liberalization scenarios than from bilateral scenarios (mostly illustrated by the implementation of FTAs between MENA countries and the E.U.). Consistent with the results found by Augier and Gasiorek (2001), other studies emphasize the superiority of multilateral trade liberalization over bilateral or regional liberalization. Thus, Egypt registers welfare gains of 4 percent of GDP from multilateral trade liberalization, while the implementation of its FTA with the E.U. adds less than 0.5 percent (Bayar 2001). Similar results have been found for Jordan (Hosoe 2001) and Morocco (Rutherford, Rutström, and Tarr 1997).

Only a few studies reviewed by Chaherli (2002) focus on changes in production. As a result of lower tariffs in agriculture, the production of import-substituting products such as field crops and livestock will tend to suffer, while export-oriented sectors such as fruits and vegetables will gain from the increase in market access. For example, Lorca and Vicens (2000) estimated that expanding the FTAs with the E.U. to agricultural products may stimulate an increase in exports of 53 percent in fruits and 20 percent in vegetables in Morocco, a 28 percent increase in fruits and vegetables in Egypt, and an 80 percent increase in olive oil exports in Tunisia. In Egypt and Morocco, sugar is another winner in that production will increase by 16 and 13 percent, respectively.

These findings are supported by Bunte (2005), who simulated the effect of the elimination by the E.U. of import tariffs on fruits and vegetables from the MENA region. This model projects a substantial increase in exports of fruits and vegetables from MENA to the E.U., along with lower consumer prices in the E.U. Morocco and Turkey will gain the most, while European horticultural producers such as France and Spain will lose.

Finally, Radwan and Reiffers (2003) presented results from a CGE analysis of agricultural trade liberalization scenarios in the context of the EMAAs. The study focused on Turkey and four MENA countries, Algeria, Egypt, Morocco, and Tunisia, and considered three alternative scenarios simulated over a five-year period, as follows:

- unilateral liberalization by the E.U.,
- reciprocal bilateral liberalization between the E.U. and partner countries (with or without progress in multilateral liberalization in agriculture), and
- asymmetrical bilateral liberalization whereby the E.U. liberalizes but the Mediterranean partner countries do not liberalize on all products and liberalize at a slower pace.

The results from the first scenario (unilateral liberalization by the E.U.) show positive but modest growth in production, exports, and employment. Only exportable products (essentially fruits and vegetables) will gain from this scenario, but for poor farmers and traditional agriculture, the situation does not change and may even become worse now that they will have to compete for resources and subsidies (such as water) with favored exports.

The second scenario tested the effects of a reciprocal bilateral liberalization between the E.U. and Mediterranean partner countries with and without agriculture liberalization in a multilateral context (under either the European Commission or the U.S. proposal).[8] Domestic trade liberalization would reduce the local prices for formerly protected agricultural commodities. On the other hand, multilateral liberalization of agricultural trade would result in higher international prices: for example, a 10.5 percent increase for wheat, 19.7 percent for maize, and nearly 7 percent for sugar.[9] The net effect would be a decrease in domestic prices but by a smaller magnitude than would occur without the multilateral liberalization of agriculture. The results would be particularly large for processed food preparations contain-

[8] These proposals are older than the ones referenced in Bouët, Mevel, and Orden (2006): The E.U. proposed to decrease import tariffs by 36 percent, exports subsidies by 45 percent, and trade-distorting domestic support by 55 percent; the United States proposed to reduce, in five years, the protection affecting trade to 5 percent of the total value of domestic production.
[9] The U.S. proposal yields slightly higher results.

ing fruits; these would sustain a price decrease of more than 40 percent, while the prices of sugar would fall by 14 percent and those of wheat by nearly 7 percent (Radwan and Reiffers 2003, 20). The net effect of this scenario suggests that tariff dismantling by Mediterranean partner countries has a larger effect than the removal of protection by OECD countries. The negative effects of a net price decrease on rural producers and therefore rural income will be greater than the positive effects on urban consumers and exporters, biasing the distribution of gains from liberalization against the more vulnerable population group. Radwan and Reiffers (2003) concluded that the liberalization should be reciprocal but gradual, starting with the reduction of domestic support by the E.U., followed by tariff reduction by Mediterranean partner countries.

The third scenario reproduces the second scenario, but, by taking into account the varying capacities to bear the changes among countries in the region, it introduces an asymmetrical implementation process whereby the E.U. would liberalize while Mediterranean partner countries would liberalize partially and at a slower rate. It also provides for structural instruments similar to those used by the Fonds Européens d'Orientation et de Garantie Agricole,[10] which remove price supports, include support for agricultural modernization, upgrade infrastructure and institutions, and support diversification in rural activities. If the implementation of these structural tools is successful, it could reduce (if not eliminate) the list of losers among the Mediterranean partner countries. The main difficulties will be to avoid rent-seeking behavior among farmers in Mediterranean partner countries and to target the support toward the sectors in rural areas that have been the most affected by the liberalization process. This last scenario seems to simulate the recent developments in the EMAAs under the Europeans Neighborhood Policy and the adoption of new action plans forging an E.U. agricultural roadmap with regard to their Mediterranean partners (see Chapter 2 for a brief summary of the EMAAs).

Unilateral Trade Liberalization

Several of the studies on bilateral trade liberalization we have reviewed have also considered the impact of unilateral trade liberalization. For example, in Tunisia unilateral trade reforms were found to be detrimental to rural households (Chemingui and Dessus 2001). These studies are usually based on country CGEs and can sometimes provide more information on the distributional effects of liberalization.

Feraboli and Trimborn (2008) used a dynamic CGE model of Jordan augmented by heterogeneous households from a household survey to examine the

[10] The Fonds Européens d'Orientation et de Garantie Agricole (European Agricultural Guidance and Guarantee Funds) have been established within the overall E.U. budget to finance the common agricultural policy.

effect of the E.U.-Jordan Association Agreement. The agreement provides for the gradual reduction of import duties on imports of E.U. industrial and agricultural products into Jordan over a period of 12 years according to a tariff reduction schedule that started in 2002 (the year of implementation) and will end in 2012. Reduction in agriculture tariffs will not start until 2006 and will proceed at a much slower rate than that for nonagricultural tariffs (Feraboli and Trimborn 2008, Table 1). As tariffs are reduced, government revenue will be reduced, which will lead in the short run to a reduction of total government transfers to households, made endogenous in the model, although the share each household will receive is fixed. The reduction in tariffs will affect the aggregate economy through decreases in the prices of imported goods (investment and consumption goods), the creation of higher incentives for investment, faster capital accumulation, and increases in output in the long run. So in the long run, the drop in government transfers to households will be partially offset by the expansion of the tax base. What the net effect will be on household income composed of labor, capital, and transfers is ambiguous because trade liberalization affects each source of income differently and each household group relies differently on the various kinds of income. In this study it appears that the net effect on welfare will be positive for most household groups and slightly higher for the poorest one. The highest income group, though, will be worse off. If the value-added tax is increased by 10 percent, the effect of trade liberalization will still be positive for households but the increase will be smaller. Although transfers will remain even higher than in the benchmark year, household welfare will be lower relative to the previous simulation due to a reduction in aggregate income (through lower investment). It has been found that trade liberalization will increase the gap in income, especially in the long run. Although low-income households will overcompensate for losses in transfers by an increase in labor income, rich households' capital income will increase much more in the long run due to an increase in investment incentives.

Lofgren (1999) analyzed the short-run equilibrium effects of alternative scenarios of reduced protection for agriculture and industry in Morocco. Because the agricultural sector represents the major income source for the poor rural population, it is also the most strongly protected in the country. The results show that lowering agricultural protection would generate aggregate welfare gains, though a significant part of the disadvantaged rural population would lose out substantially. The tariff cut would boost agricultural imports and reduce the demand, prices, and factor returns in domestic agriculture. The welfare changes for any household group primarily depend on the combined effects of changes in the prices of factors the group controls and the commodities it consumes. The incomes and resources of agricultural labor would decline significantly, especially in rainfed areas, because these depend most heavily on livestock production, which would be the best-protected sector initially. Agricultural wages would decline 14 percent if agricultural labor could not switch to nonagricultural activities. The authors assume that if labor could move among sectors, agricultural wages would decline by only 6 percent. Upgrading the skill level of the rural labor force by assuming some productivity increase would result in higher unskilled wage rates, thus benefiting the poor.

Lofgren, El-Said, and Robinson (1999) used a dynamically recursive general equilibrium model for Morocco to examine options for unilateral trade liberalization that would go beyond the terms of the EMAA. The results from unilateral trade liberalization scenarios beyond the implementation of the EMAA indicate that tariff unification (tariffs ranging between 3 and 98 percent set at 29 percent across sectors) would have small aggregate effects, while the removal of NTBs would have positive aggregate effects but favor skilled labor and capital. On average, real household income per capita would expand but in favor of urban households and nonpoor households in rural areas. Combining trade liberalization with at least one complementary domestic policy would result in a win-win outcome whereby the welfare of all household groups would increase much more rapidly than if status quo policies were followed.[11]

A third study of Morocco combined a CGE model with household survey data to obtain a detailed picture of the distributional effect of unilateral trade liberalization. Ravallion and Lokshin (2004) measured the short-term welfare impacts of the price changes attributed to removing the country's protection on cereals (they estimated cereal protection at 100 percent during 1997-98).[12] The price changes were estimated from a CGE model simulating various levels of tariff reduction (10, 30, 50, and 100 percent) for cereals and the removal of the government intervention in subsidizing cereal prices among consumers. Prices in cereals would decrease by nearly 27 percent for consumers and by around 24 percent for producers. Producer prices for fresh vegetables would also decrease, by less than 10 percent, while the prices of other agricultural products (fruits, dairy products and eggs, meat, and sugar) would decrease at the lower levels of tariff reductions on imported cereals but increase at the higher levels. In aggregate, the results show that there

---

[11] Complementary policies include (1) transfers to owners of rainfed agricultural resources (land and pasture), in each period fully compensating for losses from trade liberalization, and (2) augmentation of the stock of rural skilled labor by 5 percent in each period, with additional labor coming from the unskilled labor of rural households.

[12] The MFN tariff on cereals reported in WTO (2003) is 20.6 percent (simple average) with a range of 2.5-53.5 percent.

would be a small but negative impact on mean household consumption and a small increase in inequality, as in the case of Jordan in the study by Feraboli and Trimborn (2008). Heterogeneity in consumption behavior and in income sources has diverse impacts on households. For example, rural households have twice the budget share for cereals as urban households; also, the share of income from production accounts for a quarter of consumption in urban areas (the rest is labor earnings, transfers, and savings), while the share is 87 percent in rural areas, and about one-third of this is from cereals.

The household survey also shows that, at the national level, 16 percent of households are net producers of cereals, while in rural areas the proportion is 36 percent. The majority of the rural poor produce cereals for home consumption, and over one-third of the poorest quintile tend to produce more than they consume. These households will be worse off from a fall in cereal prices. At the national level, production losses outweigh consumption gains and the poverty rate increases overall, but the impact is felt entirely in rural areas, where losses to net producers of cereals outweigh the gains to net consumers among the poor (Ravallion and Lokshin 2004).

In a recent study of labor markets in Morocco and Tunisia, Dennis (2006b) argued that the ability of MENA countries to respond to trade liberalization is impeded by regulations that make factor markets inflexible. He cites the legal constraints on dismissing workers, the high level of legally mandated severance pay, the restrictions on the use of temporary labor, the high minimum capital requirements for starting a new business, and lengthy bankruptcy procedures. He found that Morocco and Tunisia have the least flexible labor markets among the 11 developing countries studied. To examine this issue Dennis used a CGE model to simulate the impact of a unilateral 50 percent reduction in import barriers in Morocco and Tunisia with high and low factor market flexibility. Factor market flexibility is simulated by making capital mobile and by doubling the elasticity of substitution between factors of production. Dennis found that flexible factor markets would increase the welfare gains from unilateral trade liberalization by a factor of three in Morocco and by a factor of six in Tunisia.

Summary

Most studies of global trade liberalization indicate that reducing agricultural subsidies and removing import barriers will increase world agricultural prices. The prices of agricultural commodities for which the markets are distorted (including wheat, rice, sugar, and dairy) would rise between 2 and 20 percent, with higher estimates in the case of sugar.

Almost all the MENA countries are net agricultural importers, so there is clearly some basis for concern that these countries will lose as a result of global trade liberalization. Our analysis confirms that the terms-of-trade effect of a 15 percent increase in all world agricultural prices for the MENA countries would be, on balance, US$4.3 billion, or 0.7 percent of the regional GDP. The actual impact of trade liberalization, however, is likely to be more positive for three reasons. First, this analysis does not take into account the response by producers and consumers. Second, it assumes that the price increase will be the same for all commodities. For example, Egypt could gain from global liberalization if the price of cotton (which it exports) increases more than the price of wheat (which it imports). And third, the analysis estimates the terms-of-trade effect of trade liberalization, but it does not include the efficiency gains associated with reducing distortions in domestic agricultural markets. Most studies of trade liberalization suggest that the efficiency effects will be larger than the terms-of-trade effects.

Several dozen studies have been undertaken to examine the macroeconomic impact of various types of trade liberalization in MENA. Most of these studies use CGE models to simulate the effect of alternative trade policies. The results of these studies are summarized as follows:

- Multilateral trade liberalization will generally result in net gains to countries in the region; real GDP will expand by 1–3 percent.
- The benefits of trade liberalization to a given country will depend largely on the degree of domestic liberalization carried out by the country. The effects from unilateral reforms will be larger for a specific country than those resulting from changes in trade policy in other countries. This confirms this well-known concept in studies of trade liberalization: what you do determines what you get.
- The benefits of multilateral trade liberalization will generally be greater than the benefits of bilateral trade liberalization with the E.U. or the United States and greater than the benefits of regional trade agreements within MENA.
- Trade liberalization in the MENA region will usually result in lower production and more imports of wheat but in higher production and more exports of fruits and vegetables.
- Complementary policies such as improved productivity and harmonization of standards may greatly improve the gains from trade liberalization in regional and bilateral agreements.

The distributional effects of trade liberalization are dependent on a variety of complex factors. Although, on balance, there is evidence that trade liberalization will benefit the poor, at the country level it remains an empirical matter.

CHAPTER 4

Agriculture, Trade, and Poverty in Egypt

Background

With 74 million people, Egypt is the most populous country in the MENA region. The per capita GDP of Egypt in 2006 was US$1,724 (measured in constant 2000 dollars), which makes it a lower-middle-income country in the World Bank classification system. Real per capita GDP growth averaged 2.9 percent in the 1980s, 2.4 percent in the 1990s, and 2.5 percent in 2000-06 (World Bank 2008b).

Although the contribution from the agricultural sector has declined in recent decades, the sector still plays an important role in the Egyptian economy. It accounts for about 14 percent of GDP, down from around 20 percent in the early 1980s. Agriculture also accounts for about 30 percent of total employment and 3 percent of exports. Domestic agriculture contributes to the overall food needs of the country and provides domestic industry with raw materials.

In the 1970s, Egypt's agricultural policy was characterized by heavy government intervention in production, trade, and prices. Most crops were subject to compulsory sales to state enterprises at fixed prices. The agricultural sector was highly taxed relative to other sectors of the economy. These policies had an adverse effect on agricultural development and food security. Starting in 1987, the government of President Hosni Mubarak launched a series of agricultural policy reforms to liberalize markets (Ender 2000).

As a result of broader economic reforms in the 1990s, the private sector emerged with a more important role in the economy. At the same time, the economy remained inward looking, because high tariff rates and an overvalued currency made the domestic market more attractive for Egyptian business (El-Laithy, Lokshin, and Banerji 2003). Egypt's large merchandise trade deficit is sustained by foreign aid, revenue from tourism, and remittances from Egyptians working overseas, particularly in Europe and the Gulf countries.

The Agricultural Sector

Agricultural Production

The Nile River Valley has been cultivated for at least 8,000 years, and it continues to be the focus of almost all agriculture in Egypt. About 90 percent of the agricultural area is concentrated in the Nile Delta, and most of the remainder falls within a few kilometers of the Nile and along the Mediterranean. Egypt is unusual in the MENA region in that 100 percent of its crop production is irrigated.[1] As a result, crop yields in Egypt are relatively stable and are not subject to weather-related shocks as in most countries in the region. About 97 percent of the area of Egypt is uncultivated due to the extremely limited rainfall (World Bank 2008b).

The amount of arable land per capita is just 0.04 hectares, one of the lowest figures in the world. However, the combination of warm weather, fertile soil, and irrigation allows Egyptian farmers to achieve high yields and practice multiple cropping. Also, Egypt has a relatively large number of tractors (3.9 per 100 hectare of cropland), most of which are used on a rental basis. Fertilizer use is the highest among the MENA countries, at over 700 kilograms per hectare of arable land.

In 1960 Egypt was self-sufficient in all basic food commodities with the exception of wheat, for which the country supplied 70 percent of it own needs. The self-sufficiency ratio declined dramatically for most products during the 1970s and 1980s due to a combination of rapid population growth and rising foreign currency inflows from exports (including cotton and textile products), remittances, and foreign aid. The rising dependence on imported food is a major concern among policymakers and has resulted in various attempts to restrict food imports and stimulate domestic production.

Because of irrigation, farmers can produce two or three harvests per year. In the summer growing season, the main crops are maize, rice, and cotton, while in the winter wheat, berseem (Egyptian clover), and broad beans are grown. The *nili* (autumn) season is used for growing potatoes and vegetables. Grains account for almost half (47 percent) of the cultivated area, of which wheat is the most important, followed by maize and rice. Berseem, used for animal fodder, accounts for 17 percent of the planted area, while vegetables represent 12 percent and fruit 8 percent (Siam 2005).

Domestic resource cost analysis indicates that Egypt has a strong comparative advantage in the production of cotton, wheat, and fruits and vegetables and is moderately competitive in several less water-intensive crops such as

[1] A large share of crop production in Djibouti is produced under irrigation, but no estimates are available.

maize, beans, and potatoes. It has a comparative disadvantage in producing water-intensive crops such as rice and sugarcane (Madcour and Abou Zeid 1996).

Agricultural Trade Patterns

Egypt's total imports were US$29 billion in 2004–06, of which agricultural imports represented US$4 billion, or one-eighth of the total. As in many countries in the region, wheat is the most important agricultural import (see Table 2.4). Over 2004–06, Egypt imported an average of US$873 million in wheat per year, making it the largest wheat importer in the world. Wheat is a politically sensitive commodity, because bread is the main staple food. Wheat production and marketing were strictly controlled until market reforms in the 1980s and 1990s. Agricultural input and output markets have been liberalized to some degree, but the government maintains subsidies on some types of bread and attempts to boost domestic production by restricting imports of wheat and flour. Egyptian wheat production is able to cover about 55–60 percent of domestic requirements. The second largest agricultural import is maize. Maize demand is rising due to its use as animal feed.

In 2004–06, Egypt's average total export revenue was almost US$27 billion per year (World Bank 2008b),[2] about US$2 billion of which was earned from petroleum oil exports.[3] Agricultural exports were US$1.2 billion, about 4 percent of the total and 11 percent of the merchandise exports. Fruits and vegetables are the most important category of agricultural exports, accounting for 31 percent of the total. In this category the main exports are potatoes, oranges, onions, and tomatoes, exported mainly to the E.U. Rice and cotton each represent 22–24 percent of agricultural exports. Egyptian cotton has long fibers and is considered some of the best in the world, fetching high prices on international markets. The average annual value of cotton exports was US$265 million in 2004–06, although cotton revenue has been quite volatile. Cotton is also used in Egypt's textile sector, which produces cloth and garments for domestic use and for export (see Table 2.5).

Agricultural and Trade Policy

Agricultural Policy

Agricultural policy in Egypt has been characterized by heavy intervention by the government in setting prices, granting marketing monopolies to state

---

[2] This figure refers to exports of goods and services. Excluding services (including tourism and revenue from the Suez Canal), merchandise exports were only US$15 billion.
[3] ITC (2008).

enterprises, subsidizing agricultural inputs, and restricting imports. Before 1987, most field crops were subject to compulsory purchase by state enterprises at fixed prices. The state restricted the allocation of land among crops through crop area controls. Likewise, input distribution was largely controlled by the government. The exchange rate was overvalued, and imports were tightly controlled.

Under the pressure of the growing fiscal burden and rising debt, Egypt began a process of structural adjustment in the 1980s. In 1987 the compulsory purchase of all crops was eliminated except in rice, cotton, and sugarcane. For wheat, maize, and other crops, the government switched from compulsory purchase to voluntary purchase at government-set floor prices. In 1990 there was a massive devaluation of the exchange rate, moving it toward a market rate. In 1991 rice marketing was liberalized and input subsidies were reduced significantly. Input subsidies were phased out over 1991–93. Crop area controls were largely eliminated in this period as well. In 1994–95 cotton marketing and ginning were liberalized, allowing private enterprises to compete with state enterprises (Siam 2005).

Although significant progress has been made in liberalizing agricultural markets, particularly between 1987 and 1996, the Egyptian government continues to intervene in a few areas. First, electricity and irrigation water are still heavily subsidized. Second, the General Authority for Supply Commodities continues to plays an important role in the importation of food. For example, in 2004 it imported 5.4 million metric tons of wheat and 277,000 metric tons of cooking oil, as well as significant quantities of tea, lentils, and beans. Although it does not have a monopoly on imports, it accounts for a large share of all wheat imports. Third, the government maintains a large and complex system to subsidize bread, sugar, and cooking oil. The cost of these subsidies was brought down to around 2 billion Egyptian pounds (LE 2 billion) in 2002, but expansion of the program raised the cost to LE 8 billion in 2004.[4] Wheat imports by the General Authority for Supply Commodities are sold to millers to make *baladi* bread, which is price controlled, while private-sector imports are used to make unsubsidized bread and other wheat products (WTO 2005a).

Trade Policy

Like many of its neighbors, Egypt followed a policy of import-substitution industrialization in the 1960s and 1970s. In response to a debt crisis in 1982, it became one of the first MENA countries to begin to follow a more outward-

[4] In June 2004, the exchange rate was LE 6.20 per US$1.00, so LE 8 billion was equivalent to US$1.3 billion.

oriented trade policy. The trade reforms of 1986 simplified a range of import taxes and reduced the NTBs. Generally, manufacturing benefits from the highest protection except for cotton ginning, which has negative protection. Agriculture has relatively low protection, with some important exceptions. In 1998 the government replaced import bans with high tariffs on clothing, poultry parts, meats, fruits, vegetables, and consumer appliances.

The multiple exchange rates of the 1980s were unified into one exchange rate in 1991 (Reefat 1999). In 2003 the Egyptian pound was allowed to float. In 2004 Egypt reduced the number of tariff bands, eliminated some import fees, and cut tariff rates, resulting in a decline in the average tariffs from 21 percent in 2000 to 9 percent. The tariff rates applied in 2005 are shown in Table 4.1. Although the average tariff for beverages and spirits is very high and some of the tariff rates for traditional export commodities are high, the average rate for grains, oilseeds, fats, and oils (which account for two thirds of agricultural imports) is under 10 percent.

According to the World Bank, the simple average tariff rate is low by world standards, lower than the rates in 60 percent of the countries in the world. Furthermore, Egypt's progress in trade liberalization over 2000-04 was among the strongest in the world (World Bank 2005). Egypt enjoyed a windfall from the high oil prices during the Iraq war and again during the commodity price boom of 2007-08, partly through oil export revenue and partly due to increased traffic through the Suez Canal.

Trade Agreements

Part of Egypt's liberalization has been unilateral, and part has been related to various trade agreements. Egypt signed an EMAA with the E.U. in 2001.

Table 4.1 Tariff rates in and value of imports in Egypt, 2005

Sector	Simple average tariff rate (%)	Range of tariff rates (%)	Value of imports in 2003 (millions of US$)
Grains	3.3	2-5	1,136.7
Oilseeds, fats, oils, etc.	6.4	0-32	421.9
Fruits and vegetables	15.9	2-40	212.7
Coffee, tea, cocoa, sugar, etc.	35.4	2-3,000	212.0
Live animals and animal products	18.4	5-32	218.4
Dairy products	11.5	2-32	123.8
Cut flowers and plants	4.0	2-32	9.4
Beverages and spirits	1,028.8	12-3,000	1.9
Tobacco	22.0	22	188.6
Other agricultural products	4.1	0-32	154.3

Source: WTO (2005a).

Egypt is a member of the Common Market for Eastern and Southern Africa and GAFTA. Egypt also signed the Agadir Declaration, which established a free trade area among Egypt, Jordan, Morocco, and Tunisia.

The GATT/WTO

Based on the Uruguay Round, Egypt presented base tariff rates for over 600 agricultural tariff lines and offered to bind all agricultural tariffs. For most products, the bindings were in the range of 5-80 percent, and there was a commitment to reduce them progressively. Egypt did not declare any agricultural support measures, so it is bound by the 10 percent *de minimis* restriction under which product-specific support may not exceed 10 percent of the value of that commodity and non-product-specific support may not exceed 10 percent of the value of agricultural production.

The Egypt-E.U. EMAA

Egypt's EMAA with the E.U. came into force in 2004. The agreement seeks to establish a free trade area for industrial products over a 12-year period. The restricted access to the E.U. agricultural market has been the most important barrier to the expansion of Egypt's agricultural exports. The last version of the agreement includes an enlargement of quotas and longer seasonal windows for some Egyptian exports.

The Common Market for Eastern and Southern Africa

Egypt became a member of the Common Market for Eastern and Southern Africa in 1998. The organization includes 20 countries in eastern and southern Africa that are working to reduce trade barriers. A subgroup of 9 countries formed a free trade area and were planning to phase out internal tariffs between 1992 and 2000. Two more countries joined the FTA in 2004, but Egypt is not a member of the FTA. A customs union with common external tariffs was to be established by 2003 (Siam 2002), but disagreements over the levels of external tariffs prevented this from occurring.

GAFTA

Egypt became a member of GAFTA in 1998. According to this agreement, tariffs were to be gradually phased out over the 10-year period following the signing of the agreement. Some topics are still subject to negotiation among the 14 member Arab countries, including an agricultural agenda and rules of origin.

Other Bilateral FTAs

There are several bilateral FTAs between Egypt and other countries in the region. The Egypt-Tunisia Free Trade Agreement was initiated in 1998. It provides an exemption on customs duties for specific products from both countries.

A 20 percent reduction in customs duties was granted for some other groups of commodities for five years. The Egypt-Turkey Free Trade Agreement was also signed in 1998. It was intended to boost trade, investment ties, and cooperation by using Turkey as a gateway for Egyptian products into the E.U. market. In turn, Egypt serves as a gateway for Turkish commodities in the Middle East and Africa. An FTA has been created on a bilateral basis between Egypt and Jordan.

Although one might think that the large number of FTAs implies relatively open trade policies, some have expressed concern about the proliferation of regional and bilateral agreements. The United Nations Development Programme notes that "there are difficulties in administering different rules of origin and diverse customs treatments related to various agreements. Adapting to different standards, laws and regulations may lead to delays in implementation" (UNDP 2005a, 96). The report proposes pursuing multilateral trade liberalization through the WTO and simultaneously working on trade facilitation through means such as streamlining customs procedures.

Poverty and Household Budget Patterns

This section describes the living conditions and sources of income of Egyptian households, with particular emphasis on small-scale farmers. The main source of data is the Egypt Integrated Household Survey carried out by the International Food Policy Research Institute in 1997–98. Analysis of the survey suggests that 62 percent of the households are in Lower Egypt, while the remainder are in Upper Egypt (Table 4.2). Lower Egypt's landscape is dominated by the Nile Delta at Alexandria. The delta region is well watered and crisscrossed by channels and canals. Upper Egypt is a narrow strip of land that extends from the cataract boundaries of Aswan to the area south of Cairo. Historically, the land in Upper Egypt was more isolated from activities in the north. Nationally, 54 percent of the population resides in urban areas. Lower Egypt is more urbanized, while Upper Egypt is more rural.

We define a farm household as a household relying on crop or livestock production. Only about one-third of the households in Lower Egypt are engaged in farming compared to more than half in Upper Egypt. More than three-fourths of farmers reside in rural areas; the remainder are in urban areas. Farm households represent about 70 percent of rural households and 18 percent of urban households. In terms of welfare, more than 60 percent of the poorest households are rural, and two-thirds of the poorest households are classified as farm households.

Poverty

Our study used per capita consumption expenditures to measure family well-being and poverty. As shown in Table 4.3, the national average consumption expenditure per capita in 1997/98 was LE 1,782 (US$517 at the 1998 exchange

Table 4.2 Distribution of households based on occupation and location in Egypt, 1998

		Location (percentage of all Egyptian households)	
Household group	National (%)	Urban	Rural
Total population	100.0	53.8	46.2
Nonfarmers	57.8	44.2	13.6
Farmers	42.2	9.6	32.6
Lower Egypt	62.3	37.3	25.0
Nonfarmers	40.0	32.0	8.0
Farmers	22.3	5.3	17.0
Upper Egypt	37.7	16.5	21.2
Nonfarmers	17.8	12.2	5.6
Farmers	19.9	4.3	15.6
Poorest tercile	33.4	12.1	21.4
Nonfarmers	16.1	9.3	6.8
Farmers	17.3	2.8	14.6
Middle tercile	33.3	17.7	15.7
Nonfarmers	18.6	14.4	4.2
Farmers	14.7	3.3	11.5
Richest tercile	33.3	24.0	9.2
Nonfarmers	23.1	20.5	2.6
Farmers	10.2	3.6	6.5

Source: 1997–98 Egypt Integrated Household Survey.

Note: Lower Egypt includes the following northern governorates: Alexandria, Behera, Cairo, Dakhalia, Damietta, El-Menuf, Gharbia, Ismaila, Kalyubia, Kuer, Sharbia, and Suez. Upper Egypt includes the following southern governorates: Assiut, Aswan BeniSuef, Fayoum, Giza, Menya, Qena, and Souhag.

rate of LE 3.45 per US$1.00). The figures at the regional level show that per capita expenditures are essentially equal in Lower Egypt and Upper Egypt. This is consistent with calculations of the Human Development Index that show the gap between Upper and Lower Egypt narrowing over time (UNDP 2005a). Between urban and rural areas the contrast is much sharper. The average per capita expenditure is only LE 1,368 annually among rural households but almost 60 percent higher (LE 2,137) among urban households. The results also suggest that female-headed households have per capita consumption rates 12 percent higher than those of male-headed households.

Among farm households, those producing only livestock tend to be better off than those producing crops. Within crop-producing households, those producing sugarcane are the poorest group, with per capita expenditures averaging LE 1,042. Farm households growing rice are the wealthiest, followed by households producing wheat and fruits and vegetables.

Table 4.3 Expenditure and household size of different types of households in Egypt, 1998

Household group	Household expenditure (LE/year)	Per capita expenditure (LE/year)	Household size (number)
National	8,874	1,782	5.7
Region			
Lower Egypt	8,607	1,794	5.4
Upper Egypt	9,318	1,764	6.2
Location			
Urban	9,409	2,137	4.9
Rural	8,249	1,368	6.6
Household status			
Farmer	9,368	1,485	6.9
Nonfarmer	8,515	1,998	4.8
Gender of head of household			
Man	9,264	1,751	6.0
Woman	6,664	1,962	4.2
Farm type			
Producing livestock only	8,210	1,541	5.9
Producing crops			
Cotton	11,653	1,419	8.9
Wheat	11,425	1,480	8.4
Rice	11,861	1,517	8.8
Fruits and vegetables	12,743	1,465	9.5
Sugarcane	7,533	1,042	7.4
Other crops	10,746	1,419	8.1

Source: 1997-98 Egypt Integrated Household Survey.
Note: LE, Egyptian £.

In the approach using the costs of basic needs, the poverty line represents the level of per capita expenditure at which the members of a household may be expected to meet their basic caloric needs, as well as their minimum non-food requirements. About 27 million people in Egypt, representing 42 percent of the population, were living below the poverty line in 1999-2000. Although poverty statistics are difficult to compare over time, it appears that poverty increased in the 1980s and early 1990s but declined in the second half of the 1990s (Table 4.4).

Based on the 1997-98 Egypt Integrated Household Survey, we calculated the poverty rate using the poverty line developed by Datt, Jolliffe, and Sharma (1998) according to a method similar to the approach used in World Bank (2002a). This analysis found that the poverty rate in Egypt was 38 percent in 1997/98, as shown in Table 4.5. This was comparable to but slightly below the 42 percent reported for 1999/2000 using the upper poverty line. The poverty rate is higher in rural areas than in urban areas (41 percent compared to 36

Table 4.4 Incidence of poverty and number of poor people in Egypt, 1981/82-1999/2000

Year	Share of population that was poor (%)	Number of poor people (millions)
1981/82	30.2	12.9
1990/91	39.1	20.7
1995/96	48.2	28.3
1999/2000	42.0	26.9

Source: World Bank (2002a).
Note: These poverty figures correspond to the upper poverty line in the World Bank report. The lower poverty line is the expenditure that typically allows a household to meet basic caloric needs but does not include any allowance for nonfood expenditure.

Table 4.5 Incidence of poverty for different types of households in Egypt, 1998 (percent)

Household group	National	Urban	Rural
National	38.1	35.8	40.9
Strata			
Metropolitan	41.5	41.5	–
Lower urban	38.1	38.1	–
Lower rural	38.8	–	38.8
Upper urban	25.9	25.9	–
Upper rural	43.3	–	43.2
Household status			
Farmer	39.4	39.5	39.4
Nonfarmer	37.2	35.0	44.4
Gender of head of household			
Male	38.0	35.9	40.5
Female	38.9	35.4	42.8
Farm type			
Producing livestock only	43.2	39.7	44.9
Producing crops			
Cotton	31.7	38.1	31.1
Wheat	29.8	31.0	29.7
Rice	33.5	27.4	33.9
Fruits and vegetables	27.4	33.3	26.5
Sugarcane	62.5	–	62.5
Other crops	35.0	38.6	34.6

Source: 1997-98 Egypt Integrated Household Survey.
Note: –, no households in this category.

percent). The poverty rate is highest in rural areas of Upper Egypt, followed by the rates in metropolitan areas; it is lowest in urban areas of Upper Egypt.

Farm households show a slightly higher incidence of poverty than nonfarm households, although in rural areas, where most farmers are located, the proportion of households in poverty is higher among nonfarmers. In rural areas, nonfarmers probably include landless agricultural laborers. Among different types of farmers, sugarcane growers show the highest incidence of poverty (62 percent), while fruit and vegetable growers show the lowest (27 percent). Farmers producing livestock show the second-highest poverty rate, despite the relatively high average consumption expenditures of this group. This suggests a highly skewed distribution, with many poor small-scale livestock producers and a few large-scale commercial livestock producers.

In rural areas, female-headed households tend to be slightly poorer than male-headed households, while in urban areas the difference in poverty rates is negligible. Overall, the proportion of female-headed households is about 15 percent according to the Egypt Integrated Household Survey.

Sources of Income

Although household consumption expenditures are considered the most accurate basis for assessing well-being and poverty, the Egypt Integrated Household Survey also provides information on household income and its sources. The total income of each household is divided among six sources: crop production, livestock production, wages, nonfarm business income, transfers, and other income. We include the value of home-consumed agricultural production in our calculation of income.

According to the Egypt Integrated Household Survey, almost three-fourths of Egyptian households earn wages as one source of income, implying that wages are the most widespread single source.[5] The proportion of all households with livestock income is 37 percent. About one-fifth of the population participates in crop production, and 29 percent receive transfers. As expected, the percentage of rural households with crop and livestock income is much higher than the percentage of urban households with income from these sources. Surprisingly, though, the share of rural households with wage income and nonfarm business income is almost as high as the corresponding share in urban areas (Table 4.6).

[5] Often the levels of household incomes reported in household surveys are less than the reported consumption expenditures. This is the case in the Egypt Integrated Household Survey, as shown in Tables 4.14 and 4.18. Income estimates are generally considered less accurate due to hesitancy among households to reveal this information and income fluctuations over time.

Table 4.6 Percentage of households involved in income activities in Egypt, by region, 1998

Income category	Nationwide	Urban	Rural
Crop production	19.3	3.4	37.7
Wheat	11.9	1.9	23.5
Rice	5.4	0.7	10.9
Cotton	4.2	0.6	8.4
Fruits and vegetables	0.3	0.1	0.6
Other cereals	3.4	0.6	6.7
Pulses	0.2	0.1	0.4
Tubers	0.2	0	0.5
Oilseeds	0.3	0.1	0.6
Spices	0.1	0	0.1
Sugarcane	1.3	0	2.7
Other cash crops	1.2	0.2	2.5
Clover	14.1	2.3	28.0
Livestock production	36.6	15.5	61.2
Cattle	13.9	1.0	12.9
Goats, sheep	7.7	1.2	6.5
Chickens	32.9	7.6	25.3
Wage income	73.9	75.7	71.8
Nonfarm business income	14.8	16.8	12.6
Transfers	29.4	30.2	28.4
Other income	39.0	42.2	35.2

Source: 1997-98 Egypt Integrated Household Survey.

Table 4.7 shows the composition of income for different types of households in Egypt. At the national level, crop production contributes 11 percent of household income on average. Although livestock production is carried out by nearly 40 percent of households, a large number of these households raise only poultry, so the contribution of livestock production to average household income is relatively small, less than 6 percent. Nonfarm business income represents 15 percent of the total. Almost half of these nonfarm businesses are in the retail, hotel, and restaurant sectors, followed by manufacturing and services. Transfers contribute less than 4 percent of income, although they are received by nearly 20 percent of households.

Although rural areas in developing countries are generally dependent on agriculture, the data for Egypt indicate that the rural nonfarm economy is quite important there. Wages account for 40 percent of the income of rural households, compared to 56 percent among urban households. When we break down the wages into agricultural and nonagricultural activities, most of the wages are earned from nonagricultural activities. Nonagricultural wages represent 94 percent of wage income in urban areas and 70 percent in rural areas. Crop and livestock income provide 25 percent and 12 percent of rural house-

Table 4.7 Sources of income for different types of households in Egypt, 1998

Income category	National average	Urban households	Rural households	Nonfarm households	Farm households	Wheat farmers	Rice farmers	Cotton farmers	Fruit and vegetable farmers	Sugarcane farmers
Total (LE/household/year)	6,111	6,866	5,230	5,805	6,531	9,583	11,213	11,716	11,164	7,898
Per capita (LE/person/year)	1,172	1,501	778	1,316	963	1,230	1,503	1,564	1,322	1,025
Composition (% of total)										
Crops	11.5	2.7	25.0	0.0	25.6	45.8	54.9	60.9	40.5	64.3
Wheat	1.4	0.4	2.8	0.0	3.0	7.0	7.3	7.1	3.7	11.2
Rice	2.2	0.4	4.9	0.0	4.9	9.4	21.9	8.4	3.0	0.0
Cotton	1.6	0.5	3.4	0.0	3.6	7.0	8.3	21.9	5.9	0.4
Fruits and vegetables	0.7	0.2	1.4	0.0	1.5	1.4	2.0	1.6	10.5	-0.1
Sugarcane	0.6	—	1.4	0.0	1.3	1.9	0.0	0.0	0.0	31.8
Other crops	5.1	1.2	11.1	0.0	11.3	19.1	15.3	21.8	17.4	21.1
Livestock	5.7	1.4	12.3	0.0	12.6	16.7	19.0	13.2	9.1	3.0
Wages	49.5	55.6	40.1	61.2	35.2	19.3	15.8	16.1	26.5	11.5
Agriculture	6.9	3.5	12.2	1.5	13.7	9.0	6.4	6.5	11.8	5.7
Nonagriculture	42.6	52.1	27.9	59.7	21.5	10.3	9.4	9.6	14.7	5.8
Nonfarm business	14.7	18.5	8.8	16.1	12.9	6.8	3.6	1.8	16.0	1.1
Transfers	3.6	3.6	3.6	3.9	3.2	1.3	-0.5	0.0	-0.1	6.5
Other	15.0	18.1	10.2	18.8	10.5	10.2	7.2	8.1	7.9	13.5

Source: 1997-98 Egypt Integrated Household Survey.
Notes: LE, Egyptian £; –, data not available.

hold incomes, respectively. Even among *farm* households, farm income (crops and livestock) account for less than 40 percent of income. Thus, overall, the nonfarm sector contributes almost two-thirds of rural household income. These findings are comparable with those recorded in other studies in the region. For example, nonfarm income represents the single most important source of income in rural areas of Jordan, accounting for about 51 percent of total household income (Adams 2001).

Table 4.7 also shows the composition of income for farm households growing different types of crops, especially wheat, rice, cotton, fruits and vegetables, and sugarcane. It is important to recall that these are not exclusive categories: many farmers fall into more than one category. Furthermore, it is not necessary that farmers growing a particular crop receive a large share of their income from that crop. Cotton and sugarcane farmers are the most specialized in crop production, earning more than 60 percent of their income from crops. Sugarcane farmers are fairly dependent on that crop (from which they receive 32 percent of their income), while wheat accounts for only 7 percent of the income of wheat farmers. Fruit and vegetable farmers have a higher share of their income from wages and from nonfarm businesses than do growers of other crops. Perhaps the risk and expense of horticultural production exclude households that do not have significant nonfarm income sources.

Table 4.8 shows the sources of income from rural households based on expenditure tercile and farm size. Wages play a significant role as a source of income in all terciles, but their contribution is greater among the poor (47 percent) than among the middle and upper terciles (less than 39 percent). Similarly, wheat is much more important to poor and middle-tercile households (13 percent) than to upper-tercile households (3 percent). This is not surprising given the position of wheat as the main staple food. In contrast, rice, cotton, livestock, and "other income" are more important sources of income for households in the upper terciles. Fruit and vegetable income is more important to the poorest and richest terciles compared to the middle tercile. This may reflect differences between commercial production and backyard horticultural production for households' own consumption.

Looking at the right-hand side of Table 4.8, we see that landless households are the poorest; their per capita income of LE 700 is 13 percent lower than the average rural income. Not surprisingly, large-scale farms benefit from the land they own, earning a per capita income that is more than 70 percent above the rural average. However, it is interesting to note that medium-sized farms have per capita incomes that are slightly lower than the incomes of small-scale farms.

As expected, households with no land or small farms earn the highest share of their income from wages and nonfarm businesses. Small farms also

Table 4.8 Sources of income for rural households in Egypt, by expenditure tercile and farm size, 1998

	Per capita expenditure category			Farm size category				
Income category	Poor	Middle	Rich	No land	Small	Medium	Large	Average
Total (LE/household/year)	4,144	5,743	6,074	3,450	5,690	5,523	12,055	5,230
Per capita (LE/person/year)	569	928	1,160	700	825	754	1,378	808
Composition (% of total)								
Crops	24.4	30.2	20.8	0.0	33.7	31.4	56.2	25.0
Wheat	13.0	13.3	3.2	0.0	7.7	1.8	14.6	11.3
Rice	12.9	22.5	24.9	0.0	27.6	20.9	17.1	19.6
Cotton	11.5	13.7	17.1	0.0	3.0	15.8	15.9	13.6
Sugarcane	8.5	3.0	7.0	0.0	2.9	9.2	5.6	5.7
Fruits and vegetables	8.0	3.0	6.4	0.0	4.3	12.6	4.0	5.4
Other	46.2	44.5	41.4	0.0	54.6	39.6	42.7	44.3
Livestock	6.4	11.6	11.4	1.0	12.8	20.0	15.7	12.3
Wages	46.9	37.5	38.6	63.4	36.9	34.2	15.2	40.1
Nonfarm business	9.5	8.3	9.9	15.7	6.3	2.6	3.9	8.8
Transfers	4.9	2.1	4.2	6.3	2.5	1.3	1.5	3.6
Other	7.9	10.4	14.9	13.5	7.9	10.9	7.5	10.2

Source: 1997-98 Egypt Integrated Household Survey.

Note: Per capita expenditure categories and farm-size categories are defined by terciles among rural households. Small farms have less than 0.28 hectare; medium-sized farms have 0.28 to 0.63 hectare; and large farms have more than 0.63 hectare. LE, Egyptian £.

earn a relatively large share of their incomes from rice production (28 percent compared to 21 percent and 17 percent for medium and large farms, respectively) and from "other crops." Large-scale farms earn a relatively large share of their incomes from wheat and cotton and from crops in general. Livestock and fruit and vegetable income seem to be more important among medium-sized farms. These results highlight the fact that small farmers should not be considered synonymous with poor rural households, particularly in a country where agroecological potential and cropping intensity vary widely.

Household Consumption Patterns

Table 4.9 reports average household consumption expenditures and patterns for different types of households. At the national level, the per capita consumption expenditure is LE 1,783 per year.[6] Household decisions on the allocation of resources to food spending and other needs have widespread implications for well-being. The food share in total household budgets at the national level is 57 percent. Urban and nonfarm households spend lower proportions of their total expenditures on food consumption (about 53 percent), while rural and farm households spend a larger share on food (62–64 percent). The results are consistent with the international patterns, whereby low-income households spend a larger share of their budgets on food while richer households spend a larger portion on nonfood items. Food, clothing, and footwear appear to be necessities in the sense that their budget shares decline as income rises, while education, health, recreation, and other things are luxuries in the sense that their budget shares rise with income.

It is interesting to note that the food consumption patterns are not closely related to the crops grown. For example, wheat farmers do not consume more wheat products, and rice farmers consume no more rice than other farmers. This is a sign of the relatively commercial orientation of Egyptian farmers and relatively low transaction costs, presumably due to the high population density in settled areas. It is further supported by the fact that almost all farmers are either net buyers or net sellers; few produce only for their own consumption without buying or selling.

The Impact of Commodity Price Changes on Poverty

To understand the effects on household incomes and poverty on agricultural price changes, we simulated the effect for several crops that are important in

[6] The estimated consumption expenditure in the Egypt Integrated Household Survey is greater than the estimated net income. This is a common pattern in household survey data and is probably caused by underreporting of income. In the analysis that follows, we assume that the composition of income is accurate, implying similar levels of underreporting for different types of income.

Table 4.9 Expenditure patterns for different types of households in Egypt, 1998

Expenditure category	National average	Urban households	Rural households	Nonfarm households	Farm households	Wheat farmers	Rice farmers	Cotton farmers	Sugarcane farmers	Fruit and vegetable farmers
Per capita expenditure (LE/person/year)	1,783	2,134	1,374	1,998	1,485	1,483	1,515	1,483	1,042	1,445
Poverty rate (%)	38.1	35.7	40.9	37.1	39.4	29.8	33.5	31.7	62.5	27.4
Household expenditure (LE/household/year)	8,837	9,373	8,212	8,515	9,359	11,417	11,800	11,653	7,533	13,000
Food	57.4	52.5	64.0	53.3	62.0	63.0	63.4	65.1	68.1	66.1
Wheat	6.3	4.6	8.6	4.9	8.0	8.5	8.7	6.1	9.2	10.9
Rice	3.0	2.4	3.7	2.5	3.4	4.2	3.7	6.2	4.2	1.2
Sugar	2.2	1.6	2.9	1.7	2.7	2.9	2.8	2.4	2.3	4.8
Fruits and vegetables	6.0	5.9	6.1	6.0	5.8	5.3	5.4	5.9	5.9	5.8
Other	39.9	38.0	42.7	38.2	42.1	42.1	42.8	44.5	46.5	43.4
Clothing	6.3	7.0	5.5	6.9	5.7	5.6	5.4	5.0	5.2	7.8
Health	4.0	4.3	3.6	4.5	3.4	4.0	3.5	3.4	2.0	2.9
Education	4.9	6.1	3.4	6.0	3.6	3.3	3.2	3.0	3.2	2.5
Household equipment	4.6	6.0	2.8	5.7	3.3	2.7	2.3	1.9	2.6	2.7
Other	22.8	24.3	20.8	23.5	22.1	21.5	22.3	21.6	19.0	17.9

Source: 1997-98 Egypt Integrated Household Survey.
Note: LE, Egyptian £.

Egypt. We focused on wheat, rice, cotton, fruits and vegetables, and sugarcane because they are the most important tradable agricultural commodities in the country. First we computed the consumption expenditure of each household and the percentage of these households in poverty. Next we simulated the effect on households' incomes resulting from an increase in producer prices and consumer prices, taking each household's production and consumption of each crop into account. Adding the change in income to initial consumption expenditures (under the assumption that all the change is spent on consumption), we computed a new per capita consumption expenditure level for each household and recomputed the average income and poverty measures for different types of households.[7] We used the Foster-Greer-Thorbecke poverty measures, as follows:

- the headcount index (incidence), which is the proportion of people below the poverty line;
- the poverty gap index (intensity), which is the average shortfall of the income of the poor from the poverty line, averaged over the whole population; and
- the severity index, which addresses the inequality of incomes among the poor.

The short-run simulation holds production and consumption quantities fixed at their initial levels, while the long-run simulation allows producers and consumers to respond to price changes based on plausible price elasticities. The simulation method is described in more detail in the appendix to this chapter.

Wheat

Egypt's wheat sector has been partially liberalized since 1987. Devaluation has brought local prices closer to international wheat prices. Under the Agricultural Reform Programme, wheat area restrictions, quotas, and fixed procurement prices have been removed. Egypt continues to encourage the expansion of acreage and the use of newly developed high-yielding wheat varieties. Within the past two decades, wheat production has tripled. Despite these efforts to increase local wheat production, Egypt continues to import wheat. International wheat prices are volatile and are affected by changes in the cost of ocean freight, while domestic prices are subject to stabilization measures. Household characteristics with respect to wheat production, consumption, and net sales are shown in Table 4.10. Almost all Egyptian households (97 percent) consume wheat products, and 12 percent grow wheat.

[7] Note that this method does not take into account the fact that price changes could induce a farmer to start growing a new crop or stop growing an old one.

Table 4.10 Percentage of households in Egypt that were producers and consumers of wheat, 1998

Household activity	National average	Urban households	Rural households
Percentage of households that			
Produced wheat	12.0	2.0	23.5
Consumed wheat products	97.2	97.9	96.4
Were net buyers of wheat	88.6	96.3	79.7
Were net sellers of wheat	8.2	1.6	15.9
Were self-sufficient	3.2	2.1	4.4
Percentage of wheat farmers who			
Were net buyers of wheat	31.3	19.5	32.5
Were net sellers of wheat	68.7	80.5	67.5

Source: 1997-98 Egypt Integrated Household Survey.

Even among rural households, fewer than one-quarter of the households grow wheat. Nationally, 89 percent are net buyers, while only 8 percent are net sellers, but about two-thirds of wheat farmers are net sellers.

Nationally, the annual expenditure of wheat-producing households averages LE 11,104 per household.[8] The simulation results indicated that a price increase of 10 percent will raise the average net earnings of wheat-producing households by LE 66 in the short run and LE 68 in the long run. The reason these figures are so small is that, on average, wheat accounts for only 7 percent of the income of wheat farmers (see Table 4.7). Furthermore, many wheat farmers buy wheat products, so the net gain from higher prices is reduced. One-third of the wheat farmers are actually net buyers of wheat; these deficit wheat farmers lose when rice prices increase.

As shown in Table 4.11, the poverty rate among wheat growers is 30 percent. A 40 percent increase in the wheat price will have negligible effects on the poverty rate among wheat farmers in the short run because wheat does not represent a major source of income for many of them and because some of them purchase wheat products. In the long run, wheat farmers will expand their output and substitute away from wheat consumption, so their gains will be greater. A 40 percent price increase will bring down the poverty rate from 30 percent to 27 percent in the long run. Increases in wheat prices will have small and nonlinear effects on the depth and severity of poverty among wheat farmers.

[8] Average household consumption expenditures may differ slightly from those shown in Table 4.8 due to the removal of households with incomplete data for the simulations.

Table 4.11 Estimated effects of increased wheat prices on poverty among wheat growers in Egypt

Category	Short run	Long run
Base expenditure (LE/household/year)	11,104	11,104
Change in income following a 10% wheat price rise (LE/household/year)	66	82
Incidence of poverty (P_0)		
Base	0.30	0.30
10% increase in wheat price	0.30	0.30
20% increase in wheat price	0.30	0.29
30% increase in wheat price	0.30	0.28
40% increase in wheat price	0.30	0.27
Depth of poverty (P_1)		
Base	0.075	0.075
10% increase in wheat price	0.073	0.072
20% increase in wheat price	0.074	0.069
30% increase in wheat price	0.075	0.066
40% increase in wheat price	0.076	0.074
Severity of poverty (P_2)		
Base	0.028	0.028
10% increase in wheat price	0.027	0.026
20% increase in wheat price	0.027	0.025
30% increase in wheat price	0.028	0.024
40% increase in wheat price	0.028	0.023

Source: Simulation results based on data from the 1997–98 Egypt Integrated Household Survey.
Note: LE, Egyptian £.

Rice

Rice is a preferred foodgrain among many Egyptians, and a large segment of the population in Egypt consumes rice. Rice production occurs mostly along the lower Nile, in about 10 percent of the agricultural area of Egypt. Egypt has recently been a net rice exporter. In 2005, rice production was 6.3 million metric tons, while domestic consumption was only 3.5 million metric tons. According to the Egypt Integrated Household Survey, more than 90 percent of households consume rice nationally, but only 5 percent grow rice (Table 4.12). Among rice farmers, almost 90 percent are net sellers.

The percentage of rural households that grow rice and are poor is somewhat higher than the corresponding figure among wheat growers, as shown in Table 4.13. A 10 percent increase in rice prices will lead to an average income increase of LE 272 in the short run and LE 277 in the long run. The gains among rice growers of a 10 percent price increase will be much greater than the gains among wheat growers because rice accounts for a larger share of rice growers' income and because a smaller share of rice growers are net buyers (only 10 percent).

Table 4.12 Percentage of households in Egypt that were producers and consumers of rice, 1998

Household activity	National average	Urban households	Rural households
Percentage of households that			
Produced rice	5.4	0.7	10.9
Consumed rice products	90.8	93.6	87.6
Were net buyers of rice	84.9	92.2	76.5
Were net sellers of rice	4.9	0.4	13.5
Were self-sufficient	10.2	7.4	10.0
Percentage of rice farmers who			
Were net buyers of rice	10.2	37.7	8.2
Were net sellers of rice	89.8	62.3	91.8

Source: 1997–98 Egypt Integrated Household Survey.

Table 4.13 Estimated effects of increased rice prices on poverty among rice growers in Egypt

Category	Short run	Long run
Base expenditure (LE/household/year)	11,861	11,861
Change in income following a 10% rice price increase (LE/household/year)	272	277
Incidence of poverty (P_0)		
Base	0.34	0.34
10% increase in rice price	0.32	0.32
20% increase in rice price	0.30	0.30
30% increase in rice price	0.29	0.29
40% increase in rice price	0.28	0.27
Depth of poverty (P_1)		
Base	0.078	0.078
10% increase in rice price	0.072	0.072
20% increase in rice price	0.067	0.067
30% increase in rice price	0.062	0.061
40% increase in rice price	0.058	0.056
Severity of poverty (P_2)		
Base	0.029	0.029
10% increase in rice price	0.026	0.026
20% increase in rice price	0.024	0.023
30% increase in rice price	0.021	0.021
40% increase in rice price	0.019	0.018

Source: Simulation results based on data from the 1997–98 Egypt Integrated Household Survey.

Note: LE, Egyptian £.

A 40 percent price increase will reduce the poverty rate among rice-producing households from 34 percent to 28 percent in the short run and to 27 percent in the long run. Higher rice prices will also reduce the depth and severity of poverty among rice growers.

Cotton

Cotton is one of the main agricultural exports of Egypt (along with fruits and vegetables). The crop is also important in terms of employment; among farmers, 10 percent produce cotton, and it is estimated that cotton production employs up to 1 million farm workers. Moreover, Egypt's exports of textiles and clothing products amounted to US$516 million in 2003, while its imports were US$279 million.

Table 4.14 shows the effect of cotton price increases of 10 percent to 40 percent on different measures of poverty among cotton growers. In the base scenario, 32 percent of cotton farmers are living below the poverty line, slightly higher than the rate among wheat farmers and slightly below the rate among

Table 4.14 Estimated effects of increased cotton prices on poverty among cotton growers in Egypt

Category	Short run	Long run
Base expenditure (LE/household/year)	11,653	11,653
Change in income caused by a 10% cotton price rise (LE/household/year)	306	310
Incidence of poverty (P_0)		
Base	0.32	0.32
10% increase in cotton price	0.30	0.30
20% increase in cotton price	0.27	0.27
30% increase in cotton price	0.26	0.26
40% increase in cotton price	0.26	0.25
Depth of poverty (P_1)		
Base	0.091	0.091
10% increase in cotton price	0.085	0.084
20% increase in cotton price	0.079	0.079
30% increase in cotton price	0.074	0.073
40% increase in cotton price	0.069	0.068
Severity of poverty (P_2)		
Base	0.039	0.039
10% increase in cotton price	0.036	0.036
20% increase in cotton price	0.034	0.033
30% increase in cotton price	0.031	0.031
40% increase in cotton price	0.029	0.028

Source: Simulation results based on data from the 1997-98 Egypt Integrated Household Survey.

Note: LE, Egyptian £.

rice farmers. According to the simulation analysis, a 10 percent increase in the cotton price will raise the average household income among cotton growers by LE 306 in the short run and LE 310 in the long run.

A 40 percent increase in cotton prices will bring the poverty rate down to 26 percent in the short run and 25 percent in the long run. This represents about a 16 percent reduction in the poverty level among cotton farmers. There will be even larger relative falls in the depth and intensity of poverty among cotton growers.

Fruits and Vegetables

During two decades (1982-2002), the total production of vegetables increased from 8.6 million to 16.2 million tons, an annual growth rate of 3.9 percent. The growth rate for fruits was almost 5 percent annually. In terms of area shares, fruit and vegetable production represented about 20 percent of the cropped area in 2000/01, while cereals occupied 47 percent of the area.

Table 4.15 indicates that more than 95 percent of households consume fruits and vegetables. Expenditures on fruits and vegetables account for 6 percent of total consumption and over 10 percent of food consumption expenditures nationally, according to the Egypt Integrated Household Survey. About 3 percent of all Egyptian households grow fruits and vegetables, while the figure is 6 percent among rural households. Almost two-thirds of horticultural growers are net sellers of fruits and vegetables, while more than one-third are net buyers.

According to Table 4.16, the annual average household consumption expenditures of these households are LE 12,743. The incidence of poverty among fruit and vegetable growers is 29 percent, somewhat lower than the

Table 4.15 Percentage of households in Egypt that were producers and consumers of fruits and vegetables, 1998

Household activity	National average	Urban households	Rural households
Percentage of households that			
Produced fruits and vegetables	3.0	0.7	5.8
Consumed fruits and vegetables	96.8	97.6	95.9
Were net buyers of fruits and vegetables	94.9	96.9	92.5
Were net sellers of fruits and vegetables	1.9	0.6	3.5
Were self-sufficient	3.2	2.5	4.0
Percentage of fruit and vegetable farmers who			
Were net buyers of fruits and vegetables	35.2	10.6	38.5
Were net sellers of fruits and vegetables	63.6	89.4	60.1

Source: 1997-98 Egypt Integrated Household Survey.

Table 4.16 Estimated effects of increased fruit and vegetable prices on poverty among fruit and vegetable growers in Egypt

Category	Short run	Long run
Base expenditure (LE/household/year)	12,743	12,743
Change in income caused by a 10% price rise for fruits and vegetables (LE/household/year)	164	167
Incidence of poverty (P_0)		
Base	0.29	0.29
10% increase in prices	0.26	0.26
20% increase in prices	0.25	0.25
30% increase in prices	0.24	0.24
40% increase in prices	0.24	0.24
Depth of poverty (P_1)		
Base	0.085	0.085
10% increase in prices	0.081	0.081
20% increase in prices	0.076	0.076
30% increase in prices	0.073	0.072
40% increase in prices	0.069	0.068
Severity of poverty (P_2)		
Base	0.038	0.038
10% increase in prices	0.035	0.035
20% increase in prices	0.032	0.032
30% increase in prices	0.029	0.029
40% increase in prices	0.027	0.026

Source: Simulation results based on data from the 1997-98 Egypt Integrated Household Survey.
Note: LE, Egyptian £.

figures related to other crops considered here. The results of the simulation analysis indicate that a 10 percent increase in fruit and vegetable prices will increase the net income of growers by LE 164 in the short run and LE 167 in the long run. A price increase of 40 percent will reduce the poverty rate among fruit and vegetable producers from 29 to 24 percent in both the short- and the long-run scenarios. This price increase will reduce the depth and intensity of poverty by 20-30 percent of the original values.

Sugarcane

The total production of sugar increased from 649,000 metric tons in 1982 to 1.4 million metric tons in 2000, reflecting an annual growth of 4.4 percent. The government continues to promote both cane and beet sugar production. However, given the extreme competition for Egypt's limited land and water resources, the area under sugarcane cultivation is not expected to increase. The new sugar policy is aimed at promoting beet sugar production by establishing three new sugar beet milling facilities.

Egypt is a major importer of sugar. Roughly one-third of the sugar to meet consumption needs is imported; the remainder comes from domestic production. Egypt continues to subsidize sugar consumption under the rationing system, albeit at a decreasing rate. As a long-term plan, the government is making efforts to cut the cost of the sugar program by reducing the amount of sugar available through the ration system.

Although the proportion of households that grows sugarcane is barely 1 percent, all households that produce a sugar crop are net sellers (Table 4.17). The local effect could be larger, however, because sugarcane growers are concentrated in the rural part of Upper Egypt. Furthermore, as mentioned earlier, sugarcane farmers tend to be more specialized than growers of other crops, earning almost one-third of their incomes from sugarcane. Sugarcane-producing households have per capita incomes significantly below the national average, and their poverty rate is 63 percent, far above the rural average of 41 percent.

As shown in Table 4.18, the incidence of poverty among sugarcane growers is 63 percent, far higher than the rate among growers of other major crops. A 10 percent increase in the producer price of sugarcane will raise the net average incomes of sugarcane growers by LE 461 in the short run and LE 468 in the long run. A 40 percent increase in sugarcane prices will result in a marked drop in poverty among sugarcane growers, from 63 percent to 43 percent. Overall, the long-run simulation results indicate that there will be a slightly greater poverty reduction than do the results of the short-run simulation. The depth and severity of poverty among sugarcane-producing households will also decline with higher prices. The reason for the strong relationship between sugarcane prices and the poverty rate among sugarcane growers is that these households derive a large share of their incomes from this crop.

Table 4.17 Percentage of households in Egypt that were producers of sugarcane and consumers of sugar, 1998

Household activity	National average	Urban households	Rural households
Percentage of households that			
Produced a sugar crop	1.3	0.0	2.7
Consumed sugar	91.7	91.7	96.4
Were net buyers of sugar	90.0	91.1	88.7
Were net sellers of sugar	1.3	0.0	2.7
Were self-sufficient	8.7	8.9	8.6
Percentage of sugar crop farmers who			
Were net buyers of sugar	0	–	0
Were net sellers of sugar	100	–	100

Source: 1997/98 Egypt Integrated Household Survey.
Note: –, data not available.

Table 4.18 Estimated effects of increased sugarcane prices on poverty among sugarcane growers in Egypt

Category	Short run	Long run
Base expenditure (LE/household/year)	7,533	7,533
Change in income caused by a 10% sugarcane price rise (LE/household/year)	461	468
Incidence of poverty (P_0)		
Base	0.63	0.63
10% increase in sugarcane price	0.55	0.53
20% increase in sugarcane price	0.53	0.53
30% increase in sugarcane price	0.48	0.45
40% increase in sugarcane price	0.43	0.43
Depth of poverty (P_1)		
Base	0.145	0.145
10% increase in sugarcane price	0.119	0.118
20% increase in sugarcane price	0.095	0.093
30% increase in sugarcane price	0.073	0.070
40% increase in sugarcane price	0.055	0.051
Severity of poverty (P_2)		
Base	0.044	0.044
10% increase in sugarcane price	0.031	0.031
20% increase in sugarcane price	0.022	0.021
30% increase in sugarcane price	0.015	0.014
40% increase in sugarcane price	0.010	0.009

Source: Simulation results based on data from the 1997-98 Egypt Integrated Household Survey.
Note: LE, Egyptian £.

The Impact of Crop Price Increases on Overall Poverty

Until this point we have estimated the impact of raising the price of each individual crop on the growers of that crop. In this section we estimate the impact of raising the price of each crop on the rural, urban, and overall population, including both growers and nongrowers. In the interest of brevity and because the overall effects are small, we focus on the impact on the incidence of poverty and on the simulation of 40 percent increases in the price of each crop. The results of these simulations are shown in Table 4.19.

According to our analysis, a 40 percent increase in the price of wheat will increase poverty slightly in the short run and decrease it slightly in the long run. This implies that a significant number of net buying wheat growers will respond to the higher prices by expanding their output and becoming surplus growers. Interestingly, similar patterns will hold in both rural and urban areas. This reflects the high population density in the Nile Valley, resulting in wheat farmers' living in settlements large enough to be considered urban. It is surprising that higher wheat prices would (slightly) reduce poverty in the long

Table 4.19 Estimated effects of increased commodities prices on poverty in Egypt

	Poverty rate (%)								
	Urban			Rural			National		
Simulation	Base	Short-term	Long-term	Base	Short-term	Long-term	Base	Short-term	Long-term
40% increase in wheat price	36	37	35	41	43	40	38	39	37
40% increase in rice price	36	37	37	41	41	41	38	39	39
40% increase in cotton price	36	36	36	41	40	40	38	38	38
40% increase in fruit and vegetable price	36	37	37	41	42	42	38	39	39
40% increase in sugar price	36	36	36	41	40	40	38	38	38
40% increase in prices of wheat, rice, cotton, fruits and vegetables, and sugar	36	38	n.c.	41	42	n.c.	38	40	n.c.

Source: Simulation results based on data from the 1997–98 Egypt Integrated Household Survey.
Note: The long-term effect of increasing all five prices is not calculated (n.c.) because of uncertainty regarding the cross-price elasticities of supply.

run given that 89 percent of the households are net buyers, but three factors help explain this result: (1) net sellers are poorer than net buyers, (2) the gains to the average net seller will be larger than the losses to the average net buyer, and (3) some net buyers will become net sellers in response to the higher wheat prices.

The effect of rice price increases on the poverty rate in Egypt will be quite small. A 40 percent increase in rice prices will raise the urban poverty rate by 1 percentage point. It will have this effect because urban rice consumers will be adversely affected by the higher price, but the effect will be small because rice represents just 2.4 percent of the budgets of urban households. Rice farmers will gain, but not by enough to noticeably affect the rural poverty rate. This is because, as discussed earlier, rice farmers account for just 11 percent of the rural population. The negative effect on urban households will be sufficiently large to raise the national poverty rate by 1 percentage point.

A 40 percent increase in cotton prices will reduce the rural poverty rate by 1 percentage point but will have no noticeable effect on the urban or national poverty rate. Again, the small effect is explained by the fact that cotton growers represent only 4.2 percent of all households nationally.

A 40 percent increase in fruit and vegetable prices will cause the urban poverty rate to rise 1 percentage point (recall that fruits and vegetables account for 6 percent of urban budgets). Interestingly, the higher fruit and vegetable prices will also cause rural poverty rates to rise slightly, suggesting that the rural poor are more likely to be net buyers of horticultural produce than net sellers. At the national level, the poverty rate will increase about 1 percentage point.

A 40 percent increase in sugarcane prices will reduce rural poverty by 1 percentage point but have no measurable effect on urban poverty. Because sugar-producing households are such a small part of the national population, the effect of higher sugar prices on overall poverty will be negligible.

Finally we estimate the effect of a simultaneous 40 percent increase in the prices of wheat, rice, cotton, fruits and vegetables, and sugar. In the short run, the incidence of poverty will increase by 2 percentage points in urban areas and 1 percentage point in rural areas. At the national level, poverty will rise by 2 percentage points. The rise in urban poverty is expected, but it is somewhat surprising that rural poverty will also increase, albeit by a very small margin. The implication is that many of the poor are net buyers of agricultural commodities in Egypt. The importance of wages in rural income is undoubtedly an important factor in explaining this result.

Summary

In the 1970s and 1980s, agricultural policy in Egypt intervened heavily in production, marketing, and trade. A policy of import-substitution industrialization meant that the agricultural sector was heavily taxed through low official prices and compulsory sales. At the same time, some commodities were protected by import restrictions. In the late 1980s and the 1990s, Egypt gradually liberalized its agricultural markets and reduced its level of import protection. Wheat markets remained distorted by a combination of import controls, fixed producer prices, consumer subsidies on certain types of bread, and government control over the channels leading to subsidized bread. In 2004 a series of significant tariff reductions was implemented, leading the World Bank to declare that Egypt had made more progress in trade liberalization than almost any other country. Even so, the degree of protection there is higher than in 40 percent of the countries of the world.

Full global trade liberalization would increase the prices of agricultural commodities by 5–15 percent. This would probably negatively affect the Egyptian economy because it is a net agricultural importer, though the exact effect would depend on the price changes for each commodity. Egypt would gain from higher rice and cotton prices but lose from higher wheat and maize prices. Domestic trade reform would reduce the domestic prices of imported commodities such as wheat, thus partially offsetting the adverse effect of global trade liberalization, as well as providing efficiency gains.

In this chapter we review the income and consumption patterns of Egyptian households based on the 1997–98 Egypt Integrated Household Survey and estimate the effects of changes in the prices of five agricultural commodities on incomes and poverty rates among Egyptian households. Such price changes might arise from changes in world market prices or from changes in border or subsidy policies within Egypt.

Overall, our results show that price changes can have a significant effect on poverty among the producers of specific crops, but these price changes will not have a large impact on overall rates of poverty. We simulated the effect of a 40 percent increase in the price of each commodity, which represents the upper limit of the effect of global trade liberalization, as follows:[9]

- For wheat, a 40 percent increase in the price will lower national poverty by 1 percentage point.
- For rice and horticultural produce, a 40 percent increase in the prices will raise national poverty by 1 percentage point.
- For cotton and sugar, a 40 percent increase in the prices will have a negligible effect (less than 0.5 percent) on national poverty.
- A 40 percent increase in the prices of all five product categories will result in higher poverty in urban and rural areas, though the increase will be just 1–2 percentage points.

One implication of this analysis is that agricultural trade policy is a relatively ineffective policy instrument for assisting poor rural households. Another interesting result is that, although wheat is the most politically sensitive agricultural commodity in Egypt, the effect of wheat protection on poverty is small even among wheat farmers themselves. This is because wheat farmers are not particularly poor (they are somewhat better off than the average rural household), because their incomes are fairly diversified (wheat accounts for only 8.5 percent of their incomes), and because many other households in urban and rural areas are net buyers. For example, almost 80 percent of rural households are net buyers of wheat. Although policy decisions take into account a wide range of factors not considered here, this analysis should at least weaken the poverty alleviation argument for a wheat protection policy.

Finally, the analysis suggests that some of the poorest households in Egypt are those that are involved in farming but do not own land. These households include agricultural laborers and tenants who cultivate land owned by others.

[9] At the same time, this simulation represents an underestimate of the impact of the global price crisis of 2007–08.

Agricultural trade policy can influence the well-being of these households only indirectly through the labor market.

This analysis is based on household survey data from 1997-98, more than 10 years ago. It is worth asking how this analysis might be affected if we used more recent household survey data. The share of the population in urban areas increased from 36 percent in the survey to 43 percent in 2006. This suggests that the share of farm households in the population has declined, in which case the actual effect of higher food prices is somewhat more negative than has been indicated by the analysis presented here. At the same time, per capita income has grown about 30 percent since the survey was carried out.[10] Because the share of income allocated to food declines as income rises (particularly for staple foods such as wheat), this implies that the adverse impact of higher food prices will actually be smaller than indicated by our analysis. Because these two effects offset each other, we believe that repeating this analysis with more recent household survey data would yield very similar results.

Appendix 4A: Methods for Estimating the Impact of Trade Liberalization on Egypt

Data

In our analysis we used the Egypt Integrated Household Survey carried out by the International Food Policy Research Institute in coordination with the Egyptian Ministry of Agriculture and Land Reclamation and the Ministry of Trade and Supply. The nationally representative survey provides information on income and expenditures, as well as on many household characteristics, including housing, landownership, education, employment, health and nutrition, access to facilities, migration, and credit and savings. The sample consisted of 2,500 households in 20 urban and rural governorates; the fieldwork took place during the first half of 1997. For this particular analysis, a subsample of 2,452 households has been used because the data on the rest of the households in the full sample are incomplete or missing. With this representative sample it is possible to examine the average characteristics of the poor at the national level and also through several dichotomous breakdowns, such as by urban-rural residence or residence in Upper or Lower Egypt.

Questionnaire and Sample Design

The questionnaire was divided into male and female components to reduce the time required to fill in the questionnaire. In the typical case, the male

[10] As shown in Table 1.1, per capita GDP grew 2.4 percent per year over 2000-06. Eleven years of growth at this rate yields an overall increase of 30 percent.

questionnaire was administered by a male interviewer to the male head of household (who, it is assumed, knows the most about nonfood household expenses); similarly, the female questionnaire was administered by a female interviewer to (most typically) the wife of the head of the household (who, it is assumed, knows more about household eating habits and food expenses). The male questionnaire contains most of the sections that deal with sources of income and large expenses, while the female questionnaire contains the sections focusing on information and expenditures related to tending to the household, including eating patterns, health care, and smaller, more frequent expenses.

The questionnaire was administered to 2,500 households from 20 governorates using a two-stage, stratified selection process. The sample frame used for the selection process was supplied by the Central Agency for Public Mobilization and Statistics (CAPMAS) and was based on the 1986 Egypt census and a 1993 listing of households in selected primary sampling units. This sample frame is used by CAPMAS as a master sample for most of its survey work. It consists of 492 sampling units, 296 of which are urban, while 196 are rural.

Income Calculation

Income was calculated as the sum of net revenues from the following sources: crop production, livestock production, wages, nonfarm enterprises, transfers, and other income. The net income from each crop was calculated as the value of production minus the cost of production. It covers all commodities, including by-products and home consumption. Crop production expenses (for seeds, fertilizer, chemical insecticides, labor, utilities, storage, transportation, equipment rental, and other items) were deducted to derive net crop income. Payments to landlords were also excluded from income. Livestock income included income for all types of animals and by-products. Livestock production expenses (for feeds, veterinary services, and labor) were deducted to derive net livestock income. Meat home consumption was also included as part of income. Because of uncertainty about how to calculate wage rates accurately among family members, no value was imputed for the family labor involved in crop and livestock production.

Net revenues from nonfarm enterprises were based on gross revenues minus the operating costs over the past 12 months. Wage income was calculated as the sum of annual earnings in wages for the main job; cash and in-kind wages were also examined for each household member. Transfers were derived as the net value of cash and in-kind transfers received and sent. Other income covered rents (cash and in-kind) received through ownership of assets such as housing, land, and equipment, along with interest, dividends, and pensions.

Methods

We used the data from the Egypt Integrated Household Survey to estimate the short- and long-run impact of changes in agricultural prices. In the absence of reliable estimates of the impact of multilateral and unilateral trade liberalization on agricultural prices in Egypt, we simulated the impact of four price increases (10, 20, 30, and 40 percent) for each commodity of interest. Most analyses of the impact of multilateral trade liberalization suggest that agricultural prices would rise 5-20 percent, well within the range of price increases considered here. We simulated the impact of changes in the price of wheat, rice, sugar, cotton, and fruits and vegetables. The global markets for wheat, rice, sugar, and cotton are among the most distorted, so we would expect trade liberalization to have the largest effect on the world prices of these commodities. In addition, these four commodities are important in the agricultural economy of Egypt as sources of income (wheat, rice, and cotton) and as components of the diet (wheat, rice, and sugar). The global markets for fruits and vegetables are not highly distorted, but fruit and vegetable exports from Egypt (and other countries in the region) to the E.U. are constrained by strict quality and food safety standards, as well as by seasonal restrictions to prevent competition with European growers. For this reason, we also simulated the impact on Egyptian households of improved market access to European fruit and vegetable markets, represented by increases in the prices for fruits and vegetables in Egypt.

In this analysis we simulated both the short-run and the long-run impacts of higher agricultural prices on each household in the Egypt Integrated Household Survey. The short-run impact refers to the effect on household welfare before households have had an opportunity to respond to the higher prices by producing more or consuming less. The change in per capita income of household *i* after the price change in one commodity, say wheat, can be calculated as follows:

$$\Delta y_i = \frac{1}{H_i} [(Q_{pi}\Delta P) - (Q_{ci}\Delta P)], \tag{1}$$

where Δy_i is the change in per capita income of household *i* after the price increase, H_i is the number of members in household *i*, Q_{pi} is the production of the commodity by household *i*, ΔP is the increase in the price of the commodity, and Q_{ci} is the quantity of wheat consumed by household *i*. In graphic terms, this expression is the rectangular approximation of producer surplus plus consumer surplus. If a household does not grow wheat, $Q_{pi} = 0$, and the direct effect of higher wheat prices will be negative; the magnitude will depend on the importance of wheat products in the household budget.

If a household does grow wheat, the welfare impact depends on the value of wheat production compared to the value of wheat consumption.

In the long run, farmers and consumers will respond to the higher prices by growing more and consuming less of the commodity, say wheat. The long-run effect can be estimated as follows:

$$\Delta y_i = \frac{1}{H_i}\left[(Q_{pi}\Delta P) + \left(\frac{1}{2}(\Delta P)^2 \varepsilon_S \frac{Q_{pi}}{P}\right) - (Q_{ci}\Delta P) - \left(\frac{1}{2}(\Delta P)^2 \varepsilon_D \frac{Q_{ci}}{P}\right)\right], \quad (2)$$

where ε_S is the supply elasticity of the commodity and ε_D is the price elasticity of demand for the commodity. In graphic terms, this expression is the trapezoidal approximation of the producer surplus plus the consumer surplus. The two terms with elasticities are positive regardless of whether the price change is positive or negative, implying that the long-term welfare effect of a price change is more positive (or less negative) than the short-term effect. In the absence of estimated supply and demand elasticities for the four commodities, we use 0.3 for the supply elasticities and -0.3 for the price elasticities of demand.

Because the welfare impact is calculated for each household in the Egypt Integrated Household Survey sample based on the income and consumption patterns of each household, we can estimate the change in the poverty measures caused by the change in prices. This microsimulation approach also allows us to estimate the change in income for any subgroup of households that is defined by income, farm size, or another variable. In this analysis we used the class of poverty measures identified by Foster, Greer, and Thorbecke (1984), defined as follows:

$$P_\alpha = \frac{1}{N}\sum_i \left[\frac{\mu - y_i}{\mu}\right]^\alpha, \quad (3)$$

where P_α is the poverty measure, N is the number of households, μ is the poverty line, and y_i is the income or expenditure of poor household i (the summation occurs only on poor households). When $\alpha = 0$, the poverty measure P_0 is the incidence of poverty, that is, the proportion of households whose incomes are below the poverty line. When $\alpha = 1$, the poverty measure P_1 indicates the depth of poverty, taking into account the degree of poverty, as well as the percentage of households that are poor. If $\alpha = 2$, the measure P_2 indicates the severity of poverty, incorporating information on the degree of inequality among poor households as well as the depth of poverty and the number of poor households.

CHAPTER 5

Agriculture, Trade, and Poverty in Tunisia

Tunisia is a small country (10 million inhabitants) endowed with few natural resources. In spite of these constraints, the country has diversified its economy through important investments in the agricultural, mining, energy, tourism, and manufacturing sectors. Growth in tourism and increased trade have been key elements in the economy's steady growth, although tourism has slowed since the September 11, 2001, attack.

Per capita GDP grew at a healthy rate (2.9 percent) over the 1990s, reaching over US$2,500 in 2002. This has given Tunisia the third-highest income in the MENA region, behind Turkey and Lebanon. About two-thirds of the population lives in urban areas.

Tunisia maintains relatively high tariff barriers. According to the World Bank (2005), Tunisia's simple average tariff rate puts it among the top 1 percent of countries in trade restrictions. There has been some trade liberalization, however: the average tariff rate came down from 29 percent in 2000 to about 25 percent in 2004. This progress is about average compared to that in other countries over the same period.

Meanwhile, Tunisia has a relatively favorable investment climate. The World Bank (2005) rates the investment climate in Tunisia better than that of 79 percent of the countries in the world. Furthermore, the reforms since 2000 indicate a degree of progress in the investment climate that is better than that in almost three-quarters of the world's countries. In particular, Tunisia has streamlined its procedures for opening and registering new businesses and for closing businesses. Tunisia, along with Morocco, has the highest ratio of foreign direct investment to GDP, over 3 percent.

Agriculture and Food

The Tunisian economy has undergone significant structural changes, including industrialization, the growth of the service sector, and the development of tourism. Nonetheless, the agricultural sector remains economically and socially important for its contribution to food security, employment, regional balance, and social cohesion. The contribution of agriculture and the fisheries sector has remained in the range of 11–14 percent of GDP since the mid-1990s. The value added in the food processing sector has remained at around 3 percent of GDP. Together, these sectors account for about 15 percent of GDP (Table 5.1).

Based on the gross value of output, livestock is the largest component of the agricultural sector in Tunisia, representing 36 percent of the total (Table 5.2). This is followed by fruits and vegetables, which together account for about 33 percent of the total. Agricultural production in Tunisia remains vulnerable to drought, however, as indicated by the annual variation in the value of output. The value of grain and fruit output has been particularly volatile.

According to a 2004/05 agricultural survey, wheat accounts for 23 percent of the planted area in Tunisia, barley 13 percent, olive trees 32 percent, fruit and nut trees 17 percent, forage crops 9 percent, and vegetables 4 percent. Agriculture in the north is dominated by grains and horticulture, in the center by olive production, and in the south by fruit, nuts, and olives. Table 5.3 shows the cropping pattern by farm size. The share of cultivated area allocated to grains ranges from 32 percent among farms with less than 5 ha to 45 percent among farms with more than 100 ha, reflecting the fact that grains are less labor-intensive than other crops. Hard wheat (used for couscous and pasta) represents roughly half the grain area across farm size categories, while soft wheat is more important on large farms and barley is more important on small farms. Large farms devote a larger share of their cropland to hard wheat, soft wheat, and forage crops, while small farmers allocate a larger share to barley, vegetables, and tree crops, most of which are olive trees (MARH 2006).

Tunisian exports were US$9.4 billion in 2002. One source of growth in exports has been textiles and apparel, which earned US$2.9 billion in 2002. Tunisia enjoyed preferential access to European markets as a result of the quota system under the Multi-Fiber Arrangement. However, the Multi-Fiber Arrangement expired in January 2005, so Tunisian exporters will now compete more directly with exporters from Asia, particularly China, India, and Pakistan.

As discussed in Chapter 3, Tunisian agricultural exports in 2002 were about US$500 million, or about 5 percent of total exports. The largest agricultural export over 2000–02 was olive oil, although the value of olive oil exports fluctuated considerably over this period. Other important agricultural exports include dates, wheat flour, tomato paste, and pasta, reflecting the importance of the food processing sector.

Tunisian imports were worth about US$10 billion in 2002, while agricultural imports were at US$1.2 billion, or 12 percent of the total. As in many other MENA countries, wheat is the most important agricultural import. Wheat imports account for 60–80 percent of domestic consumption, depending on

Table 5.1 Contribution of agriculture and food processing to GDP in Tunisia, 1995-2001

Category		1995	1996	1997	1998	1999	2000	2001
GDP	Nominal prices (millions of TND)	17,052	19,066	20,898	22,561	24,672	26,685	28,757
	1990 prices (millions of TND)	13,074	14,009	14,771	15,477	16,415	17,181	18,028
Agriculture	Nominal prices (millions of TND)	1,938	2,615	2,760	2,866	3,211	3,298	3,347
	1990 prices (millions of TND)	1,573	2,038	2,098	2,077	2,306	2,283	2,249
	Contribution to GDP (%)	11.4	13.7	13.2	12.7	13.0	12.4	11.6
Food processing	Nominal prices (millions of TND)	556	586	701	708	817	863	903
	1990 prices (millions of TND)	426	434	517	501	566	608	593
	Contribution to GDP (%)	3.3	3.1	3.4	3.1	3.3	3.2	3.1

Sources: Tunisian Ministry of Agriculture and Central Bank of Tunisia.

Notes: TND, Tunisian dinars. The exchange rate was TND 1.10 per US$1.00 in 1997, TND 1.16 per US$1.00 in 1998, TND 1.21 per US$1.00 in 1999, TND 1.34 per US$1.00 in 2000, and TND 1.50 per US$1.00 in 2001, according to the June 30 rates in www.oanda.com.

Table 5.2 Composition of the Tunisian agricultural sector, 1995-2001

	Value of agricultural production (millions of TND at nominal prices)							
Sector	1995	1996	1997	1998	1999	2000	2001	2001 share (%)
Overall	2,291	2,986	3,167	3,285	3,684	3,761	3,862	100.0
Grains	162	650	275	429	460	285	364	9.4
Fruits	593	647	1,116	810	951	1,119	804	20.8
Vegetables	389	444	442	515	599	600	462	12.0
Livestock	898	964	1,091	1,182	1,317	1,379	1,390	36.0
Fisheries	184	202	241	248	249	273	278	7.2

Sources: Tunisian Ministry of Agriculture and Central Bank of Tunisia.
Note: TND, Tunisian dinars.

Table 5.3 Share of crop area allocated to different crop categories in Tunisia, by farm size (hectares), 2006

Crop	0-5 ha	5-10 ha	10-20 ha	20-50 ha	50-100 ha	>100 ha	Overall
Grains	31.8	32.8	33.7	37.1	41.3	45.1	36.5
Hard wheat	16.9	18.0	18.5	19.3	23.5	22.6	19.3
Soft wheat	0.6	1.0	1.0	2.2	3.7	11.3	3.7
Barley	14.0	13.4	13.8	15.2	14.0	10.4	13.1
Other grains	0.0	0.3	0.3	0.4	0.0	0.9	0.4
Pulses	1.8	1.9	1.8	1.4	1.6	2.1	1.8
Forages	7.2	6.8	7	7.6	9.6	13.5	8.7
Vegetables	5.5	5.6	3.5	2.4	2.2	1.2	3.7
Industrial crops	0.5	0.5	0.3	0.4	0.8	0.6	0.5
Tree crops	53.2	52.4	53.6	51.2	44.4	37.5	48.9
Total	100.0	100.0	100.0	100.0	100.0	100.0	100.0

Source: MARH (2006).

the weather and the size of the wheat harvest. Other major agricultural imports are maize, barley, soybean cake, cooking oil, and sugar. As in most other MENA countries, in Tunisia the value of agricultural imports exceeds the value of agricultural exports.

Agricultural and Trade Policy

The implementation of a structural adjustment program for the agricultural sector between 1986 and 1996 began the liberalization of Tunisian agriculture, the improvement in the competitiveness of agro-food industries, and their adaptation to the qualitative and sanitary requirements of international markets. With the exception of activities related to wheat, agricultural production activities have been substantially liberalized. Agricultural input subsidies and interest rate subsidies have been practically eliminated. Although irrigation water is still subsidized, fees continue to be adjusted. Agricultural marketing boards have lost some of their monopoly powers.

Agricultural and Food Policy

Concerning domestic support, Tunisia declared to the WTO a current total aggregate measurement of support of zero for the year 2002 relative to a maximum commitment of 61 million Tunisian dinars (TND 61 million, or US$5.5 million) on the following products: durum and soft wheat, barley, milk, olive oil, and sugar beets. The support declared for 2002 was *de minimis*. It consisted of fixed producer buying prices for wheat and intervention prices for other products. Tunisia reported that a similar amount was spent on green box measures exempt from the reduction commitment; these mostly went toward water and soil conservation and forestation programs.

In addition, Tunisia has declared an additional TND 8.3 million (US$750,000) as an irrigation subsidy. In fact, farmers in publicly irrigated areas still pay for water at below the real cost. Additionally, farmers and agro-food enterprises are entitled to special electricity and diesel tariffs. Tunisia also subsidizes exports of agricultural products. These subsidies consist of payments intended to reduce the cost of processing and air freight.

Agricultural Pricing Policy

The agricultural and fisheries sector has been subjected to two forms of price control: controls on producer prices and controls on prices for agricultural inputs. Since 1986, Tunisia has been conducting a program of structural adjustment aimed at reforming the agricultural sector by shifting prices closer to those on world markets and reducing producer subsidies. Although subsidies on inputs have been removed totally (except for those on water), support for agricultural production through investment subsidies remain at a high level for some activities (see the next subsection).

Concerning the control of producer prices, prices for all products are freely determined except those for grain and milk, which continue to benefit from guaranteed public prices. Instead of supporting farm prices, Tunisian agricultural pricing policy has had the effect of holding farm prices down. When domestic production is limited for a given product, mainly for vegetables and meats, prices tend to rise. Public authorities implement a set of maximum prices on wholesale or retail markets without any compensation to farmers. However, when prices are at low levels due to the abundance of local production, no instrument of support for farmers is applied. This policy, intended to control inflation, has heavily affected farm incomes during the past few years. Small farmers producing vegetables are the most affected by the policy.

Taxation

In addition to tariffs, supplementary taxes are levied on the consumption of a whole range of food products, in particular maize and soybean cake, preserved food, fruits and vegetables, and fish. The taxes are earmarked for the Fund for the Development of Competitiveness in the Agriculture and Fishing Sectors. These taxes are applied to locally produced goods, as well as to imports.

The tax code is used to encourage agricultural development. More specifically, the investment incentives code includes the following provisions:

- deduction of amounts invested from taxable profits,
- exemption from customs duties and the suspension of the value-added tax and consumption tax due on imports of capital goods for which there are no locally manufactured equivalents,
- the suspension of the value-added tax on locally manufactured capital goods, and
- the exemption of investments from income tax for 10 years.

Financial benefits include an (investment) subsidy of 7 percent of the cost of the investment (maximum TND 300,000, or US$33,500) and another subsidy of 1 percent of the total cost of investment, with a ceiling of TND 5,000, as the state's contribution to project design costs. In 2002, Tunisia spent TND 91 million (US$8.2 million) through its development programs to encourage investment in agriculture by subsidizing the cost of private investment in selected activities.

Consumer Food Subsidies

The consumer price for each product for which the producer price is subject to administrative control is also controlled. This is particularly true for grains and milk. By means of the General Compensation Fund (Caisse Générale de Compensation), the Tunisian government has subsidized the consumption of basic foodstuffs since 1970. The subsidies have been applied uniformly to whoever chooses to buy subsidized products in whatever quantity. The subsidies of the fund have been introduced to satisfy a somewhat contradictory host of objectives: (1) stabilization of fluctuating prices for basic products, (2) preservation of the purchasing power of underprivileged households, and (3) the redistribution of incomes in favor of low-income groups.

Since 2000, the products covered by the subsidies of the fund are grains and products derived from them, vegetable oil, and milk. Although the size of the food subsidies has gradually been reduced since 1996, the subsidies still represent about 2 percent of government expenditures (Table 5.4).

The cereal subsector accounts for the most politically sensitive, complex, and costly part of the system of subsidies. Subsidies are injected at three levels in the marketing channel: the collection of local production, importation, and flour milling. The Grain Board (Office des Céréales) manages the payment of subsidies in the cereal subsector for the General Compensation Fund. The Grain Board has a monopoly on the importation of grains and on the collection of locally produced cereals by farmers. Together with the Grain Board, two technically private, well-regulated cooperatives work in the name of the Grain Board according to the same mechanism. The National Edible Oils Board (Office National de Huiles) controls the importation and refining of vegetable oil and the subsidies for it. The consumption price of vegetable oil is set below cost, and the board is refunded the difference through the General Compensation Fund. Presently, the milk subsector represents only a small share of the consumption subsidies. This has been the result of the development of local production and improvements in the productivity of private industry.

Trade Policy

Tunisian authorities use tariffs and NTBs to protect domestic production from outside competition. These began to be modified in 1995 with the implementation of the URAA, but the two instruments are still widely used in Tunisia.

Table 5.4 Structure and importance of food subsidies in Tunisia, 1999-2004

Category	1999	2000	2001	2002	2003	2004
Composition of food subsidies (%)						
Grains	64.2	73.9	80.5	72.5	64.4	70.7
Oil	29.3	20.4	15.1	23.7	32.6	26.7
Milk	5.5	5.7	4.4	3.8	3.0	2.5
Sugar	1.0	0.0	0.0	0.0	0.0	0.0
Food subsidies/government expenditures (%)	2.1	2.0	2.1	1.8	1.7	1.9
Food subsidies/GDP (%)	0.8	0.8	0.8	0.7	0.6	0.7
Subsidies/person (TND/year)	21.1	19.5	21.0	18.1	17.3	19.4

Source: Authors' calculations using data from the Central Bank of Tunisia (2005) and the INS (2005).

Notes: TND, Tunisian dinars. The exchange rate was TND 1.21 per US$1.00 in 1999, TND 1.34 per US$1.00 in 2000, TND 1.50 per US$1.00 in 2001, TND 1.38 per US$1.00 in 2002, TND 1.36 per US$1.00 in 2003, and TND 1.25 per US$1.00 in 2004 according to the June 30 rates at www.oanda.com.

Tunisian customs duties are still among the highest in the world. In fact, in 2002 nondiscriminatory duties rose to 34.5 percent, on average, against an average rate of 12.8 percent among middle-income countries in the same year. The agricultural and food processing sectors continue to be highly protected. Because the partnership agreement with the E.U. has bearing only on non-agricultural and manufactured food products, agricultural trade continues to be governed by the commitments that Tunisia has made within the multilateral framework of the WTO. Quantitative restrictions have been converted to customs duties, but, as in many member states, bound tariff rates have been fixed at very high levels. Although on the eve of the signing of the GATT in Marrakech in 1994 nominal protection rose to an average rate of 39 percent and 46 percent, respectively, for the agricultural and food processing sectors, the respective rates rose to 136 percent and 88 percent in 1997. They have been reduced through the years in conformity with the agreement on agriculture but still remain at very high levels, 89 percent on average for agricultural products and 72 percent for agro-industry products (Table 5.5).

For agricultural and food processing products, the tariffs vary greatly. Customs duties and other import taxes are generally high for fruit, forest cultivation products, tobacco, meat, dairy products, products derived from the processing of cereals, canned foods, and beverages. They are not so high for cereals, livestock, oils, and sugar, four categories that, together, account for 60 percent of agricultural imports. Nevertheless, Tunisia preserved preferential customs duties as part of its proposals for the GATT agreements in 1994, which are applied to certain products within the limits of quotas set by public authorities. Preferential rates are much lower than the bound tariffs (Table 5.6).

Table 5.5 Nominal protection by major economic activity in Tunisia, 1995-2003 (percent)

Sector	1995 E.U.	2000 E.U.	2001 E.U.	2002 E.U.	2002 rest of world	2003 E.U.	2003 rest of world
Agriculture and fishing	39	126	100	98	98	89	89
Manufacturing	43	39	36	33	45	29	42
Other sectors	11	11	3	3	9	1	3
Total	34	42	36	35	43	31	39
Total, except agriculture and food processing	30	21	16	15	24	12	22

Source: Chemingui and Lahouel (2006).
Note: E.U., European Union.

Table 5.6 Tariff rates in and out of quotas, 2005, and use of tariff quotas in Tunisia, 2001-04

Product	Average in-quota tariff rate (%)	Average out-of-quota tariff rate (%)	Tariff quota commitments (tons)	Quota use rate (%)			
				2001	2002	2003	2004
Durum wheat	17	73	300,000	100	100	0	0
Soft wheat	17	73	600,000	100	100	85	100
Barley	17	73	200,000	100	100	100	100
Beans	25	60	1,300	0	0	0	0
Sugar	15	42	100,000	100	100	100	228
Shelled almonds	43	60	1,335	70	100	0	0
Tomato concentrate	43	100	155	0	0	0	100
Milk powder	17	76	20,000	10	19	35	43
Butter	35	100	4,000	60	88	48	49
Cheese	27	139	1,500	100	100	100	100
Calves and bullocks	27	82	3,000	0	0	0	97
Bovine meat	27	88	8,000	0	0	0	100
Sheep and goat meat	27	125	380	0	0	0	100

Source: WTO (2005b).
Note: The quota use rate refers to the level of imports as a percentage of the quota.

Import operations at preferential tariffs are generally granted to state enterprises. Accordingly, wheat, maize, and barley are imported under tariff quotas exclusively by the Grain Board, vegetable oil by the National Edible Oils Board, and tea and coffee by the Tunisian Trade Board. Special authorization is required to import products subject to tariff quotas. This license is issued by the Ministry of Trade. Private operators are rarely able to import within the framework of the preferential quotas.

Effective protection has decreased over time but remains high. It increased during the first years of the dismantling of tariffs on European manufactured products because of the dismantling sequence, which began with inputs and finished products that do not compete with local production. This situation has been redressed with the entry of the fourth list of competing products in the dismantling phase of customs duties (Table 5.7). Concerning agricultural and agro-industrial products, effective protection has followed a declining tendency, albeit very limited. In fact, effective protection in this sector decreased from 162 percent in 2000 to 108 percent in 2003.

The monopolies on the importation of certain food and agricultural products by state enterprises (the Grain Board, the Tunisian Trade Board, and the National Edible Oils Board) continues to represent the main tool for protection of the agricultural and food sector in Tunisia. These monopolies cover an important share of Tunisian imports. The Tunisian Trade Board maintains the

Table 5.7 Effective protection in Tunisia, by major economic activity, 1995, 2000-03 (percent)

Sector	1995 E.U.	2000 E.U.	2001 E.U.	2002 E.U.	2002 rest of world	2003 E.U.	2003 rest of world
Agriculture and fishing	45	162	123	120	118	110	108
Manufacturing	85	68	60	57	92	49	87
Other sectors	12	15	3	4	11	1	1
Total	41	63	50	49	60	44	54
Total except agriculture and food processing	34	30	20	19	34	16	29

Source: Institute of Quantitative Studies (2003).
Note: E.U., European Union.

monopoly on importing products considered basic, such as sugar, coffee, tea, black pepper, cocoa beans, rice, kidney beans, and dry yeast, as well as some fresh and dry fruits and vegetables and tinned foods. For other agricultural and food products that might otherwise be freely imported, obtaining authorization (rather than simply a license) makes importation almost impossible. Without offering any justification, the Tunisian administration often rejects import requests.

Technical barriers also represent an indirect tool for the protection of domestic production. In general, technical barriers aim at verifying the conformity of imported products with sanitary and food safety norms. Technical control has been consolidated since the accession of Tunisia to the WTO in 1995. Although it was applied to only around a quarter of the customs categories in 1994 (37 percent of the value of imports), the percentage of customs categories subject to this control rose to more than 30 percent in 2001 (43 percent of the import value). Most of this increase involved the control of consumption goods through certification, but systematic control remains very important, applying to almost 14 percent of the imports in terms of customs value. It is this kind of control that mostly causes deadline and efficiency problems. The sanitary, phytosanitary, and technical standards are legitimate under WTO rules and are practiced in most countries, but often technical control is used for protectionist ends in Tunisia.

Customs clearance is another obstacle to importation, particularly for imports destined for the local market. Imports of agro-food products that are exclusively destined for the domestic market still suffer from long clearance delays, estimated at three weeks on average, compared to only a few days in other countries.

The tariff equivalent of NTBs provides an indicator of the scale of this type of protection. In order to assess this for the main agricultural products imported into Tunisia in 1992, Chemingui and Dessus (2001) used the price gap approach, which involves comparing local prices and border prices. Of 19 agricultural and food products studied, 6 were subjected to significant levels of NTBs. Sugar had the highest nontariff protection, with a tariff equivalent of 28 percent, followed by hard wheat (20 percent). The other protected products were barley, soft wheat, vegetable produce, and canned goods.

Trade Agreements

Tunisia is currently involved in many regional trade agreements in addition to its commitments under the WTO. Overall, Tunisia has concluded trade agreements with about 60 countries; some of these agreements provide for preferential arrangements. Since its last trade policy reform was implemented in 1994, Tunisia has signed the WTO agreement, a bilateral agreement with the E.U., bilateral agreements with the members of the Arab League, and agreements with Turkey and the European Free Trade Association. All of these agreements are classified as FTAs. In what follows we describe the content of these trade agreements regarding agricultural products.

The WTO

Tunisia acceded to the GATT in 1990 and has been a member of the WTO since March 1995. The commitments of Tunisia emerging from the Uruguay Round involve binding 4,005 tariff lines in the agricultural and industrial sectors or 66 percent tariff lines under the Harmonized System. In the agricultural sector, the commitments made by Tunisia involve binding 1,503 tariff lines (25 percent of the total) at rates that vary between 25 and 250 percent, along with a commitment to reduce these rates by 24 percent over 10 years (1995–2004). The commitments of Tunisia also involve insuring the opening up of tariff quotas for the importation of agricultural and food processing products at lower customs duty rates. Furthermore, Tunisia committed to reducing the level of its domestic support for agriculture by 13.3 percent over 1995–2005.

The EMP Agreement

The E.U. is Tunisia's main trading partner: 76 percent of Tunisia's trade goes to or comes from the E.U. Imports of European agricultural and food products account for a little under half of all imports of products in these two categories. The European market takes up about 70 percent of Tunisia's agricultural trade and food exports.

Tunisia is one of the most important exporters of several products, including olive oil, dates, citrus fruit, seafood, and various organic fruits and vegetables. Exports of these products are slowly being supplanted by increases in exports of melons, table grapes, table olives, and, potentially, tomatoes and strawberries. At the same time, Tunisia is a net importer of other agricultural products, mainly wheat, sugar, and vegetable oils. For these products, the E.U. is a leading exporter country. Both the imports and exports of agricultural products by Tunisia are sensitive to the common agricultural policy of the E.U. In fact, import prices for agricultural products are significantly determined by the level of European subsidies on exports under the common agricultural policy; likewise, exports of Tunisian agricultural products are subject to the protection instruments implemented through this policy.

Trade relations between Tunisia and the E.U. in agricultural and food products are governed by the EMP Agreement signed in 1995. This provides for the establishment of a free trade area following a 12-year transitional period. The foundation of the partnership agreement is the principle of reciprocity. It provides for the removal of tariffs on all products, with the exception of agricultural products. Agricultural products are excluded from the agreement and are subject to specific arrangements. In fact, trade in agricultural and food products remains affected by barriers to entry in both markets. In the case of the E.U. market, the Common Agricultural Policy has introduced many barriers to the importation of Tunisian agricultural and food products.

Although agriculture was excluded from the 1995 agreement, the agreement provided for the E.U. and Tunisia to review the trade regime for agriculture in 2000. In December 2000 the E.U. and Tunisia agreed on measures to liberalize trade in agricultural products beginning in January 2001. As an illustration, Tunisia has obtained better access to the E.U. market for olive oil (an increase in the annual quota and a duty set to zero), cut flowers, tomato concentrate, new potatoes, and oranges, for which an increase in the free duty quota has been agreed. The E.U. has obtained improved access for vegetable oils and wheat with the application of the preferential tariffs.

In accordance with Protocol 3 of the association agreement, Tunisia applies preferential tariff quotas to several agro-food products originating in the E.U. With respect to meat, dairy products, cereals, and sugar, which are also covered by WTO tariff quotas, exports from the E.U. may draw either on the WTO quota or on the preferential quota. However, E.U. exports under preferential tariff quotas are zero-rated; moreover, these quotas also cover other agricultural products such as eggs, poultry, potatoes, hazelnuts, maize (corn), meal, malt, starch, certain flours, fats, oils, glucose, and dog and cat food.

For Tunisian agricultural exports to the European market, a new regime of trade implemented on March 8, 2001, ratified the association agreement between the parties through the modification of the agricultural protocols annexed to the 1995 association agreement. In this respect, export quotas, tariff reductions, and schedules for products exported by Tunisia to the E.U. are indicated in the first draft (protocol) of the agreement. For olive oil, the agreement clauses specified (1) the institutionalization of the quota regime and permanent integration of these products into the association agreement and (2) an increase in the quota from 50,000 metric tons as of January 1, 2001, to 56,000 metric tons on January 1, 2005, with a complete exemption from customs duties.

Protocol 2, which concerns fishing products, stipulates that fishing products from Tunisia may be admitted to the E.U. with no quantitative limit and totally exempt from customs duties. Furthermore, the two parties agreed to examine in 2005 the possibility of granting each other mutual concessions in order to liberalize their trade in agricultural and fishing products. These negotiations are still in progress, and no agreement has been reached to date.

It is important to note that the agricultural sector in Tunisia is affected by the general scarcity of water and arable land, occasional drought, and natural resource degradation, all of which limit the ability of Tunisian farmers to take advantage of further concessions by the E.U. (Olive oil, however, is one product for which E.U. concessions could generate immediate benefits for Tunisian farmers.) Furthermore, the integration of agricultural products into the FTA cannot be separated from the issue of the support paid by the E.U. to its farmers. Without a substantial reform of the common agricultural policy, most agricultural activities in Tunisia will not be able to overcome the European competition, particularly in products that are highly subsidized in Europe.

GAFTA

The executive program of the Convention on the Facilitation and Development of Inter-Arab Trade entered into force in January 1998; it is currently being applied by 17 of the 22 members of the League of Arab States. GAFTA is a new Arab League initiative that aims to revive previously unsuccessful attempts at regional integration. According to the agreement, all Arab products moving among the members will be afforded the status of national goods in accordance with the principle of gradual liberalization through an annual reduction of 10 percent of the customs duties and taxes that have equivalent tariff effects. Initially, goods were scheduled to be traded duty free among the members by 2007, but at its 69th meeting, in Cairo, the Economic and Social Council decided to accelerate the establishment of GAFTA, setting 2005 instead of 2007 as the deadline for the launch. In 2004 it was planned that all the Arab countries that had joined GAFTA would reduce their customs duties on bilateral trade by 80 percent and completely eliminate all tariffs by 2005.

Provisions for agricultural trade under the agreement offer members the opportunity to suspend tariff reductions on some products during peak harvest seasons. In this regard, each member is allowed to submit a list of 10 products for suspension, with a total exemption of all these products for 45 months.

The FTA with the European Free Trade Association

The member states of the European Free Trade Association—Iceland, Lichtenstein, Norway, and Switzerland—signed an FTA with Tunisia in Geneva on December 17, 2004. Negotiations on the European Free Trade Association-Tunisia Free Trade Agreement were launched in Tunis in October 1996 and were concluded in 2004 after six rounds of negotiations. The agreement covers trade in industrial goods, as well as processed agricultural products.

The agreement takes into consideration the different levels of economic development of the members of the European Free Trade Association on the one hand and Tunisia on the other by providing for asymmetric tariff reduction. The states of the association will eliminate duties and other restrictions for covered products upon entry into force of the agreement, while Tunisia will gradually abolish its duties during a transition period. The agreement contains rules of origin on the model of the Euro-Mediterranean accumulation system. Trade in basic agricultural products is covered by arrangements concluded bilaterally between each association state and Tunisia.

The FTA with Turkey

The association agreement establishing a free trade area between Tunisia and Turkey was signed on November 25, 2004. The agreement covers provisions on preferential trade, state monopolies, competition and state aid, intellectual property rights, public procurement, and economic and technical cooperation. With this agreement Tunisia and Turkey aimed at strengthening their cooperation, removing trade barriers, including agricultural trade, establishing appropriate conditions for competition, and promoting bilateral investments. A free trade area will be created within nine years following the entry into force of the agreement.

Protocol II of the agreement establishes a preferential trade regime that will be applied to agricultural trade. Concessions are exchanged for a given number of agricultural, fishing, and processed agricultural products on the basis of tariff quotas. This agreement entered into effect in June 2005.

Poverty

Tunisia has made significant progress in reducing poverty (Figure 5.1). The incidence of poverty (defined using the national poverty line) was cut from

Figure 5.1 The evolution of poverty reduction in Tunisia, 1990-2000

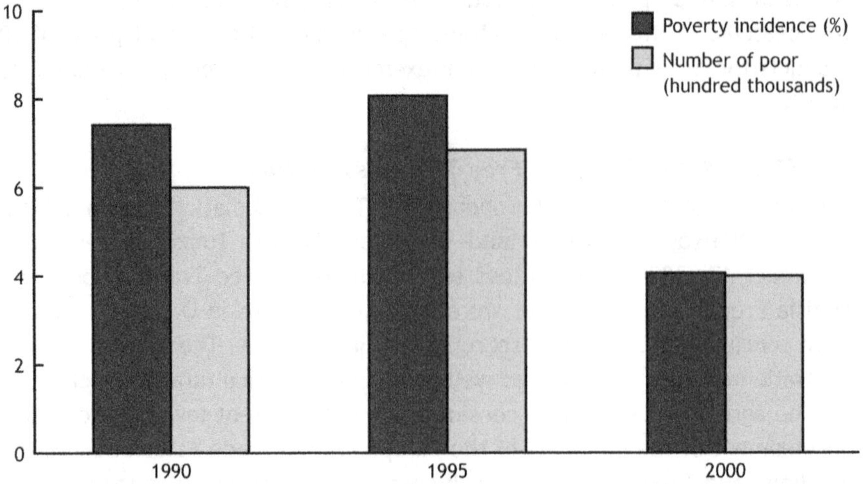

Source: World Bank (2003a).

40 percent in 1960 to 11 percent in 1985 and to 7.4 percent in 1990. The poverty rate stagnated between 1990 and 1995 (8.1 percent)[1] but resumed its decline between 1995 and 2000, when its incidence reached the lowest level (4.1 percent). At the same time, the population growth rate declined and life expectancy increased markedly, regional disparities were reduced, and improvements were achieved in education, access to health care, and basic infrastructure. The distribution of income improved until 1990, as the Gini coefficient fell from 0.434 in 1985 to 0.401 in 1990. It was estimated at 0.417 in 1995 and 0.409 in 2000. Average per capita expenditures for the lowest deciles of the population moved closer to mean expenditures for the country as a whole. In absolute terms, the number of the poor increased from 600,000 in 1990 to 690,000 in 1995 and fell to 400,000 in 2000 (World Bank 2003a). Given that the distribution of consumption is quite steep near the poverty line, many households are vulnerable to sliding back into poverty.

Regarding the characteristics of the poor in Tunisia, poverty remains primarily a rural phenomenon. In 2000, the incidence of rural poverty was 8.3 percent compared to 0.8 percent in metropolitan areas and 2.3 percent in other urban areas (Table 5.8). Rural areas, with less than 40 percent of the total population, accounted for 74 percent of the poor in 2000 compared to 76 percent in 1990 (World Bank 2003a).

[1] Using a new World Bank and Institut National de la Statistique poverty line (World Bank 2003a).

Table 5.8 Poverty lines and poverty incidence in Tunisia, 1990, 1995, and 2000

Population group	Year	Lower poverty lines (core poverty) (TND)	Poverty incidence (%)
Metropolitan	1990	236	2.8
	1995	306	1.8
Other urban	1990	210	3.5
	1995	272	4.2
	2000	318	2.3
Rural	1990	194	14.8
	1995	252	15.8
	2000	294	8.3

Source: World Bank (2003a).
Note: TND, Tunisian dinars.

There is a strong association between poverty and lack of schooling in both rural and urban areas. Over 60 percent of poor household heads have no formal education compared to about 40 percent of nonpoor household heads. Poor rural households engaged in production activities typically have access to land, but their land holdings are small (averaging 2 hectares), are rarely irrigated, and often exhibit low productivity, especially in rainfed areas.

The urban poor are mostly wage earners in low-skill occupations. According to data from the Institut National de la Statistique (INS 2002), between 1990 and 1995 the incidence of poverty increased in the agricultural, fishing, and construction sectors and fell in tourism and commercial activities. In 2000, the poorest households were still concentrated in the construction and agricultural sectors.

The Impact of Trade Liberalization on Poverty

This section presents the results of a microsimulation analysis of the impact of trade liberalization on Tunisian households.[2] First we briefly describe the methods used to generate the estimates (a more detailed description is found in the appendix to this chapter). Then we describe the results of the simulations of four different types of trade liberalization. The impact is assessed in terms of macroeconomic variables, sectoral production, imports, exports, and the incidence of poverty in urban and rural areas.

[2] The model used here has been developed through a study funded by the Poverty and Economic Policy Research Network (see Chemingui and Thabet 2006).

Methods

This analysis involves using a CGE model to simulate the effects of four types of trade liberalization on the Tunisian economy and households. The CGE model is built on a social accounting matrix (SAM) calibrated to describe the Tunisian economy in 1996. It is a standard neoclassical CGE model, with imperfect substitution in consumption between imported and domestic goods and imperfect substitution in production between exports and production for the domestic market. Production combines raw materials and factors of production in fixed proportions, while the use of different factors varies according to relative factor prices. There are five categories of labor:

- farmers,
- unskilled agricultural wage earners,
- skilled agricultural wage earners,
- unskilled nonagricultural workers, and
- skilled nonagricultural workers.

Other factors are land, physical capital, and natural resources. The model covers 17 commodities and 17 activities, of which 14 are related to agriculture and food processing. It assumes perfect mobility of physical capital among the different sectors. The model also assumes an exogenous real trade balance, fiscal deficit, and fiscal expenditure. Increases in import demand are offset by depreciation of the exchange rate, which stimulates exports and maintains the trade balance. Reductions in import tariff revenue are offset by increases in the value-added tax (VAT).

What distinguishes this model is that it includes a fully integrated microsimulation model. In order to estimate the distributional impact of trade policy, data from 397 households are integrated into the CGE model. These 397 households are a representative sample from the 1995 Tunisian household expenditure survey. The survey contains detailed expenditure data but not income data. Thus, it was necessary to generate estimated income data based on survey information on the main economic activity of each member of the household. The household survey data, the SAM, and the CGE model are described in more detail in the appendix to this chapter.

It is important to note that this is a static model in that it does not take into account the effect of trade liberalization on investment or on the rate of adoption of new technology. To the extent that trade liberalization encourages investment or accelerates the adoption of technology, as some studies suggest, the model will understate the welfare benefits of liberalization.

Results

We analyze the impact of four alternative types of trade liberalization. Each scenario provides empirical estimations of the potential trade liberalization of agricultural products either with a single partner or with various partners at the same time. The four simulations are as follows:

1. elimination of tariffs on imports of industrial products entering Tunisia from the E.U. as specified in the partnership agreement signed between the two partners,
2. elimination of tariffs on Tunisian imports of industrial *and agricultural* products from the E.U.,
3. elimination of tariffs on Tunisian imports of industrial and agricultural products from the E.U. *and the rest of the world,* and
4. elimination of tariffs on imports of industrial and agricultural products from the E.U. and the rest of the world, *together with multilateral trade liberalization,* which it is assumed would increase international prices for all agricultural products by 15 percent.

The model is used to simulate the impact of these alternative policies on macroeconomic variables, production, international trade, and the incidence of poverty.

Simulation 1

In this scenario, Tunisia eliminates tariffs on industrial products from the E.U. in accordance with the provisions of the EMP (note that this simulation does not capture the effect of E.U. import liberalization on Tunisian exports). According to Table 5.9, this trade policy change would have a relatively weak macroeconomic impact. Real GDP would increase by 0.2 percent relative to the base year. The total output of goods and services would show a more important improvement, at a rate of 3.7 percent. Total final consumption would increase by 0.4 percent relative to the base scenario.

Agricultural production would not be stimulated by the increase in the openness of the Tunisian economy to trade with Europe, which is not surprising because agriculture remains outside the liberalization process in this scenario. Moreover, "other manufacturing" and nonmanufacturing industry would expand, drawing mobile production factors (physical capital and unskilled labor), which would cause a drop in production in most agricultural activities. There would be a 71 percent decline in tariff revenue, but the model maintains the original level of fiscal revenue by a 99 percent increase in the VAT, from 4.2 percent to 8.3 percent (Table 5.10).

Total imports would expand by 16 percent as a result of import liberalization, but most of this would occur in nonagricultural goods. Imports of food and agricultural commodities would generally decline or increase only modestly because the lower tariffs on nonagricultural imports would stimulate the demand for foreign currency, thus raising the cost of agricultural imports (Table 5.11).

Table 5.9 Estimated impact of trade liberalization on macroeconomic variables in Tunisia

Category	Base scenario	Simulation (% change relative to base scenario)			
		1	2	3	4
Real GDP (millions of TND)	38,673	0.2	0.3	0.2	0.2
Total output (millions of TND)	39,910	3.7	4.1	5.6	5.2
Total investment (millions of TND)	4,760	8.5	8.5	10.9	9.6
Consumer price index	100	-2.3	-3.5	-4.1	-4.3
Tariff income (millions of TND)	1,328	-71.0	-79.8	-100.0	-100.0
Adjustment in average VAT (%)	4.2	98.8	119.3	149.6	193.7
Total real final consumption (millions of TND)	14,586	0.4	1.9	2.6	2.9
Total imports (millions of TND)	8,326	15.9	18.0	22.0	22.5
Total exports (millions of TND)	8,030	23.2	26.1	32.0	33.7

Source: Authors' calculations.

Notes: Simulation 1 is the removal of tariffs on industrial goods from the European Union. Simulation 2 is the removal of tariffs on all goods from the European Union. Simulation 3 is the removal of tariffs on all goods from all countries. Simulation 4 is the removal of tariffs on all goods from all countries plus multilateral trade liberalization. TND, Tunisian dinars; VAT, value-added tax.

Table 5.10 Estimated impact of trade liberalization on production in Tunisia

Sector	Base value (millions of TND)	Simulation (% change relative to base scenario)			
		1	2	3	4
Cereals	591	-0.5	-0.1	-1.8	-1.8
Legumes	32	-1.8	-0.8	-0.1	-5.5
Other crops	220	-1.6	-8.7	-9.9	35.0
Fruits	840	-0.7	-0.6	-0.8	0.5
Vegetables	526	-0.9	0.0	0.0	-5.6
Other agricultural activities	29	7.5	4.3	6.9	-2.4
Livestock	1,011	-3.2	-6.7	-7.7	-2.7
Forestry	72	-1.2	-1.4	-1.5	-1.8
Fishing	276	-6.4	-6.6	-8.6	-9.6
Meat	633	-4.1	-8.2	-8.7	-3.5
Milk	191	0.1	-14.7	-20.4	8.4
Sugar	141	-1.3	-2.9	-6.6	64.0
Beverages	228	-4.0	-7.6	-7.7	-3.1
Other food processing	2,765	-1.5	0.1	0.7	-12.6
Other manufacturing	11,404	16.4	18.3	23.6	23.5
Nonmanufacturing industry	2,362	8.7	9.7	15.9	14.4
Services	18,587	-0.9	-0.9	-0.8	-1.3

Source: Authors' calculations.

Notes: Simulation 1 is the removal of tariffs on industrial goods from the European Union. Simulation 2 is the removal of tariffs on all goods from the European Union. Simulation 3 is the removal of tariffs on all goods from all countries. Simulation 4 is the removal of tariffs on all goods from all countries plus multilateral trade liberalization. TND, Tunisian dinars.

Table 5.11 Estimated impact of trade liberalization on food and agricultural imports in Tunisia

Sector	Base year (millions of TND)	Simulation (% change relative to base scenario) 1	2	3	4
Cereals	186.0	-4.9	-1.1	11.4	-17.2
Legumes	70.6	-4.5	-4.5	13.6	-13.6
Other crops	63.0	0.3	13.6	11.2	-0.8
Fruits	8.0	-7.0	62.8	203.0	214.3
Vegetables	13.0	-5.8	13.9	12.8	15.3
Other agricultural activities	7.6	0.8	24.2	37.3	51.3
Livestock	7.3	-2.3	22.8	24.0	25.0
Forestry	5.1	-6.9	-10.9	-12.1	-5.6
Fishing	1.6	2.4	1.6	4.0	0.8
Meat	9.9	-2.3	163.4	165.1	50.3
Milk	27.9	-4.8	59.6	76.4	-1.1
Sugar	87.4	-3.4	-1.6	11.4	-40.9
Beverages	7.2	4.2	103.6	105.2	-10.3
Other food processing	258.3	1.4	9.6	17.8	153.1
Other manufacturing	6,280.0	17.6	17.8	20.3	19.9
Nonmanufacturing industry	669.2	74.0	76.0	116.6	112.4
Services	623.8	9.2	9.2	15.3	14.6

Source: Authors' calculations.

Notes: Simulation 1 is the removal of tariffs on industrial goods from the European Union. Simulation 2 is the removal of tariffs on all goods from the European Union. Simulation 3 is the removal of tariffs on all goods from all countries. Simulation 4 is the removal of tariffs on all goods from all countries plus multilateral trade liberalization. TND, Tunisian dinars.

Although total exports would increase significantly (by 23 percent) relative to the base scenario, the increase would be due largely to the industrial sector. Agricultural export performance would be mixed: among the major exports, fruit exports (including olives) would expand but fishery product exports would decline. These gains are due to the reduction in prices of imported input products and the increased demand for foreign currency (Table 5.12).

Overall, poverty would decline slightly, from 8.1 to 7.7 percent. The gains in poverty reduction are entirely attributed to improvements in rural area; the urban poverty rate would increase slightly. The total number of poor people would decline by 4.7 percent, or more than 34,000 people (Table 5.13). Presumably, the import liberalization would lower the cost of imported goods for consumers, thus increasing their purchasing power, and would reduce the cost of productive inputs, which would increase agricultural returns.

Table 5.12 Estimated impact of trade liberalization on food and agricultural exports in Tunisia

Sector	Base year (millions of TND)	Simulation (% change relative to base scenario)			
		1	2	3	4
Cereals	1.5	20.8	47.1	78.4	149.5
Legumes	1.9	5.7	20.0	28.6	107.1
Other crops	1.0	13.9	41.8	54.1	1,121.1
Fruits	57.1	3.2	5.4	6.2	8.7
Vegetables	5.8	11.2	22.7	25.3	-0.2
Other agricultural activities	3.0	18.2	28.6	39.0	-2.4
Livestock	6.2	-5.3	0.6	2.6	19.7
Forestry	0.0	0.0	0.0	0.0	0.0
Fishing	21.3	-19.8	-20.2	-27.5	-25.9
Meat	1.6	-8.5	-2.8	-2.8	318.3
Milk	1.8	12.5	17.5	21.3	908.8
Sugar	3.6	3.2	14.5	14.0	1,650.0
Beverages	16.9	1.6	3.3	4.7	11.2
Other food processing	271.3	0.8	9.5	12.2	9.4
Other manufacturing	4,449.9	42.0	45.9	56.1	56.3
Nonmanufacturing industry	641.8	11.9	13.0	19.6	18.9
Services	2,545.6	-8.2	-8.4	-10.8	-10.2

Source: Authors' calculations.

Notes: Simulation 1 is the removal of tariffs on industrial goods from the European Union. Simulation 2 is the removal of tariffs on all goods from the European Union. Simulation 3 is the removal of tariffs on all goods from all countries. Simulation 4 is the removal of tariffs on all goods from all countries plus multilateral trade liberalization. TND, Tunisian dinars.

Table 5.13 Estimated impact of trade liberalization on incidence of poverty in Tunisia

Type of household	Base poverty	Simulation			
		1	2	3	4
Poverty incidence (P_0)					
National	8.1	7.7	7.7	7.6	5.4
Urban areas	3.2	3.5	3.5	3.5	3.7
Rural areas	15.8	14.3	14.3	14.1	7.9
Number of poor					
National	735,215	-4.7	-4.9	-5.7	-33.7
Urban	178,005	10.3	9.8	9.8	16.4
Rural	557,210	-9.5	-9.5	-10.6	-49.7

Source: Institut National de la Statistique and the authors' calculations.

Notes: Simulation 1 is the removal of tariffs on industrial goods from the European Union. Simulation 2 is the removal of tariffs on all goods from the European Union. Simulation 3 is the removal of tariffs on all goods from all countries. Simulation 4 is the removal of tariffs on all goods from all countries plus multilateral trade liberalization.

Simulation 2

In this scenario the model is used to simulate the elimination of all tariffs on imports from the E.U., including tariffs on industrial and agricultural products. This scenario can be seen as extending the EMP into agricultural trade liberalization (though the effect of E.U. import liberalization is not included). As shown in Table 5.9, this simulation also has a weak macroeconomic impact: real GDP would expand by 0.3 percent compared to the base scenario, an additional 0.1 percentage points compared to Simulation 1 (the liberalization of industrial imports from the E.U.). Real consumption would grow by 1.9 percent compared to the base scenario, more than in Simulation 1. The loss in tariff revenue would be almost 80 percent of total government tariff revenue in the base year, somewhat more than with nonagricultural trade liberalization in Simulation 1. The model compensates by raising the VAT to maintain government revenue. Tunisian imports would expand more than in Simulation 1, responding to the broader import liberalization. Exports would expand in response to the greater demand for foreign currency.

Overall output would increase by 4.1 percent relative to the base (0.4 percentage points above Simulation 1). This increase in production shows the extent to which lowering tariffs might improve the efficiency of factor allocation through movement toward more profitable and more competitive activities. However, the production of "other crops," meat, dairy, and beverages would decline as a result of the reduced protection from imports from the E.U. There would be little change in the output of cereals, pulses, vegetables, and fruits, including olives (see Table 5.10).

Imports of fruits, vegetables, meat, dairy products, beverages, and tobacco would increase substantially due to the reduction of import barriers on agricultural products. Nonagricultural imports would also increase by only slightly more than in Simulation 1 (see Table 5.11). Most agricultural exports except fishery products and meat would also expand (see Table 5.12). This illustrates the concept in international trade economics that a tax on imports is an implicit tax on exports. In this case, removing agricultural import tariffs would increase the demand for foreign currency, causing a depreciation of the exchange rate and stimulating exports, including agricultural exports.

In general, the effect of this reform on poverty would be quite similar to that of Simulation 1. As in Simulation 1, a small increase in the urban poverty rate would be more than offset by the decrease in rural poverty rates. The change in poverty rates would be almost the same as in Simulation 1, though the number of poor people would decline slightly more than in Simulation 1.

Simulation 3

In this scenario we extend the elimination of Tunisian tariffs on E.U. imports to imports from non-E.U. countries as well. Real GDP would increase by 0.2

percent relative to the base year, while real consumption would grow by 2.6 percent, indicating an additional gain of 0.5 percentage points compared to Simulation 2. Total imports would increase by 22 percent, while exports would grow by 32 percent, a significant increase relative to the previous simulation. The elimination of tariffs on imports from the rest of the world would increase the demand for imports and, hence, foreign exchange. The resulting depreciation would make exports more competitive. This reform would induce a complete (100 percent) loss in tariff revenue. The model compensates by increasing the VAT from 4.2 percent in the base scenario to 10.5 percent.

At the sectoral level, this reform would entail a drop in domestic production in most agricultural activities. This decrease is explained by the lower prices associated with agricultural import liberalization, the increase in unskilled wages, and the limited mobility of land between agricultural activities.

The effect of this reform on poverty would be similar to that of Simulations 1 and 2 except that the decline in rural poverty would be slightly greater. The number of poor people would fall by 5.7 percent (about 42,000 people) compared to the base scenario. Farmers' incomes would be improved by higher prices for exports, lower costs for imported consumer goods, and lower costs for imported inputs such as seed and cattle feed.

Simulation 4

Along with the import liberalization in Simulation 3, this last scenario simulates an increase in the prices of the main basic agricultural products as a result of a multilateral liberalization of trade in agricultural products. Agricultural protectionism in importing countries and production subsidies in high-income countries would depress world agricultural prices, which would penalize all surplus farmers. Here we simulate a 15 percent increase in the world prices of basic agricultural products, assumed to be the result of global trade liberalization and the removal of all producer subsidies. This is a plausible change in light of previous studies of the impact of removing all distortions in the agricultural sector (see Chapter 3).

In this simulation we see that total output in Tunisia would rise by 5.2 percent relative to the base year, a reduction of 0.4 percentage points compared to Simulation 3. Real GDP would rise by 0.2 percent, while total consumption would rise by 2.9, the largest gain among the four simulations. Total imports would rise by 22 percent and exports increase by 34 percent relative to the base year.

Global agricultural trade liberalization would enhance the competitiveness of "other crops" and sugar, causing a sharp increase in production. The increase in world prices would be transmitted to local markets, resulting in a rise in the retail prices of cereals, vegetables, and other crops, which would induce a reduction in the internal demand (see Table 5.10).

The higher world prices of agricultural commodities would also cause reductions in most of the important agricultural and food imports (cereals, legumes, "other crops," and sugar) while expanding the most important agricultural exports (fruit, consisting mainly of olives).[3] In spite of the higher agricultural prices, the consumer price would decline relative to the base scenario, reflecting the importance of nonfood items in the consumption basket. Thus, global trade liberalization is associated with higher food prices, reduced agricultural imports, and higher agricultural exports (see Tables 5.11 and 5.12).

This situation was actually observed for olive oil in Tunisia during the 2005 agricultural year, when high world prices led to a rise in domestic retail prices, which curbed local demand and, consequently, stimulated exports. This scenario would thus result in a favorable income gain for olive-producing farm households because of the rise in producer prices.

Global trade liberalization, with the 15 percent increase in world agricultural prices, would cause poverty to decline from 8.1 percent in the base scenario to 5.4 percent. This is the largest drop among the four simulations, and it would be entirely the result of progress in rural areas, where the poverty rate would fall by half, from 15.8 percent in the base scenario to 7.9 percent. The fact that rural poverty would decline from 14.1 percent in Simulation 3 (import liberalization for all goods from all countries) to 7.9 percent in Simulation 4 suggests that the higher agricultural prices would be responsible for the poverty reduction in rural areas, as well as the modest increase in urban poverty. Compared to the base scenario, the number of poor people in Tunisia would decline by one-third, or 248,000 people.

Summary

Tunisia has carried out a number of reforms as a result of its structural adjustment program, but its level of agricultural protection remains one of the highest in the world. At the same time, Tunisia has a relatively good investment climate, which contributed to significant inflows of foreign direct investment and a healthy growth rate through the 1990s.

Like many MENA countries, Tunisia is a net agricultural importer. Its main exports are olives and dates, and its principal imports are wheat and maize. Multilateral liberalization is expected to raise agricultural prices. If all agricul-

[3] Although some commodities would show dramatic percentage increases in imports, these are commodities with very modest or negligible import volumes.

tural commodity prices rise proportionately, Tunisia will face declining terms of trade because it is a net agricultural importer. On the other hand, it would benefit from domestic liberalization due to efficiency gains. The combined effect is likely to be positive for Tunisia as a whole because most estimates show that efficiency gains would be larger than terms-of-trade effects.

However, the combination of global and domestic liberalization would probably reduce agricultural prices because the effect of the loss of high levels of protection (89 percent on average) would be greater than the modest increase in world prices (5–20 percent) due to global liberalization.

Simulations using a CGE model linked to household survey data suggest that the removal of industrial tariffs on imports from the E.U. (which approximates Tunisian import liberalization under the EMP agreement) would cause both imports and exports to expand significantly, although almost all the change would be in nonagricultural trade. Real GDP would increase slightly (0.2 percent) because of the efficiency gains associated with the removal of distortions. Poverty would decline from 8.1 to 7.7 percent. Significant gains in rural poverty reduction would more than offset the small increase in urban poverty.

The removal of *all* tariffs on imports from the E.U. (approximating the Tunisian side of an extended EMP agreement) would cause large increases in imports of meat, beverages and tobacco, fruit, dairy products, and vegetable oil as import barriers on these goods were lifted. The effect on GDP and poverty would be similar to that in the first simulation.

The elimination of tariffs on imports from *all* countries would increase the imports of almost all agricultural commodities, as well as stimulate agricultural exports to maintain the trade balance. The reduction in poverty would be slightly greater in this case than in the case of the first two simulations: poverty would decline from 8.1 percent in the base scenario to 7.6 percent. The rural poor would again be the main beneficiaries of these changes in trade policy.

Finally, the elimination of all Tunisian tariffs plus global trade liberalization (represented by a 15 percent increase in world agricultural prices) would not do much for the overall economy. This is partly because, as a net agricultural importer, Tunisia would lose out due to higher world agricultural prices. Nonetheless, the agricultural sector would gain from the higher prices. Exports of fruit (mainly olives) would expand significantly, as would exports of a number of other agricultural commodities. As a result, poverty would decline to the lowest level among the four scenarios. Compared to the base scenario, rural poverty would be cut in half (from 15.8 to 7.9 percent) according to this simulation.

Overall, it appears that trade liberalization would have only modest effects on the level of GDP, but it would have a significant effect in reducing poverty. Furthermore, the combined effect of global and domestic liberalization would be more pro-poor than the effect of domestic liberalization alone.

We draw two general implications from the Tunisia case study. First, the impact of trade liberalization on rural poverty may be quite different from the impact one might assume based on simple indicators. As a net importer of agricultural commodities, Tunisia may be expected to experience terms-of-trade losses from higher world agricultural prices. Furthermore, because Tunisia has a high level of agricultural import protection, we would expect its agricultural sector to lose from trade liberalization that would remove this protection. Yet the simulations suggest that trade liberalization would reduce rural poverty. Three factors explain these results:

- For cereals, import liberalization would reduce prices more than global trade liberalization would increase them. But poor farm households would not lose much from lower cereal prices because cereal production is concentrated on medium and large farms (see Table 5.3). Furthermore, many rural poor households are likely to be net buyers who benefit from lower cereal prices.
- Global trade liberalization would boost the world prices of agricultural commodities, including olives. This would benefit olive growers, and Table 5.3 shows that tree crops (primarily olive trees) are concentrated among smaller farms.
- The shift from producing cereals to more labor-intensive activities such as raising fruit, dairy products, and sugar would increase the demand for unskilled agricultural labor, thus increasing wage income among the rural poor.

Second, the positive outcome of these simulations would be partly based on the ability of farmers to replace activities that were once protected, such as wheat and livestock production, by activities involving export commodities, such as the raising of olives, dates, and citrus. The need to facilitate the replacement of one set of activities with another highlights the importance of farmer training, marketing information systems, and extension services, as well as farm-level investments and the public infrastructure necessary to expand the newly competitive crops.

Appendix 5A: Method for Estimating the Impact of Trade Liberalization on Tunisia

Background on Micro-Macro Linkages

The most comprehensive way of modeling the overall impact of policy changes on the economy is through a CGE model, which incorporates many of the important general equilibrium interactions in an economic system. To measure distributive impacts, CGE models often map factor incomes among different types of households. The models have been applied in the analysis of policy changes in several developing countries. The change in the cost of living among segments of a population is then used to assess the impacts on income distribution. These studies provide an upper-bound measurement of the increase in income required for each group to purchase the same quantities of goods that they purchase in the base situation.

Decaluwé et al. (1999) have evaluated the relevance of different types of macroeconomic general equilibrium modeling for measuring the impact of economic policy shocks on the incidence of poverty and on the distribution of income. Three approaches have been identified in the literature and implemented using an archetypal economy, as follows:

1. The first is based on a traditional form of the CGE model that specifics a large number of households, thus allowing the capture of only intergroup income inequalities.
2. The second uses survey data to estimate the distribution function and average variations by group, thereby allowing for estimates of the evolution of poverty.
3. The third approach involves directly incorporating individual datasets into the general equilibrium model according to the principles of microsimulation.

Studies have demonstrated the importance of intragroup information and therefore the relevance of microsimulation exercises. Even if we disaggregate the population of households into a few representative groups, we will still not be able to obtain relevant results regarding the evolution of total inequality. Indeed, decomposable income indexes show that intragroup inequality often contributes more to total inequality measures than does intergroup inequality. Accordingly, the most promising direction consists in seeking true integration between the CGE model and the observed heterogeneity of households as observed in a household survey.

There are two main ways to achieve consistency between a macroeconomic framework and microeconomic surveys, as follows:

1. The first, proposed by Cogneau and Robilliard (2000), has been labeled the "fully integrated micro-macro framework." It is based on a standard CGE model wherein representative households and workers are replaced by a full sample of households and workers whose behavior is observed through household and labor force surveys. The advantage of this method is its ability to capture the impact of macroeconomic changes on workers and households and also the feedback effects of microsimulation on the

macroeconomic portion of the model. However, the method is very demanding in computational resources and imposes the construction of a relatively simple CGE model.

2. The second approach is the "sequential micro-macro framework." The macroeconomic part of the model is an extended CGE model that is supposed to describe the functioning of the economy under analysis. The link with the microsimulation model occurs through a vector of prices, wages, and aggregate employment. If one understands the change in the link variables resulting from a shock in the macroeconomic part of the model, one may modify the microeconomic household database in a way that is consistent with the link variables. This approach combines a standard multisector CGE model with a microsimulation model that describes real income generation behavior among a representative sample of households. The microsimulation model will be used to generate changes in individual wages and employment status in a manner that is consistent with the set of macroeconomic variables in the macroeconomic or CGE model. When this is done, the full distribution of the real household income corresponding to the shock or policy change initially stimulated in the macroeconomic model may be evaluated (Bourguignon, Robilliard, and Robinson 2002).

In building a CGE microsimulation model to assess the impact of trade policy reforms and external shocks on poverty in Tunisia, we have chosen to adopt the first approach, the fully integrated micro-macro framework, which involves directly incorporating a representative sample of households into the CGE model.

Tunisian Household Budget and Expenditure Surveys

The microsimulation approach requires data on income and expenditure patterns among households in a sample. In the case of Tunisia, the quantitative data available from household budget surveys are limited to the expenditure side. Quantitative information on income sources, as well as on the level of savings (or debt), are not collected in Tunisian household budget surveys. However, important qualitative data allow an estimation of the different income sources. We believe that the mistakes linked to problems of estimating the different income positions of households are much less important than the mistakes relative to ignorance of the income effects in the analysis of the evolution of poverty.

Seven national household expenditure surveys have been carried out, in 1968, 1975, 1980, 1985, 1990, 1995, and 2000. Eight national household expenditure surveys have been carried out, in 1968, 1975, 1980, 1985, 1990, 1995, 2000, and 2005. The information gathered through direct observation of household consumption allows changes in living standards and welfare among households to be measured.

The method of data collection consists of interviewing households during many visits. The direct observation of the expenditures of each sample household lasts four weeks. Nonetheless, for large expenditures that are made less frequently, such as the purchase of durable goods, the observation period lasts one year; in this case, the month-long enquiry is supplemented with retrospective accounts of the 11 months preceding the start of the survey. The part of the survey that is devoted to food consumption relies on measuring the food intended for household consumption ration by ration and day by day during a week for each sample household.

The survey questionnaire on household budgets and expenditures consists of a main questionnaire aimed at recording collective household expenditures and a complementary questionnaire aimed at registering the individual expenditures of each household member with an income.

For the part of the main questionnaire relative to expenditures, information is requested on the expenditures each household member makes to satisfy his or her needs and the needs of those household members in his or her charge, notably, the expenditure categories of a collective nature (such as food, housing, services). The main survey questionnaire is composed of four sections: the household roster, a list of the economic activities of members aged 15 years and over, another list of the economic characteristics of active workforce members, and information on regular household expenditures (INS 2002).

Estimation of the Micromodule

As we have explained, every five years the Institut National de la Statistique (INS) carries out a survey on household budgets and consumption. The survey conducted in 2000 covered a sample of 12,018 households. Although the data from this survey were not available for this analysis, we were able to obtain raw data on approximately 400 households from the 1995 household expenditure survey. The exploration and manipulation of these data revealed many inconsistencies, which give us some reservations regarding the quality of the data. The sample of 400 households is considered representative of the whole sample of 10,415 households surveyed in 1995.

Table 5.14 provides details on the composition of the households according to the occupation of the head of household for the original sample and for the subsample used in this analysis. This indicates that the subsample is representative of the larger sample and, presumably, the population as a whole.

We assume that the total revenue of each household is equal to its total expenditures; we ignore savings and debt. Indeed, a homogeneous savings level for all households in the sample will eventually be determined when the

Table 5.14 Representativeness of the sample in Tunisia, by occupation of head of household, 1995

Socioprofessional category of the household head	Number and percentage of households in the whole sample		Number and percentage of households in the subsample		Number and percentage of households at the national level		Total population	
Managers and professionals	2,853	27.4	108	27.2	490,100	28.8	2,570,500	28.5
Those in other nonagricultural activities	2,955	28.4	111	28.0	490,300	28.9	2,725,500	30.3
Farmers	1,349	13.0	52	13.1	200,700	11.8	1,218,100	13.5
Agricultural wage earners	882	8.4	33	8.3	130,800	7.7	752,100	8.4
Retirees and the unemployed	2,376	22.8	93	23.4	387,500	22.8	1,735,300	19.3
Total	10,415	100.0	397	100.0	1,699,400	100.0	9,001,500	100.0

Source: Authors' calculations based on data from the Institut National de la Statistique.

SAM is balanced out. Once the total income of each household is estimated, we move to the estimation of the different sources of income. The qualitative information collected on the professional status of the household head through the Tunisian household survey, as well as information on the other household members, allows us to sketch out a table of the income sources of each member and of the whole household. After constructing a table on the working members of each household in the available sample, we estimate the income of each household member. For this purpose we establish three main income sources: salaries, rents, and transfers. The main source of income in the majority of Tunisian households is salaries. Thus, based on the results of the employment survey conducted annually by the INS, we estimate the income derived from the salaries received by all members of each household with reference to the salary grid for 1996 and 1997 (INS 1998), which shows each professional category and the main economic activities. For independent workers who do not earn salaries, we estimate a salary equivalent equal to the salary level for the same activity carried out by a salaried worker with the same qualifications.

To simplify the estimation process, we assume that only poor households receive transfers, mostly in the form of government aid or transfers from other household members who work abroad (and who represent an important support for this category of households in Tunisia). Moreover, we suppose that poor households do not receive rents. These rents represent the income from capital invested by capital owners (such as in land). For independent workers engaged in a specific economic activity, two household categories may be distinguished: poor households (in which the total income is below the national poverty line) and nonpoor households (in which income is above the national poverty line).

Finally, it is important to specify that the salaries and rents received by each household are differentiated according to the economic activities carried out by the members of the household who work as wage earners or as independent workers. Any amount left over in the total income of each household after accounting for the salaries (or equivalent salaries) represents transfers among poor households and rents among nonpoor households.

The SAM for Tunisia

In order to reduce the inconsistencies between the SAM and the 1995 household survey data, we chose to build another SAM for the year 1996.[4] This allows us to balance out the SAM using an entropy program that makes the minimal adjustments necessary in the two datasets so that they are consistent with each other. The data used to build the detailed 1996 SAM on Tunisia are drawn from various sources, including input-output tables, national accounts, the government budget, and trade statistics. The microeconomic SAM for 1996 was constructed in several steps.

In the first step we constructed a microeconomic SAM covering more than the 19 activities and commodities in the original input-output table established by the INS. The disaggregation of activities and commodities was carried out in order to match the commodity structure in the household expenditure data. Thus, the disaggregation involved mainly agriculture and agro-food processing commodities, given the importance of these commodities in household expenditures in Tunisia. The macroeconomic SAM and the input-output table were fully consistent and balanced. Additional data on the various components of supply and demand have been provided by the INS. These cover sectoral imports and exports, final consumption, duties on imports, investment, stock variations, and other indirect taxes. Transfers among institutions and direct tax payments have also been provided by the INS.

In the second step in building the microeconomic SAM, labor and capital accounts were disaggregated, the labor account into five categories (three in the agricultural sector and two in nonagricultural activities) and the capital

---

[4] The year 1996 is the survey year that is most proximate to the 1995 household expenditure survey, for which a SAM is already available.

account into three (land remuneration, other resources, and physical capital). Table 5.15 lists the different accounts in the SAM for Tunisia used in this study.

When the micromodule is superimposed on the 1996 SAM table using otherwise unchanged column coefficients, all sector accounts are, as expected, out of balance. An estimation approach is needed to generate a balanced SAM table. We selected a cross-entropy approach given the practical advantages and the theoretical basis of this approach in information theory (see, for example, Golan, Judge, and Miller 1996). Cross-entropy is a technique for solving underdetermined estimation problems. It has been applied to the estimation of input-output tables (Golan, Judge, and Robinson 1994) and SAMs (Robinson and El-Said 2000; Robinson, Cattañeo, and El-Said 2001), as well as a wide range of other problems inside and outside economics. The underlying philosophy of entropy estimation is that all available relevant information should be used but no other information (Golan, Judge, and Miller 1996). More concretely, this means that the user may impose control values (in our case, by drawing on what is known for 1996). However, it is not necessary to impose values for what may not be known. Control values may be imposed exactly, or they may be imposed with allowance for measurement errors.

In our case, the problem is to estimate a new micromodule with minimum entropy distance relative to the previous micromodule by drawing on the information presented in the 1996 SAM, subject to the constraint that the row and column totals of the new SAM should be equal for all accounts and that control values should be satisfied (exactly or by accounting for errors). The entropy distance depends on the differences between the two tables in terms of column coefficients and control values. Control values may be imposed exactly, or they may be imposed with allowance for measurement errors.

Table 5.15 Dimensions of the Tunisian SAM

Activities	Production of cereals, legumes, other crops, fruits, vegetables, other agriculture products, livestock; meat, dairy, sugar, beverages; forestry; fishing; other food-processing industries; other manufacturing industries; nonmanufacturing industries; and services
Labor factors	Nonwage agricultural workers, skilled wage workers in agriculture, unskilled wage workers in agriculture, skilled workers in nonagriculture, and unskilled workers in nonagriculture.
Other factors	Land, other natural resources, and physical capital
Institutions	Government, 397 households, European Union, and the rest of the world
Other accounts	VAT, subsidies on production, subsidies on consumption, taxes on income, changes in inventory, and saving-investment

Note: VAT, value-added tax.

CGE Model Structure

The CGE model used here for Tunisia is a standard neoclassical static model with imperfect substitution between domestic and foreign goods. Domestic prices are endogenous on each market (goods and factors). They equalize supply (imports and production for the domestic market) and demand (the final demand of households, the government, investors, and foreign partners; the intermediate demand of producers; and factor demand) so as to obtain equilibrium.

Supply is modeled using the nested constant elasticity of substitution functions, which describe the substitution and complement relations among the various inputs. Producers are cost minimizers, and constant return to scale is assumed. Output results from two composite goods (intermediate consumption and value added), which are combined in fixed proportions. The intermediate aggregate is obtained by combining all products in fixed proportions. The value added is then decomposed into two substitutable parts: labor and capital. The labor market is further disaggregated into five categories (nonwage agricultural workers, skilled wage workers in agriculture, unskilled wage workers in agriculture, skilled workers in nonagriculture, and unskilled workers in nonagriculture) and capital into three categories (physical capital, reserve of natural resources, and land). Substitutions among labor categories are implemented through a nested constant elasticity of substitution structure for two main activities: agricultural activities and nonagricultural activities. For agricultural activities, the first level of the constant elasticity of substitution function describes the substitution between wage workers and nonwage workers, while the second level describes substitution between skilled and unskilled wage workers. For nonagricultural activities, there is substitution only between skilled and nonskilled wage workers.[5]

The labor market is modeled according to labor type. For nonwage agricultural workers (farmers), we assume that an economywide wage variable is free to vary to ensure that the sum of demand from all activities equals the quantity supplied, which is fixed. Each activity pays an activity-specific wage that is the product of the economywide wage and an activity-specific wage (distortion) term. For the remaining four labor categories, we assume that there is unemployment and that the real wage is fixed. This assumption is appropri-

---

[5] This static model is intended to capture the short- and medium-term allocative effects of various trade policies. However, it does not incorporate some of the expected dynamic effects of trade policies, notably those on productivity, because factors availability and average efficiency are fixed in this version of the model. This feature is ignored because, in the long run, household features have to be changed, and the calibration of the model requires more than one household survey.

ate in the Tunisian case because there is considerable unemployment among all wage-worker categories. Compared to the modeling of nonwage workers, the only change is that the economywide wage variable is fixed (or exogenized), while the supply variable is flexed (or endogenized). Each activity is free to hire any desired quantity of workers at the fixed activity-specific wage (which, implicitly, is indexed to the model *numéraire*).

Income from labor and physical capital accrues to households using fixed shares derived from the SAM once the micromodule is fully integrated, as do all rents created by specific capital factors (natural resources and land). Total household demand is derived by maximizing the utility function subject to the constraints of the available income and consumer price vector. Household utility is a positive function of the consumption of the various products and savings; the income elasticity for each product is set to unity. Government demand and investment demand are disaggregated into sectoral demands once the total value is determined according to fixed coefficient functions.

The model assumes imperfect substitution among goods originating in different geographical areas. Import demand results from a constant elasticity of substitution function aggregating domestic and imported goods. Export supply is symmetrically modeled as a constant elasticity of transformation function. Producers decide to allocate their output to domestic or foreign markets in response to relative prices. At the second stage, importers (exporters) choose the optimal demand (supply) across regions as a function of relative import (export) prices and the degree of substitution across regions. The substitution elasticity between domestic and imported products is set at 2.2, while it is set at 5.0 among imported products according to origin. The elasticity of transformation between products intended for the domestic market and products for export is 5.0, while it is set at 8.0 among the different destinations for export products.[6]

Finally, several macroeconomic constraints are introduced into this model. First, the small country assumption holds. Tunisia is unable to change world prices; thus, its import and export prices are exogenous. Capital transfers are exogenous as well, implying that the trade balance is fixed so as to achieve balance of payments equilibrium. Second, the model imposes a fixed real government deficit and fixed real public expenditures. Public receipts thus

[6] In the absence of the trade elasticities estimated for Tunisia, we use trade elasticities from the empirical literature devoted to CGE models. For example, see Burniaux, Nicoletti, and Oliveira-Martins (1992); Konan and Maskus (1997); or, more recently, Gallaway, McDaniel, and Rivera (2000).

adjust endogenously in order to achieve the predetermined net government position by shifting the income tax of households.[7] Third, investment is determined by the availability of savings from households, government, and abroad. Because government and foreign savings are exogenous in this model, changes in investment volumes reflect changes in household savings and changes in the price of investment. Policy impacts are compared relative to the situation observed in the base year in terms of macroeconomic aggregates, trade volumes, sectoral outputs, household welfare, and poverty indicators.

[7] This closure policy can be understood as a net transfer from households to government (or the reverse). With one representative household, it is considered the most neutral way to assess trade reform. Other closures could be tested (by adjusting indirect taxes, for instance), but this would risk introducing new distortions, thereby making it more difficult to conceptually isolate the impact of the trade policy on income distribution and poverty.

CHAPTER 6

Agriculture, Trade, and Poverty in Syria

The Syrian Arab Republic has approximately 17 million inhabitants, of whom about half live in urban areas. Its per capita GDP is US$831, above that of the poorest MENA countries (Djibouti and Yemen) but below the others. The agricultural sector is relatively large, accounting for 23 percent of total GDP.

The Syrian government adopted socialism in the late 1950s and kept control of major industries, though private services and retail trade were allowed. The economy has been adversely affected by various conflicts in the region, including the Arab-Israeli wars of 1967 and 1973 and the Syrian intervention in Lebanon from 1976 until 2005. Limited economic reforms and a major expansion in oil exports stimulated economic growth in the early 1990s, but growth has been sluggish since then. Although international trade and the exchange rate have been partially liberalized, the government still imposes significant controls on the economy, including price controls, state monopolies in certain sectors, agricultural subsidies, and a large number of state-owned enterprises. Overall, Syria's per capita GDP grew at 2.2 percent per year during the 1990s, an improvement over its performance during the 1980s, when it fell in real terms.

Like Jordan, Syria was adversely affected by the end of the United Nations Oil for Food program in Iraq and the subsequent war in Iraq, which disrupted trade flows. More recently, Syria has benefited from the conflict in Iraq and from high oil prices.

The Agricultural Sector

Agricultural Production

Wheat is the most important food crop in Syria. Unlike most MENA countries, Syria is self-sufficient in wheat. As discussed later, its self-sufficiency in wheat is the result of policies that impose high barriers on imports. Barley and maize are also grown, but domestic production is not sufficient to satisfy demand. Cereal production is subject to weather-related fluctuations because rainfall is unreliable. Syria also produces grapes, apples, and olives in the highlands and citrus fruits along the coast. Horticultural production is often irrigated. About 23 percent of Syrian cropland is irrigated, much of this because of the Euphrates Dam built in the 1970s.

The main production units in Syrian agriculture are small and medium-sized farms, because the agrarian reform caused the practical disappearance of traditional large-scale landowners. Between the two agricultural censuses for which data are available, conducted in 1981 and 1994, there was a 26 percent increase in the total number of farm households, from 486,000 in 1981 to 614,000 in 1994 (Table 6.1). The percentage of farmers whose main occupation was agricultural and who owned land was 71 percent of total farm households with land in 1994 compared to 64 percent in 1981. Furthermore, 57 percent of farmers without land stated that their main occupation was farming, compared to only 15 percent in 1981. These changes show the growing numbers of farm households both with land and without land whose main occupation is farming. This is the direct result of the segmentation of land and the slow growth in the demand for labor in the nonagricultural sectors.

Agricultural Trade Patterns

The total exports of Syria were US$7.6 billion in 2002. Oil and fuel account for over half of the total value of exports, although it is estimated that the existing oil reserves will be exhausted within 12 years at the current extraction rates. Syrian agricultural exports are about US$1 billion, and the main commodities are cotton, sheep, tomatoes, and anise/fennel. As a group, fruit

Table 6.1 Characteristics of farm households in Syria, 1981 and 1994

Farm household type	1981 census	1994 census
Total number of farm households (1)	485,691	613,657
Farm households with land (2)	409,492	573,193
Farm households without land (3)	76,199	40,464
Farm households with land whose main occupation is agriculture (4)	261,386	409,142
Farm households without land whose main occupation is agriculture (5)	11,224	22,860
Percentage of farm households with land (2/1)	84	93
Percentage of landowners for whom agriculture is the main occupation (4/2)	64	71
Percentage of landless for whom agriculture is the main occupation (5/3)	15	56

Sources: 1981 census and 1994 census.

and vegetable exports earn over US$300 million per year. Syrian wheat exports averaged US$48 million in value per year over 2000-02.

Syria's total imports in 2002 were US$5.9 billion, of which agricultural imports were US$860 million. The main agricultural imports are sugar, maize, and tea. Unlike most MENA countries, Syria has a modest surplus in agricultural trade, although this is partly due to the tight restrictions on food and agricultural imports. According to the U.S. Department of Agriculture, imports of processed foods, frozen foods, snack foods, meat, fruits, and vegetables are, in general, prohibited (USDA 1999).

Syria's principal trading partners are the E.U. and other Arab countries. The E.U. represents the main market for Syrian exports, accounting for some 60 percent of exports. The E.U. is a particularly important market for Syrian oil but also accounts for a significant share of Syria's manufactured exports, such as cotton and textiles (the E.U. accounts for almost 40 percent of its manufacturing exports). The Arab countries are the second-largest market for Syria exports, accounting for slightly over 20 percent of total exports, followed by the United States (9.5 percent). Of the Arab countries, Iraq has historically been the major trading partner, although this trade has been disrupted by the conflict there. Exports to the Arab countries are mainly concentrated in foodstuffs, notably cereals, fruits, and vegetables.

The E.U. is the most important source of Syrian imports; an average of 31 percent of total merchandise imports originated in the E.U. during 1994-2000. Syria also maintains strong commercial links with former communist countries in Eastern Europe and with Russia and China, which together accounted for 18 percent of total imports during 1994-2000. Arab countries supplied Syria with only about 8 percent of its merchandise imports.

Agricultural and Trade Policies

Agricultural Policy

Syrian agricultural policy is characterized by a high level of government intervention. Before 1987, the prices of many agricultural products, such as cereal, fodder, industrial crops, potatoes, garlic, and some fruits, were determined by the government. Since 1987, a gradual process of economic reform has been under way, and some regulations on production, prices, and marketing have been relaxed. This process has intensified since 2002, when the government introduced a package of reforms aiming to reduce distortions and public intervention in the economy.

On the basis of these changes, the orientation of Syrian economic policy in general and of agricultural policy in particular has focused on price deregulation, a reduction in public intervention, and a gradual reduction in subsidies. We analyze below the main components of Syrian agricultural policy, focusing on recent reforms, as well as on obstacles that still affect the agricultural sector and farm incomes.

Land-Use Planning

In Syria, agricultural production is centrally planned by means of land-use plans, which vary from region to region. The land-use plans are prepared by the state based on its strategic goals and the technical characteristics of farms. The land-use plans often determine other aspects of Syrian agricultural policy, namely, price and credit policy. The state seeks to ensure the achievement of the objectives assigned to the agricultural sector in the national economic development plan without taking into account farmer preferences. The discrepancy between government objectives and farmer objectives has always been manifested by the flouting of the rules on land use. This situation has made it difficult for farmers to acquire the necessary inputs whenever their plans differ from the government land-use plans. In addition, the situation results in weak performance by farms as a result of the lack of credit and support for unapproved production.

Procurement by State Monopolies

Wheat, cotton, tobacco, and sugar beets are considered strategic commodities. In order to stimulate production and control distribution, the state has a marketing monopoly over these products. The prices of these commodities are fixed using a well-established procedure. First, the cost of production is estimated jointly by the Ministry of Agriculture, the general trade union of farmers, the Ministry of the Economy, the Ministry of Trade, the Ministry of Industry, and other institutions. Once the average cost has been estimated, a margin of benefits is fixed for each crop on the basis of the relative importance of the crop in the Syrian economy as measured by the importance of each product in the final consumption of households and the demand for these crops as industrial inputs. These continually revised prices are published each year before the beginning of the agricultural season. This price-fixing mechanism has led to increases in producer prices that far exceed the rise in consumer prices, typically fixed by the state for the same products. One consequence of these policies is the accumulation of large stocks by state enterprises and large financial costs in the state budget.

Administered Prices

Another category of agricultural commodities is subject to administered prices but without a state monopoly on marketing. This is the case for barley, lentils, maize, and sunflowers. Farmers have the option of selling to state marketing boards at the official prices, but they can also sell on the private market. Indeed, like procurement prices, these prices are fixed on the basis of a study jointly conducted by representatives of the government, farmers, and processors. Prices are set according to the estimated average production cost plus a profit margin that is smaller than that accorded strategic products. Thus, the proposed prices are considered minimum guaranteed prices for farmers so as to protect them from unusually low market prices.

Consumer Price Policy

This category of prices is also fixed by the state administration and is meant for consumption products such as vegetables, fruits, milk, meat, eggs, rice, and oil. These prices are considered simple indicators that should not be applied in transactions between producers (and importers) and consumers, except for products that public institutions buy. These prices are also fixed by a committee that is generally made up of the Ministry of the Economy and the Ministry of Trade, as well as other departments involved in the sector.

This pricing policy has undergone significant reforms during recent years. Many products, notably vegetables, have witnessed liberalization in prices and imports. Furthermore, state monopolies in the importation of certain products have been relaxed, opening the door to private importers. However, pricing policies have not undergone changes relative to many other products, leading to high fiscal costs because of the gap between producer prices and (lower) export or retail prices.

Input Policy

Syria's agricultural input policy is based on the principle that all necessary inputs for agricultural production should be made available through the establishment of state monopolies in the production of inputs. However, the private sector participates in some marketing activities without authorization from the state administration. There is a state monopoly on the importation and distribution of chemical fertilizers. State trading enterprises import fertilizers on behalf of the cooperative agricultural bank, which distributes the fertilizers to farmers. Payment is made either in cash or by means of loans granted by the same institution on the basis of conditions fixed in advance by the Ministry of Agriculture. In addition, there is a state monopoly on the production, importation, and distribution of seeds. The private sector is authorized to market pesticides with the approval of the Ministry of Agriculture and to import and distribute agricultural machinery.

The partial liberalization of the importation and distribution of pesticides and agricultural equipment has helped increase the level of agricultural pro-

Table 6.2 Budget cost of food and agricultural subsidies in Syria, 1995-2003

Product	1995	1996	1997	1998	1999	2000	2001	2002	2003
Sugar subsidy (millions of SYP/year)	2.45	3.74	4.24	4.93	0.00	3.80	0.00	3.50	3.40
Rice subsidy (millions of SYP/year)	0.00	0.22	0.56	1.14	0.00	0.33	0.00	0.32	0.07
Wheat subsidy (millions of SYP/year)	0.00	0.00	4.52	4.33	1.90	2.24	9.73	8.43	7.97
Wheat products subsidy (millions of SYP/year)	17.26	0.00	23.50	25.48	23.24	26.01	22.09	19.99	20.61
Cotton subsidy (millions of SYP/year)	0.00	7.37	10.87	14.73	15.39	14.09	15.84	13.17	9.64
Wheat subsidies as a percentage of agricultural subsidies	88	0	64	59	62	61	67	63	69
Wheat subsidies as a percentage of government expenditures	11	0	13	13	10	10	10	8	7
Wheat subsidies as a percentage of GDP	2	0	3	3	3	3	3	3	3

Source: State Planning Council.

Notes: The wheat subsidy refers to the cost of supporting the producer price of wheat, while the wheat products subsidy is paid to millers to maintain the consumer price of bread and other products at below-market levels. The official exchange rate was SYP 41 per US$1 over 1995-2000, SYP 46 per US$1 in 2000, SYP 53 per US$1 in 2001, SYP 50 per US$1 in 2002, and SYP 44 per US$1 in 2003, based on the June 30 rates recorded at www.oanda.com. SYP, Syrian £.

duction in the country. However, the continued monopoly on the importation and distribution of fertilizers has had negative effects. In addition to long delays in fertilizer delivery and the rationing of fertilizer among farms, this policy has led to additional costs, estimated at 30 percent of the farmgate price (Bakour 2004).

The Cost of Agricultural Subsidies

The cost of agricultural subsidies estimated by the State Planning Council is shown in Table 6.2. The value of subsidies is calculated as the difference in the value of these products at domestic prices and the opportunity costs of these products, measured by the international price after adjusting for transport costs and distribution margins up to the mill. The table shows that subsidies are equivalent to about 3 percent of GDP and that wheat subsidies account for about two-thirds of the total cost of food and agricultural subsidies.

Another analysis, whose results are shown in Table 6.3, includes both direct subsidies and the losses of public enterprises in charge of marketing and processing agricultural commodities. Under this broader definition, subsidies for agricultural and food products in 2003 amounted to 6.8 percent

Table 6.3 Cost of government price intervention in Syria, 1998/99

	Value of subsidies	
Subsidy type	**(billions of SYP)**	**(% of GDP)**
Wheat (1999)		
Public enterprise loss	26.29	3.24
Subsidy to farmers	9.04	1.11
Subsidy on standard flour	3.76	0.46
Cotton (1998/99)		
Public enterprise loss	6.42	0.79
Subsidy to farmers	9.88	1.22
Tax on domestic spinners	2.3	0.28
Sugar (1999)		
Public enterprise loss	3.72	0.46
Subsidy to farmers	1.55	0.19
Subsidy to consumers	1.63	0.20
Total		
Losses	36.43	4.49
Subsidy to farmers	20.47	2.52
Subsidy to consumers	5.39	0.66
Tax on domestic industry	2.30	0.28

Source: Westlake (2003).

Notes: The official exchange rate on June 30, 1999, was SYP 41.85 per US$1 according to www.oanda.com. SYP, Syrian £.

of GDP. The table also shows the distribution of benefits between farmers and consumers. Sugarcane farmers and sugar consumers benefited in roughly equal amounts from the subsidies on sugar. In the case of wheat, some 85 percent of the total price subsidies went to farmers.

These figures are calculated at the aggregate level, without reference to the size distribution of the holdings and the land tenure status of farmers. Little is known about the distribution of these gains among small-scale farmers and large-scale farmers. In absolute terms, it is safe to say that large-scale wheat farmers capture a disproportionate share of the subsidies because the subsidy benefits are proportional to wheat production. However, the percentage contribution of these subsidies to farm incomes among different farm groups depends on the importance of the subsidized crops within their incomes.

Recent Agricultural Policy Reforms

It is important to point out that the 1970s saw an increase in the use of public monopolies in the marketing of many agricultural products in Syria. This involved the purchase and distribution of these products on local and foreign markets. These marketing monopolies were directed at various cereals, the main fruits, and crops and harvests for industrial processing. Disciplinary and penal sanctions were applied against individuals who did not respect the monopoly regulations, whether producers or traders.

However, the beginning of the 1980s witnessed the introduction of a reform in the marketing policy for agricultural products. This reform involved the following:

- the elimination of the system of compulsory importation of certain products (wheat, barley, lentils, chickpeas, maize, and others) by public enterprises and the elimination of the restriction on cereal purchases by the state trading enterprise from farmers who choose to sell;
- the preservation of the state monopoly on the exportation of strategic products while granting concessions to the private sector to involve it in the exportation of cereals on condition of a prior agreement with the Grain Board;
- the encouragement of the private sector to participate in export operations in fruits and vegetables through greater freedom in the use of foreign currency receipts, exemptions from the tax on agricultural production, and a reduction in the income tax;
- authorization for public enterprises to process agricultural products and to obtain goods directly on the market at market prices without the obligation to pay official prices, which are often higher than market prices; and

- authorization for agricultural enterprises to market any of their production that is not under state monopoly on local and foreign markets according to the best interests of the enterprises.

Certainly these changes represent a movement toward liberalization in the marketing of agricultural products and in exportation. However, the results of these reforms have been modest for various reasons. First, the state monopoly on distribution has been maintained for strategic products, primarily those for which the processing industries belong to the state. This covers mainly cotton, tobacco, and sugar beets. Second, there is an absence of export mechanisms able to facilitate trading relationships with foreign clients and foster new outlets. In addition, weaknesses in the marketing infrastructure and the high transaction costs in marketing have reduced the supply response in agriculture.

Agricultural policy continues to be a subject of debate. Some are calling for the maintenance of the state marketing system based on administered prices, while others are calling for a more flexible system that responds to changes in supply and demand both in marketing and in fixing agricultural prices. In the latter case, public enterprises that process or export certain agricultural products must obtain their goods directly on the market through contracts with producers, cooperatives, or agricultural companies and wholesalers.

Trade Policy

Foreign trade is subject to a significant intervention, particularly through import barriers such as tariffs, quantitative restrictions, and technical barriers to trade (NTBs). These import barriers are discussed in detail in the following paragraphs.

Tariffs

Syria's current import tariffs range from 6 to 235 percent and average 35 percent, including other duties and surcharges. There are 10 tariff bands. Statutory tariffs range from 0 to 200 percent. These are supplemented by a unified duty that ranges from 6 to 35 percent, with the applied surcharge increasing with the level of the applicable tariff rate. The highest tariffs apply to the imports of certain types of vehicles. Tariffs of 100 percent or more apply to imports of certain fruits, vegetables, and processed foods, as well as textiles, ceramics, and glass products, all of which are produced locally. As discussed later, many of these products are also subject to quantitative restrictions on trade. Goods originating in GAFTA countries are duty free.

The average tariff, weighted by the composition of imports, is currently only 8 percent, which is relatively low compared to the tariffs applied in other countries in the region before they joined WTO or signed an EMP agreement. But this low average tariff rate is misleading as an indicator of openness for two reasons. First, because it is an import-weighted tariff at the mean, it gives less weight to those commodities on which the tariff rates are the highest. Second, it does not take into account the pervasive system of quantitative restrictions, which raises effective protection (and thus the implicit tax on exports) substantially.

If account is taken of the tariff equivalent of quantitative restrictions, the overall weighted average rate of protection exceeds 25 percent, making Syria one of the countries least open to trade in the MENA region (World Bank 2004).[1]

Quantitative Restrictions

A quantitative restriction is any measure that limits the volume of trade directly rather than through import taxes. Examples include quotas, licensing requirements, and safeguard levies. In Syria, quantitative restrictions are implemented principally by the regulation of imports through four lists, as follows:

- The first list comprises all products forbidden for importation for environmental, security, or sanitary reasons. Officials indicate that this list is similar to ones used in OECD countries.
- A second list encompasses all products forbidden for importation from non-GAFTA countries because of their negative impact on Syrian industry. All products on this list have an equivalent produced in Syria. The list covers a large number of agricultural and industrial products: flowers, animal products, forestry products, vegetable oils, sugar-based products, quarrying products, plastic and rubber products, leather and leather products, wood products, paper products, silk, textiles and clothing, craft products, glass products, electrical machinery and materials, and so on.
- The third list includes products that may be imported only by the public sector. This list includes, notably, oil and oil-related products, alcohol and beer, arms, cotton, some cereal products, tobacco, pharmaceutical products, salt, black cement, fish, fruits, olive oil, veterinary medicines, and phosphates.
- The fourth list comprises products that were once imported only by particular public entities and that may now be imported by anyone provided that a commission is paid to the relevant public entities. This commission generally represents 3-5 percent of the import value before taxes. The most important products on this list are cars and transport machinery,

[1] See Nashashibi (2002) for a comparison of trade openness among MENA countries.

steel and steel products, wood, white cement, yarn for the textile industry, coffee, tea, rice, canned fish and meat, raw sugar, fertilizers, raw leather, and paper.

Both public entities and private agents may theoretically import any products not included on these four lists. According to Syrian officials, there is thus no positive list of imports that are allowed in Syria. These Syrian officials made no mention of the existence of quotas, tariff quotas, or calendar restrictions or of the need to comply with particular standards.

Measuring the impact of quantitative restrictions on prices is a difficult task. The most common method is the price-gap approach, which compares the domestic price of imported goods with the international price after adjustment for tariffs, shipping costs, costs of domestic transportation, and customs procedures and the impact of import and export financing schemes (Chemingui and Dessus 2004). The remaining price differentials between domestic and world prices thus measure the impact of quantitative restrictions on the domestic price of importable goods. This approach does have limitations because it is difficult to obtain accurate information on domestic and world prices at a sufficiently disaggregated level. In most cases, the estimated tariff equivalent of quantitative restrictions covers a set of products.[2] In addition, it is impossible formally to assign the origin of the estimated residual price gap to an existing import regulation; for instance, corruption or quality differences might also partially explain the price gap.

Given these qualifications, Table 6.4 presents estimates of the tariff equivalents of quantitative restrictions for selected agricultural commodities. Across all product categories (agricultural and nonagricultural), tariff rates are positively correlated with the tariff equivalents of quantitative restrictions, which suggests that both are used to support the same objective. Chemingui and Dessus (2004) estimate that across all product categories, the weighted average tariff equivalent of quantitative restrictions is 19 percent, compared to the weighted average tariff rate of 8 percent. Thus, quantitative restrictions probably represent the main source of trade protection in Syria.

Other Barriers to Trade

Two other barriers to trade tend to raise the cost of international trade between Syria and the rest of the world: (1) the use of a multiple exchange

[2] The calculations carried out by Chemingui and Dessus (2004) cover, on average, 60 percent of the products within each group of imported products (and 50 percent on a weighted average). By default, the authors assumed that the share of imports not covered in each group faces the same tariff equivalent as the share of imports covered by their estimates.

Table 6.4 Tariff equivalents of quantitative restrictions and tariffs on agricultural products in Syria, 2004 (percent)

Sector	Tariff equivalent of quantitative restrictions	Tariffs on agricultural products
Fish products (SITC 03)	3.9	19.5
Fruits and nuts (SITC 057)	27.4	54.0
Other food, live animals, oils, fats, and waxes (rest of SITC 0-4)	19.9	7.8
Tobacco and beverages (SITC 1)	309.3	110.1

Source: Chemingui and Dessus (2004).
Note: SITC, Standard International Trade Classification.

rate system in trade finance and (2) cumbersome customs procedures and inefficient trade logistics.[3]

Syria's import (and export) regime is complicated and rendered nontransparent because of the multiple exchange rates for private and government entities. The exchange rate system in Syria has been tightly managed, with a total of 11 rates applied for different transactions. In the 1990s, many of these rates were unified, most recently in 2002, when the three exchange rates used for the valuation of imports were harmonized and, in 2004, with the unification of the rate used for budget calculations with the rate applied to other public sector operations.

Until 2007, there were three exchange rates:

- the official rate, determined by the Central Bank of Syria, valued at 46.5 Syrian pounds (SYP 46.5) per US$1, which was used by the public sector for imports;
- a free market rate, approximately SYP 53 per US$1, which was determined by supply and demand mainly on the Beirut foreign exchange market and was used for both commercial and noncommercial purposes; and
- the so-called export proceeds rate, valued at SYP 51 per US$1, which was used to value foreign exchange that exporters are required to surrender.

As a result, imports were implicitly subsidized at different rates depending on the end user, while exports were implicitly taxed by an overvalued exchange

[3] The term *technical barrier to trade* used here does not perfectly match the international definition. In particular, the multiple exchange rate system in place may also be considered a nontariff measure because it directly affects the price of imports and exports. But because it also entails additional transaction costs, one is equally justified in considering it a technical barrier to trade.

rate, again at different rates depending on the export sector. Estimates carried out by Chemingui and Dessus (2004) suggest that the average implicit subsidy on imports stemming from this system amounted to the equivalent of 2.7 percent of the value of imports. Similarly, the implicit tax on exports amounted to 8.9 percent of the total value of exports. These estimates are a function of the difference between the exchange rate that applies to public- and private-sector entities, as well as the magnitude of the foreign exchange surrender requirement.

Customs procedures and regulations constrain trade through a lack of consistency, a manual system for processing customs data, and the inadequate distribution of information on procedures and requirements. One additional implication of the complex system of customs tariffs and duties and the nontariff regime is that enforcement requires complicated and burdensome procedures. Estimates by Chemingui and Dessus (2004) suggest that the tax equivalent of the transaction costs related to the clearance of goods is around 15 percent.[4] They also suggest that the implicit tax on exports due to transaction costs is around 15 percent. Moreover, the incidence of the system varies not only by sector but also by type of firm or product, depending on whether the producers or importers are public or private.

Recent Trade Policy Reform

A number of actions have been taken over the past few years to liberalize the trade regime. The fact that imports may be undertaken by the private sector has been a significant change, as has been the gradual unification of the various exchange rates that apply to private and public transactions. The foreign exchange surrender requirement was further reduced to 10 percent in 2004. Traders in possession of import licenses are now also allowed to import directly. (They were previously required to use local agents.) Furthermore, it is no longer necessary to finance imports using foreign exchange generated from exports. There has also been a reduction in the number of prohibited imports, and explicit export taxes have been eliminated. Syria is gradually becoming integrated into the world economy at the regional and multilateral levels.

The Effect of Policy on Agricultural Prices

The pricing and commercialization policies applied in Syria, together with the trade policy, have protected Syrian farmers from the negative effects

[4] This is consistent with the survey-based information in Zarrouk (2003), described earlier. Relative to the import procedures of other countries in the region, Syria's are considered among the more problematic and costly by international traders.

of volatility in world markets, particularly in the case of wheat, cotton, and sugar. Furthermore, government-administered pricing commands a significant role in the rural economy because of its large-scale sequencing impact on resource allocations and farmer incomes down to the farm level (UNDP 2005b).

According to a recent study carried out by the Food and Agriculture Organization of the United Nations (FAO 2003), if farm incomes were not supported by government purchasing at official prices, farmers growing strategic crops, because of their high costs of production, would take losses in a normal-rainfall year, and, in the case of irrigated wheat and sugar beets, the losses would be higher. These losses would induce farmers to switch to other crops until only the lowest-cost producers remained in the market. The generous subsidies paid to producers and received by consumers are at the expense of the huge losses incurred by state-owned enterprises that purchase and process wheat, seed cotton, and sugar beets.

It is important to note that the seven crops that the government considers strategic crops and on which it continues to set producer prices account for over half the total value of national crop production and occupy about three-quarters of the 4.6 million hectares that are under cultivation in Syria. Wheat and cotton are, by far, the most important of the strategic crops in terms of farmgate value and employment creation.

By comparing the equivalent import or export price at the farmgate, one may estimate the magnitude of support provided to farmers for strategic crops in Syria. This kind of analysis was carried out by Westlake (2003) using 1999 data on six of the seven strategic crops. For sugar beets, the producer price in the late 1990s was almost three times import parity, rendering beets much more protected than any other crop in the country. Soft wheat producer prices were 66 percent higher than import parity. Cotton producer prices exceeded export parity by 31 percent as result of a steady decline in international prices for cotton fiber from 1995 to 1999. For barley, official prices were roughly equal to import parity but well above export parity. In the case of lentils and chickpeas, official prices were below the estimated export parity price. The analysis also showed that, to the extent that farmers may switch among crops in response to relative profitability, government price intervention has artificially stimulated the production of wheat, cotton, and sugar beets at the expense of barley, lentil, and chickpea production (Table 6.5).

Trade Agreements

At the regional level, in February 1997 Syria signed the agreement leading to GAFTA. In 1998 and 1999 it signed bilateral FTAs with Lebanon and Jordan,

Table 6.5 Comparison of official and parity producer prices in Syria, 2003

Product	Official producer price (millions of SYP/year)	Import parity price at the farmgate (millions of SYP/year)	Official price as a percentage of the import parity price
Import product			
Soft wheat	10,800	6,497	166
Barley	7,500	7,316	103
Sugar beets	2,150	746	288
Export product			
Lentils	16,000	18,799	85
Chickpeas	17,800	28,852	62
Cotton	29,290	22,291	69

Source: Westlake (2003).
Note: SYP, Syrian £.

respectively, and in 2005 it signed an FTA with Tunisia. In October 1997, Syria formally started negotiations on the association agreement with the E.U. An agreement was reached in 2004 but has not yet been ratified by the European countries and so has not entered into effect. At the multilateral level, in October 2001 Syria requested accession to the WTO, but few advances have been achieved toward accession.

The FTA signed between Syria and the E.U. (which has not entered into effect) calls for reinforcement of the trade relationship between Syria and the E.U. This will require significant reform in Syrian trade policy and in the application of instruments of protection in Syria. The main provisions of the Syria-E.U. association agreement relate to trade in agricultural products and are in four sections. The first section relates to E.U. imports of Syrian agricultural products. Accordingly, annual tariff quotas have been set for Syrian exports of selected horticultural products (Table 6.6).

For fresh tomatoes, a reduction of 60 percent applies to the MFN duty for quantities above the quota, although for products to which entry prices apply, this entry price is maintained. For other products, at the entry into force of the agreement the ad valorem duty will be set at zero for unlimited quantities. A list of these products has been annexed to the agreement. For a certain number of other products, at the entry into force of the agreement the ad valorem duty will be set at zero under a tariff quota covering traditional trade. A list of these products has also been annexed to the agreement. Finally, for a number of products, at the entry into force of the agreement the

Table 6.6 Proposed changes in European Union quotas for Syrian exports

Commodity	Season	Initial quota (metric tons)	Increase in quota
Potatoes	January 1-April 30	25,000	Annual increase of 1,000 metric tons for two years
Potatoes	June 1-July 31	5,000	No change
Fresh tomatoes	All year	15,000	Annual increase of 3% for two years
Oranges	January 1-May 31	25,000	Annual increase of 3% for two years
Small citrus	November 1-February 28	13,000	Annual increase of 3% for two years
Lemons	October 1-March 30	7,000	Annual increase of 3% for two years
Fresh grapes	November 1-July 31	3,000	Annual increase of 3% for two years
Fresh apples	All year	20,000	No change
Olive oil	All year	10,000	Annual increase of 1,000 metric tons for two years

Source: Draft European Union-Syria Euro-Mediterranean Partnership agreement.

ad valorem duty will be reduced to a certain level. A list of these products has been annexed to the agreement.

The second section includes regulations on the import by Syria of agricultural products originating in the E.U. For these products Syria will dismantle its tariffs to reach a zero tariff sequentially according to the following schema: 0-5 percent at entry into force, 5-10 percent in year 4, 10-40 percent in year 7, 40-100 percent reduced to 40 percent at entry into force and then a linear reduction to zero in year 12, above 100 percent reduced to 70 percent at entry into force and a linear reduction to zero at year 12. Additionally, annual tariff quotas at zero duty have been set for European exports for the following products without entry price: oranges (1,500 tons), small citrus fruits (750 tons), and fresh apples (2,500 tons).

The third section concerns processed agricultural products. Syria will grant annual tariff preference quotas for the following categories of these products: mineral water, soft drinks, spirits, cigarettes, and homogenized tobacco. Within the quotas, the applied tariff will be reduced by 40 percent when the agreement comes into force.

Finally, Syrian tariffs on fish will be dismantled over 12 years, with 0-10 percent reductions immediately, 10-30 percent in 5 years, 30-80 percent in 7 years, and all above 80 percent brought down to 80 percent at entry into force and dismantled over 12 years. On the other hand, all imports into the E.U. are to be dismantled by the third year after entry into force, with the exception of tuna, on which an annual quota of 100 metric tons will apply. (Currently, Syria does not export fish to the E.U.)

Poverty

According to the United Nations Development Programme, 11.4 percent of the Syrian population is unable to meet their basic food and nonfood needs. Furthermore, measured by the lower household-specific expenditure poverty lines, poverty in Syria rises to 30.1 percent, representing almost 5.3 million individuals. Measured according to the international measure of US$2 a day, 10.4 percent of Syrians are poor (UNDP 2005b).

Although poverty is generally more prevalent in rural Syria than in urban areas, the greatest difference is geographical. As shown in Table 6.7, in the northeastern region both rural and urban areas suffer from the greatest incidence, depth, and severity of poverty; the southern urban region has very low levels of poverty; and the middle and coastal regions have intermediate levels of poverty. The same report shows that poverty decreased between 1996-97 and 2003-04 for Syria as a whole, but regional patterns differ. The incidence of poverty declined rapidly in the middle and southern regions, especially in rural areas. Poverty declined moderately in urban areas of the northeastern and coastal regions. However, poverty actually rose in rural parts of these regions. Over this period, inequality in Syria as a whole rose slightly: the Gini coefficient rose from 0.33 to 0.37. However, a large increase in average per capita expenditure outweighed the effects of this increased disparity.

Results from the 2003-04 surveys show that lack of education is the characteristic with the strongest correlation to poverty in Syria. More than 18 per-

Table 6.7 Poverty measures in Syria, by region, 2003-04

Population group	Poverty measures			Percentage share		
	P_0	P_1	P_2	Poor	Nonpoor	Overall
Urban						
Southern	5.8	1.23	0.45	10	21	19
Northeastern	11.2	1.79	0.44	20	21	21
Middle	9.0	1.64	0.46	5	7	7
Coastal	9.3	1.95	0.60	3	4	4
Rural						
Southern	10.7	2.03	0.64	10	11	11
Northeastern	17.9	3.51	1.01	38	22	24
Middle	11.1	1.81	0.49	9	9	9
Coastal	9.7	1.92	0.57	4	5	5
All Syria	11.4	2.13	0.62	100	100	100

Source: UNDP (2005b).

Note: Poverty estimates are based on the lower poverty line.

cent of the poor population was illiterate, and poverty was most widespread, deepest, and most severe among these individuals. Poverty was inversely correlated with educational attainment, so even a moderate improvement in education could reduce the ranks of the poor. In urban areas the poverty headcount ranged from 11.7 percent among illiterate persons to only 1.5 percent among university graduates. The corresponding rates in rural areas were 16.5 and 5.0 percent (UNDP 2005b).

The same study shows that the highest poverty rates were among those self-employed in marginal and unskilled activities and among nonwage workers. Agriculture and construction were overrepresented within poor groups. Moreover, the poor were more likely to work in the informal sector, which employed 48 percent of the poor. Unemployment rates correlated with poverty; the poverty incidence among the unemployed was higher than average in urban areas. Table 6.8 shows that more than 50 percent of the poor in rural areas are farmers, while only 38 percent of the nonpoor in rural areas are farmers.

Table 6.9 presents the main poverty indicators for heads of household working in agriculture. Only 9.3 percent of urban heads of household working in agriculture are poor, while 18 percent of agricultural households in rural areas are poor. It is worth noting that 17 percent of agricultural households are poor compared to 11 percent of all Syrian households.

Table 6.8 Distribution of the population in Syria, by location, poverty status, and agricultural or other pursuits, 2005 (percent)

Population group	Agriculture	Other activities	Total
Urban			
Poor	5.7	94.4	100.0
Nonpoor	5.2	94.8	100.0
Total	5.3	94.8	100.0
Rural			
Poor	50.4	49.6	100.0
Nonpoor	38.2	61.8	100.0
Total	40.0	60.0	100.0
All Syria			
Poor	33.9	66.1	100.0
Nonpoor	21.5	78.5	100.0
Total	22.9	77.1	100.0

Source: UNDP (2005b).

Table 6.9 Poverty measures for households in Syria whose heads are working in agriculture, 2005

Population group	Poverty measure P_0	P_1	P_2	Percentage of population
Urban	9.3	1.7	0.4	5.4
Rural	18.0	3.5	1.1	40.6
All Syria	17.0	3.3	1.0	23.5

Source: UNDP (2005b).

The Impact of Wheat Market Liberalization on the Poor

Background

Syria's recently adopted five-year plan (2006–10) gives high priority to meeting the challenge of reducing the fiscal deficit by 7 percentage points of GDP over the period. The main strategy for achieving this objective is to reduce expenditure by phasing out subsidies and to increase revenue by adopting a value-added consumption tax.

Phasing out subsidies would have a significant effect on the fiscal deficit. First, the cost of agricultural and energy subsidies is large, about 18.9 percent of GDP. Second, unlike raising taxes, this measure can yield significant efficiency gains given the large deadweight loss associated with this policy. Third, the policy reform is an opportunity to make government subsidies more equitable, converting them to a powerful instrument for redistribution and poverty reduction. Fourth, the short-term contractionary impact on the economy will be smaller and the contribution to the adjustment of external accounts larger than using other fiscal measures. Finally, by pushing for greater efficiency in resource allocation and protecting budgetary spending on education, health, and infrastructure, this reform will improve the economy's long-term growth and balance-of-payments prospects (Chemingui and Fetini 2006).

In this section we examine the economic and distributional effects of the removal of wheat subsidies. We focus on wheat because of its importance in agricultural policy: wheat output represents 12 percent of total agricultural production, but this sector receives two-thirds of the total support to farmers. There is a close link between the removal of wheat producer subsidies and trade liberalization in the sense that restrictions on wheat imports facilitate the government policy of supporting wheat prices. In other words, it would be difficult to sustain the high support prices for wheat if imports were liberalized. In this sense, simulating the reduction in wheat subsidies corresponds to a policy of reducing agricultural trade protection.

For this analysis we have developed a static CGE model linked to data from the Syrian household expenditure survey. The model is used to assess the direct and indirect implications of reducing the producer price of wheat to international levels and increasing the consumer prices of wheat products through a reduction in subsidies. The assessment will focus on the overall economic structure and on household consumption and welfare.

Methods

The model used in this study is a static CGE model based on the standard static CGE model developed by Lofgren, Harris, and Robinson (2002). The Syrian standard CGE model explains all of the payments that are recorded in the SAM with which it is associated. The model is based on a SAM that was, in turn, based on the input-output table built by Chemingui and Fetini (2006) to assess the effect of phasing out subsidies on energy products. The model includes ten households, each representing one decile of the Syrian population. This allows us to examine the impact of alternative policies on different income groups in the country. A more detailed description of the model is provided in the appendix to this chapter.

The model is used to simulate three scenarios:

- a reduction in the subsidies on wheat production and wheat consumption by 20 percent,
- a reduction in the subsidies on wheat production and wheat consumption by 50 percent, and
- the elimination of the subsidies on wheat production and wheat consumption.

The decrease in the wheat producer price and the increase in the consumer prices for wheat products would have multiple effects on the economy and on households. The change would affect virtually all households as consumers and some households as producers as well. The most immediate and publicly visible impact of the proposed reform of subsidies would be on the cost of living for wheat-consuming households, which would face higher prices for wheat products such as bread. In addition, the decline in the producer price of wheat would negatively affect the income of wheat-producing farmers. In addition to these two direct effects, there would be indirect effects whereby the new set of relative prices would induce a reallocation in resources; farmers would reallocate land and labor from wheat to competing crops, and consumers would substitute other foods for wheat products. Other households would be affected by the reallocation of consumer spending and by the reallocation of factors of production.

We calculated the incremental effects on sectoral production and prices and the overall cost of living caused by the proposed reform in wheat prices and the prices of wheat derivates. We did this by combining a SAM that shows the input structure for the production of all final goods and a consumer expenditure survey that shows the amount of each final good purchased by households differentiated by decile welfare groups. It is important to note that the current version of the SAM does not differentiate farmers from non-farmers; household categories are defined only by their level of per capita consumption. The income sources for each category of household are composed of labor income, capital income, remittances, and other transfers.[5]

Results

The macroeconomic effects of the reduction or elimination of the wheat subsidies would be relatively modest, as shown in Table 6.10. Aggregate consumption, imports, and exports would change by less than 1 percent even with the full elimination of the subsidies (Simulation 3). The positive (albeit small) effect of the subsidy removal would be due to the elimination of a policy distortion that creates an inefficiency loss in the economy. The largest macroeconomic effect would be on government savings, which would increase by 2.77 percentage points of GDP as a result of the elimination of the subsidies. In other words, government savings would increase from 0.78 percent of GDP to 1.99 percent of GDP. Private savings would decline by 3.65 percentage points of GDP as a result of the subsidy removal.

Table 6.11 shows the impact of subsidy reduction or removal on the prices and output in various sectors of the economy. Not surprisingly, the sectors most affected would be the wheat and food processing (including milling) sectors. The producer price of wheat would decline by 4 percent with a 20 percent reduction in subsidies and by 16.5 percent with the complete elimination of the subsidies. The lower producer prices imply a decline in the profitability of wheat production and some substitution toward other crops. Because of the relatively inelastic supply of wheat, even complete elimination of the subsidy would cause a decrease in wheat production of less than 2 percent. Thus, farmers will be the direct losers from this reform, at least in the short run.

---

[5] A more detailed analysis would involve disaggregating production factors to include land rents and agricultural wages among the income sources for each decile.

Table 6.10 Estimated impact of wheat subsidy removal on macroeconomic indicators in Syria

Indicator	Base year value	20% reduction in wheat subsidies (% change)	50% reduction in wheat subsidies (% change)	Elimination of wheat subsidies (% change)
Real absorption	1,184.90	0.13	0.31	0.49
Real household consumption	764.01	0.19	0.48	0.76
Total real exports	431.95	0.17	0.46	0.77
Total real imports	403.74	0.19	0.49	0.82
	Percentage of GDP	**(% change)**	**(% change)**	**(% change)**
Investment	20.58	-0.02	-0.06	-0.10
Private savings	25.32	-0.89	-2.25	-3.65
Trade deficit	-4.21	0.00	0.01	0.02
Government saving	-0.78	0.70	0.01	2.77
Tariff revenue	1.52	0.00	1.74	0.02

Source: Simulation results using a computable general equilibrium model for Syria.

The policy reforms would have mixed effects on the wheat milling industry. The sector would benefit from the lower price of wheat, but, on the other hand, it would lose subsidies for wheat processing, and the volume of wheat production (and thus processing) would decline. Thus, the food processing sector, which includes wheat milling, would face better prices but a smaller volume (see Table 6.11). It appears that the net effect on the sector would be slightly positive in that the price increase would be greater than the volume decrease. The impact of these policy changes on output in other sectors would generally be positive because of the elimination of the distortion in the economy but small because the effects would be indirect.

The magnitude of the welfare loss for the average consumer would not be very great because the share of wheat in household expenditures is low and because a relatively small share of households grow wheat.[6] Disaggregat-

[6] The impact on welfare (welfare loss) is a relative concept in that it measures what is needed in terms of money to keep expenditures per group at the same level as before the increase in prices. A subsidy reduction by SYP 1 would matter more to the poorest consumers than to the richest and would contribute to a higher welfare loss for the former than for the latter. In absolute terms, the impact would differ according to the amount of expenditure by different household groups in the wheat product and the other products linked to it, so those households consuming more of a subsidized product (and therefore allocated more subsidies) would lose more if the prices for consumer goods were increased.

Table 6.11 Estimated impact of wheat subsidy removal on prices and production in Syria (percent change)

Sector	Producer price: 20% reduction in wheat subsidies	Producer price: 50% reduction in wheat subsidies	Producer price: Elimination of wheat subsidies	Output level: 20% reduction in wheat subsidies	Output level: 50% reduction in wheat subsidies	Output level: Elimination of wheat subsidies
Wheat	-4.045	-10.222	-16.505	-0.427	-1.136	-1.94
Other agricultural production	-0.435	-1.207	-2.165	0.059	0.139	0.21
Mining	-0.144	-0.421	-0.799	0.008	0.019	0.03
Food processing	1.791	5.044	9.238	-1.747	-4.814	-8.56
Paper, publishing, and printing	-0.283	-0.794	-1.446	0.076	0.19	0.31
Nonmetallic industries	-0.365	-0.982	-1.709	0.199	0.502	0.81
Chemical and textile activities	-0.103	-0.315	-0.625	0.124	0.315	0.51
Metallic industries	-0.251	-0.692	-1.235	0.153	0.386	0.62
Other manufacturing	-0.236	-0.657	-1.186	0.135	0.344	0.56
Electricity	-0.477	-1.272	-2.191	0.165	0.415	0.67
Water	-0.143	-0.434	-0.854	0.160	0.401	0.64
Other services	-0.333	-0.904	-1.589	0.208	0.530	0.87

Source: Simulation results using a computable general equilibrium model for Syria.

Table 6.12 Estimated impact of wheat subsidy removal on welfare in Syria, by income decile

Population decile	Change in household welfare (equivalent variation as a percentage of income) 20% reduction in wheat subsidies	50% reduction in wheat subsidies	Elimination of wheat subsidies
Poorest	-0.06	-0.19	-0.42
2	-0.06	-0.22	-0.47
3	-0.02	-0.10	-0.26
4	-0.01	-0.08	-0.21
5	-0.02	-0.03	-0.12
6	0.04	0.03	-0.01
7	0.05	0.08	0.08
8	0.09	0.11	0.13
9	0.53	0.23	0.34
Richest	0.19	1.35	2.20

Source: Simulation results using a computable general equilibrium model for Syria.

ing the welfare losses resulting from the reduction in wheat subsidies shows that the richest 10 percent of the population would gain the most from the reforms and the top 50 percent would gain something, while the poorest 50 percent of households would lose (Table 6.12). This difference reflects the original unequal distribution of benefits from subsidies among different consumers and producers of these products and the similar distribution of income sources among categories. However, the effects would be quite small; the welfare changes associated with full subsidy removal would be less than 1 percent for all groups except the richest 10 percent of households.

Summary

The Syrian agricultural sector is characterized by a high degree of government intervention, including fixed prices, state marketing boards, state monopolies in the marketing of strategic crops, state monopolies in the distribution of fertilizer, and high barriers to the importation of agricultural commodities and food products. Reforms to liberalize the agricultural sector have been introduced in recent years, but the sector remains one of the most highly regulated agricultural sectors in the MENA region.

On the one hand, agricultural policy toward the main strategic crops has been successful in achieving national self-sufficiency in wheat and rapid growth in the production of the country's main agricultural export commodity, cotton. It has also prevented the development of large disparities in the incomes of rural and urban households. On the other hand, the policy has achieved these objectives at a high cost in terms of government budgetary resources and the efficiency of resource allocation within the agricultural sector. Subsidies in agriculture and energy have also contributed to an unsustainable budget deficit. With the depletion of oil reserves over the coming 10-15 years, the government will need to find alternative sources of economic growth and fiscal revenue. The latest five-year plan envisages the phasing out of subsidies and the implementation of a value-added tax.

Broad domestic liberalization of the agricultural sector would result in substitution away from wheat, sugar beets, and cotton and toward barley, lentils, and chickpeas. Completion of the EMP agreement with the E.U. will expand the exports of fruits, vegetables, and olive oil if Syrian producers can meet exacting quality and food safety requirements.

About two-thirds of the agricultural subsidies are devoted to maintaining a high producer price for wheat and low consumer prices for bread and other wheat products. By banning the private importation of wheat and by not importing through the state marketing board, government policy keeps the domestic price of wheat 66 percent higher than the import parity price. Wheat is the most important staple food, as well as an important source of income for farmers, so the government is particularly sensitive to the impact of reducing or removing import protection and subsidies for wheat. Using a CGE model that simulates the effect of policy changes on households in 10 income categories, we examined the effect of liberalizing wheat markets by removing import protection and eliminating subsidies. The macroeconomic effects would be relatively modest, although government savings would increase by almost 3 percent of GDP. Complete liberalization would reduce the producer price of wheat by about 17 percent and production by about 2 percent. The effects of subsidy removal on the welfare of Syrian households would be regressive in the sense that high-income households would gain while lower-income households would lose. The magnitude of the effects, however, would be quite small: less than 1 percent of the base incomes for all but the richest income group.

It is important that one keep three factors in mind in interpreting these results. First, the impact on farmers (particularly wheat farmers) will be larger than the impact on the poorer deciles because each decile includes both farmers and nonfarmers, thus diluting the adverse impact of the reforms on wheat farmers. If one-third of the poorest decile are farmers and we assume that there would be no impact on nonfarmers, the impact on poor wheat farmers would be a decline of 1.3 percent (0.42/0.33) in welfare.

Second, the distributional impact will vary among farmers. Farmers growing and selling large quantities of wheat will lose the most in absolute terms from the elimination of protection and subsidies. Smaller farmers will lose less. The impact of the reforms in terms of percentage changes in real incomes will depend on net sales of wheat as a percentage of household incomes. If net sales are a large share of incomes, the negative effect will be large. More information on the share of incomes from wheat and other crops would be needed to explore the distributional impact among farmers.

Third, the impact of liberalization on the poor depends partly on complementary policies. For example, if the wheat market reforms were implemented along with a reduction in energy subsidies, the combined effect would be more pro-poor. The study recently carried out by the World Bank (Chemingui and Fetini 2006) shows that, in the case of subsidies on energy products, 80 percent of the people will be better off; the maximum gain would accrue to the poorest decile, which would obtain a net gain equivalent to 35 percent of the decile's overall consumption. Only the two richest deciles would experience a net loss (equivalent to 2.5 percent and 5.5 percent of decile consumption, respectively). Alternatively, the wheat subsidy reduction could be implemented in conjunction with a safety net program that used a portion of the fiscal savings for targeted programs for the poor.

One aspect of agricultural policy that is more important in Syria (and Egypt) than in the other countries under consideration is that the support for wheat farmers is provided in large part through direct subsidies from the government rather than through the taxation of consumers through import tariffs. This increases the feasibility of a political solution whereby a portion of the savings from reducing these subsidies could be used to compensate those who would lose from the reforms. One possibility would be to use some of the fiscal savings to implement a direct income-support program that would compensate wheat farmers for losses associated with the reforms. The compensation should be a fixed amount based on historical production or area and could be phased out over a number of years, giving wheat farmers the time and resources necessary to develop alternative income sources (see Olhan 2006 and Chapter 8).

Appendix 6A: Methods for Estimating the Impact of Trade Liberalization on Syria

The model used in this study is a static CGE model and directly inspired by the prototype developed by Lofgren, Harris, and Robinson (2002). The Syrian standard CGE model explains all of the payments that are recorded in the SAM with which it is associated. The model is based on a SAM that was, in turn, based on the input-output table built by Chemingui and Fetini (2006) to assess the effect of phasing out subsidies on energy products.

Regarding domestic supply, each producer (represented by an activity) is assumed to maximize profits, defined as the difference between revenue earned and the cost of factors and intermediate inputs. Profits are maximized subject to constraints that capture the production technology and optional rigidities in factor employment. At the top level, the technology is specified by a constant elasticity of substitution function or, alternatively, by a Leontief function of the quantities of value added and aggregate intermediate input. Value added is itself a constant elasticity of substitution function of primary factors, whereas the aggregate intermediate input is a Leontief function of disaggregated intermediate inputs. Each activity produces one or more commodities according to fixed yield coefficients. As noted, a commodity may be produced by more than one activity. Revenue from the activity is defined by the level of the activity, yields, and commodity prices at the producer level. Factor incomes are distributed to domestic and foreign institutions in fixed shares that are defined by factor and activity. The value added is then decomposed in two substitutable parts: aggregate capital-labor and land. The aggregate capital-land is further disaggregated into land and capital. Land is used only by agricultural activities as described in the SAM. Labor is further disaggregated into agricultural labor and urban labor. Agricultural labor is fully employed and perfectly mobile across agricultural activities, while urban labor is also fully employed and perfectly mobile across nonagricultural activities.

In the CGE model institutions are represented by households (deciles), enterprises, the government, and the rest of the world. The households (disaggregated as in the SAM) receive incomes from the factors of production (directly or indirectly via the enterprises) and transfers from other institutions. More specifically, each household receives fixed shares of factor income flows (disaggregated by factor and source, either domestic activities or the rest of the world). Transfers from the rest of the world to households are fixed in foreign currency.

The households use their incomes to save, consume, and make transfers to other institutions. In the current model, direct taxes and transfers to other institutions (both domestic and the rest of the world) are defined as fixed shares of household income, whereas the savings share is flexible for selected households. Household consumption at market prices (adjusted for taxes and subsidies) is allocated across different commodities according to linear expenditure system demand functions derived from the maximization of a Stone-Geary utility function. Instead of being paid directly to the households, factor incomes may be paid to one or more enterprises.

Enterprises may also receive transfers from other institutions. Enterprise incomes are allocated to savings and transfers to other institutions. Enterprises do not consume. Apart from this, the payments to and from enterprises are modeled in the same way as the payments to and from households. The government collects taxes and receives transfers from other institutions. In the current model, all taxes are at fixed ad valorem rates. Transfers from the rest of the world are exogenous in foreign currency, whereas transfers from domestic institutions are fixed shares of the net (posttax and savings) incomes of these institutions. The government uses this income to finance its own consumption, commodity and activity subsidies, and transfers to other institutions. Government consumption is fixed in real (quantity) terms, whereas government transfers to domestic institutions (households and enterprises) are indexed to the consumer price index. Government savings (the difference between government income and spending) is a flexible residual. The final institution is the rest of the world.

Commodities pass through a chain, the first stage of which consists of the generation of aggregated domestic output from the output of different activities for a given commodity. These outputs are imperfectly fungible as a result of, for example, differences in timing, quality, and location among different activities. A constant elasticity of substitution function is used as the aggregation function. The demand for the output of each activity is derived through the problem of minimizing the cost of supplying a given quantity of aggregated output, subject to this constant elasticity of substitution function. Activity-specific commodity prices serve to clear the implicit market for each disaggregated commodity. At the next stage, aggregated domestic output is allocated between exports and domestic sales on the assumption that suppliers maximize sales revenue for any given aggregate output level, subject to imperfect transformability between exports and domestic sales, expressed by a constant elasticity of transformation function.

On international markets, export demand is infinitely elastic at given world prices. The price received by domestic suppliers for exports is expressed in domestic currency (to the border) and export taxes (if any). The supply price for domestic sales is equal to the price paid because of domestic demand (from the supplier to satisfy demand) per unit of domestic sales. If the commodity is not exported, total output is passed to the domestic market.

Domestic demand is made up of the sum of the demand deriving from household consumption, government consumption, investment, and intermediate inputs. If the supply of a commodity destined for domestic use is made up of both imports and domestic output, all domestic market demand is a composite commodity made up of imports and domestic output, the demand for which is derived on the assumption that those who account for domestic demand minimize their costs, subject to imperfect substitutability. Total market demand is directed toward the imports of commodities the demand for which is not satisfied by domestic production and toward the domestic output of nonimported commodities. Demand prices are adjusted for commodity taxes and subsidies. The derived demand for imported commodities is met through international supplies that are infinitely elastic at given world prices. The import prices paid because of domestic demand also include import tariffs (at fixed ad valorem rates). Similarly, the derived demand for domestic output is met by domestic suppliers. Flexible prices balance between the demand for and the supply of domestically marketed domestic output.

Finally, several macroeconomic constraints are introduced in the model. First, the small country assumption holds; the Syrian economy is unable to change world prices, so its imports and exports prices are exogenous. Capital transfers are exogenous as well, and therefore the trade balance is fixed so as to achieve the balance-of-payments equilibrium.

The SAM used here is based on the input-output table built by Chemingui and Fetini (2006) to assess the effect of phasing out subsidies on energy products. This input-output table is converted to a SAM using additional information on income formation and transfers among different institutions. The activity structure of the SAM has been updated for this study by adding new sectors and commodities (wheat and wheat derivatives) and by aggregating others (mainly energy products). The specification of the agricultural sectors has also been rendered consistent with the need for meaningful mapping between input-output sectors and household expenditure items so as to be able to measure the effects of subsidy reforms on household welfare. The specification of the input-output structure has been based on detailed microeconomic data at the sectoral level but also at the enterprise level in some cases.

Substitution elasticity between domestic and imported products is set at 2.2. The elasticity of transformation between products intended for the domestic market and products for exports is 5.0. Trade elasticities come from the empirical literature devoted to CGE models. They are not specific to Syria. See, for instance, Burniaux, Nicoletti, and Oliveira-Martins (1992); Konan and Maskus (1997); or the more recent Gallaway, McDaniel, and Rivera (2000). Devarajan, Go, and Li (1999) econometrically estimated substitutions elasticities for Syria and obtained results close to 0.1 for both Armington and CET elasticities. These elasticities are not distinguished by product, which explains their low levels to a large extent. Nor are they statistically significant.

Substitution elasticities in the production function are the following: 0.5 between intermediate consumption and value added, 1.0 between aggregate capital and labor, 0.0 between the physical capital and land, and 0.4 between various types of labor.

Chemingui and Dessus (1999) and Chemingui (2007) tested the influence of changing the values for international trade substitution elasticities as well as substitution elasticities between fixed and mobile factors. For trade elasticities, halved values for imports and exports are tested. This cut in substitutability between domestic and foreign products reduces the magnitude of the impact of a cut in tariffs, but consumers do not turn toward foreign products. When substitution elasticity between capital and labor and between different types of capital (physical and land) are doubled, the cost of trade liberalization is lower, but the direction of the impact does not change.

CHAPTER 7

Agriculture, Trade, and Poverty in Morocco

The Kingdom of Morocco has approximately 30 million inhabitants, about half the population of Egypt. A little more than half (57 percent) of the population lives in Casablanca, Rabat, and other urban areas. It is a lower-middle-income country, with per capita GDP of about US$1,667, close to the average for the MENA countries.[1]

Since joining the WTO in 1995, Morocco has been liberalizing its agricultural trade policies. The state monopoly on the importation of staple foods has been dismantled except for the import of common wheat flour. Quantitative import restrictions have been converted to tariffs, resulting in tariffs as high as 339 percent. The tariffs on agricultural imports average 33 percent. Consumer subsidies are being maintained on common wheat flour and sugar. Variable import duties are used to stabilize and support the farmgate prices of wheat, barley, maize, rice, and sorghum (WTO 2003).

Morocco joined the WTO in January 1995 and signed the EMP agreement with the E.U. the following year. The EMP agreement calls for the elimination of Moroccan industrial duties between 2000 and 2012. Morocco is among the first MENA countries with existing agreements with the E.U. to have signed the EMP in 2005. Under the EMP, the E.U. is committing to allow greater access to its markets and contribute greater financial assistance to its Mediterranean partners (World Bank 2009). In 2003 Morocco signed an FTA with the United States; this will be implemented over 10 years.

In spite of these agreements, Morocco retains a relatively high tariff structure. The World Bank estimates that the simple average tariff rate is among the highest 1 percent among the world's countries. Morocco's progress in reducing tariffs over 2000-04 has been about average compared with that of other countries in the world (World Bank 2005).

[1] This is the per capita GDP in 2006, measured in constant 2000 U.S. dollars (World Bank 2008b).

The Agricultural Sector

Agricultural Production

Morocco's agricultural sector contributes 16 percent to its GDP, provides 45 percent of its total employment, and accounts for 6 percent of its total exports. Morocco has more agricultural potential than many MENA countries because of suitable soils and rainfall combined with irrigation potential. Currently, agriculture satisfies about one-half to two-thirds of Morocco's grain requirements through the cultivation of wheat, barley, and maize in the rainfed areas. Wheat is the main agricultural import, followed by sugar and soybean oil.

Because grains are grown under rainfed conditions, harvests and thus import requirements vary sharply from one year to the next. In 2002 Morocco produced 5.0 million metric tons of barley and wheat and imported about 3.9 million tons, which represents a self-sufficiency ratio of about 56 percent. The following year, favorable rains increased wheat and barley output to 8.3 million tons, causing imports to decline to 2.3 million tons, representing 78 percent self-sufficiency. The government has several programs to extend and upgrade irrigated areas so as to make agricultural supply less vulnerable to weather, in particular by strengthening a national program to encourage local irrigation and use water more efficiently (FAO 2004).

Agricultural Trade Patterns

Morocco's total exports were US$22 billion in 2006, while its agricultural exports were US$1.3 billion, or 6 percent of the total. Unlike in most other MENA countries, agricultural exports in Morocco are dominated by fruits and vegetables. Citrus fruits, tomatoes, olives, potatoes, and other horticultural crops are grown, often under irrigation, and exported to Europe. Exports are facilitated by the short distance across the Straits of Gibraltar to Spain. Fruit and vegetable exports account for about 65 percent of Moroccan agricultural exports.

Morocco's total imports were US$25 billion in 2006, of which agricultural imports accounted for US$2.3 billion, or 9 percent. As in many MENA countries, the largest agricultural import in Morocco is wheat. Over 2004-06, Morocco imported an average of US$460 million in wheat. Imported wheat competes with domestically produced wheat, which accounts for 50-60 percent of consumption, depending on the year. Morocco also imports raw sugar, soybean oil, and maize. Maize is mainly supplied by imports; there is no sizeable domestic production. There is substantial domestic production of barley, but not at a level sufficient to supply local needs (World Bank 2008b; FAO 2009a).

Agricultural and Trade Policies

Moroccan agricultural policy has gone through three main phases. The first phase, from the time of its independence in 1956 until the middle of the 1980s, was characterized by significant intervention by the government in all activities and throughout the production process. The second phase, from the mid-1980s until 1995, involved the implementation of a structural adjustment program that reduced government intervention in the economy and encouraged the expansion of the private sector. In the third phase, since 1995, Morocco has increased its integration into the world economy, consolidated by a series of trade agreements. These three phases of agricultural and trade policies are described in detail in the following sections.

The Preadjustment Period

Since its independence, Moroccan agricultural policy has been conceived to achieve ambitious but contradictory objectives. In fact, on the one hand the policy has aimed to exploit the comparative advantages of the Moroccan agricultural sector in exports, but it has also attempted to meet internal demand through domestic production by encouraging import-substitution production.[2]

The agricultural policy of the mid-1960s is associated with the "policy of dams," which, as a symbolic objective, aimed at the irrigation of a million hectares by 2000. The state promoted the construction of dams through public investment, subsidies, elimination of taxes, loans, price policies, supervision, and distribution. Public investment in the basic infrastructure was massive, with investment in water resource mobilization reaching close to 30 percent of public investments during this period. The agricultural investment code, promulgated in 1969, regulated the use of irrigated lands and encouraged the modernization of farming and the intensification of agricultural production. To help farmers come into line with the state policy in agriculture, an extensive system of subsidies and incentives was provided to foster modernization. Irrigation water was heavily subsidized.

The production pricing policy was selective. The state regulated the prices of certain basic products for the internal market, such as grains, milk, and some industrial crops. However, there was no regulation of the prices of fruits (including citrus), vegetables, or olive oil products, which were promoted as export crops. At the beginning of the 1970s, agricultural policy attempted to maintain income levels among farmers through subsidies without raising consumer prices for agricultural products. For some commodities (sugar, oilseeds and milk), the government supervised the entire supply chain.

---

[2] This section is largely based on Akesbi (2002).

The results of these policies did not meet expectations. Furthermore, the fiscal burden of the agricultural and consumer subsidies increased over time. While the world prices of basic products (grains, oil, meat, and milk) decreased, producer prices in Morocco rose, and consumer prices remained stable. These budgetary imbalances were the main cause of a crisis in Moroccan public finances in the middle of the 1980s and the subsequent adoption of a structural adjustment plan under the supervision of the World Bank and the International Monetary Fund.

The Structural Adjustment Period

In the middle of the 1980s, Morocco undertook a wide-reaching program of economic reform aimed at stabilizing the national economy and laying the groundwork for greater growth in the medium and long terms. As in many developing countries, the adjustment program was adopted in Morocco to escape a situation of crisis and insolvency and to gain access to international credit. The worsening fiscal deficits and mounting debt were the main results of the costly and inefficient policies. The structural adjustment program aimed to reduce the budget deficit, establish a coherent pricing policy, move the real exchange rate closer to equilibrium, and correct the country's trade imbalance. One of the main elements of this effort to reconstruct the national economy was the Sectoral Adjustment Program for Agriculture.

In the medium term, the objectives of this sectoral adjustment program were to stimulate the agricultural sector to raise economic growth, reduce the trade deficit, and create employment. This was to be achieved by liberalizing agricultural markets and encouraging private investment. Within this framework, priority was given to increasing the production of agricultural products in which Morocco had a comparative advantage. The components of the program included

- adjusting and liberalizing producer prices and progressively eliminating subsidies to create a favorable environment for the participation of the private sector and the liberalization of activities;
- rationalizing state intervention, progressively disengaging the state from trade activities that could be adequately run by the private sector, and consolidating the state's main role as a regulator; and
- improving the efficiency of public expenditures and investment in line with development objectives and the priorities in agricultural policy.

Specific policies included the concession of some state land to the private sector, the redefinition of the role of public enterprises, the elimination of barriers to internal and foreign trade (namely, monopolies, quotas, and marketing regulations), the elimination of most subsidies for agricultural inputs and consumption, and the reform of the agricultural credit system. Subsidies for irrigation water and for agricultural equipment were maintained, as was the large public investment in water resources.

Producer pricing controls on agricultural commodities were eliminated for hard wheat, barley, maize, rice, milk, and cattle feed. Consumer pricing for dairy products and grains was liberalized. Only the prices of soft wheat flour, sugar, and vegetable oil remained controlled and subsidized by the state. Except for a few sensitive or strategic products (grains, sugar, oil, meat, and dairy products), the marketing channels for agricultural and food products were liberalized. Likewise, importation and exportation operations for agro-food products were liberalized except for sensitive products.

The Global Integration Period

The adoption of a structural adjustment program was only the beginning of a much more thorough reform of the Moroccan economy. Starting in the mid-1990s, the government signed a number of trade agreements that committed Morocco to greater liberalization in trade, thus consolidating the reforms carried out under the structural adjustment program.

In 1994 Morocco signed the GATT, agreeing to the different commitments incumbent on the developing countries. A year later, like other southern Mediterranean countries, Morocco signed a partnership agreement with the E.U. that provided for the creation of a free trade area between the two partners over a period of 12 years. Trade liberalization through the adhesion of Morocco to free trade areas was also manifest in GAFTA, implemented beginning in 2005. Morocco likewise signed FTAs with the countries of the Agadir initiative (Egypt, Jordan, and Tunisia), the European Free Trade Association, Turkey, and the United States (see Table 2.9 and Figure 2.3).[3] Some of the more important trade agreements are discussed in the next section.

Trade Agreements

GATT and the WTO

The commitments of Morocco under the GATT and WTO are limited to market access. In fact, Morocco does not provide export subsidies, which are the focus of a commitment for reduction. In addition, its level of aggregate market support is well below the allowable level. Concerning market access, Morocco has changed all NTBs into tariffs. For products such as grains, sugar, milk, meat, and oilseeds and their by-products, which were subject to NTBs,

[3] The European Free Trade Association includes Iceland, Liechtenstein, Norway, and Switzerland.

tariff equivalents have been set. The bound tariff rates for these products allow for high levels of import protection. For products that were subject to tariff barriers alone, the bound rates have been set at 60 percent. This product category covers all fresh or processed agricultural products except basic products.

In both cases, Morocco has committed itself to progressively reduce these tariff rates by 2.4 percentage points per year over 10 years. The products that are currently targeted for minimum access are mainly meat, milk, and cereals. Because the bound tariff rates are quite high, the level of protection remains high. Because the tariff reductions over 10 years are fairly small, the impact of the GATT and WTO on protection in Morocco has been quite modest.

The EMP Agreement with the E.U.

Morocco's partnership agreement with the E.U. is based on the principle of reciprocity. It provides for the gradual elimination of tariffs on all industrial products. Agricultural products, as defined by the E.U., are excluded from the EMP implementation agreement.[4] However, the schedule for tariff elimination is not the same for all products. The agreement provides for the rapid dismantling of the tariffs on products that are not produced domestically and on equipment. In contrast, it provides for slower tariff reductions on goods that compete with domestic production.

The E.U. and Morocco signed an additional agreement at the beginning of 2004 relative to trade in agricultural products. This agreement promotes the access of Moroccan products to the European market and sets up high preferential quotas for European agricultural products on the Moroccan market depending on the level of production of these products in Morocco. The EMAA for Morocco is set to be further enhanced by the new EMP action plans that will increase political, social, and trade relations between the E.U. and Morocco and back the ambitious programs with financial assistance (European Commission 2009).

The Morocco-United States Free Trade Agreement

The FTA between Morocco and the United States was established to enhance the economic and trade relations between the two countries. In terms of foreign trade, the United States is the fourth most important trade partner of Morocco. On the Moroccan side, the agreement goes beyond tariff reduction to include measures to improve the environment of trade and economic

[4] A complete list of the agricultural products is found in Annex I of the Rome Treaty and was updated after the signing of the Amsterdam Treaty in 1997. It comprises all land-based, breeding, and fishing products as well as the related primary processed products.

exchanges with a view to attracting more foreign investment in the country. The U.S. market is considered a potential outlet for Moroccan products, notably for agricultural and textile and clothing products. But, as in the case of the European market, access to the U.S. market is constrained by quality norms as strict and rigorous as those applied at Morocco's entry into the European market.

In Morocco there is a concern that opening the Moroccan market to subsidized U.S. grain will undercut local grain production, thus increasing rural poverty and causing excessive migration to urban areas. During the FTA negotiations, the Moroccan side recommended that a special framework be established for the grain sector before total liberalization, given the repercussions on the living standards of grain producers, an important segment of the Moroccan population. The United States argued that the advantage of the agreement for Morocco resides in the structural changes in Moroccan agriculture that will make it more competitive and exploit its comparative advantages. But Moroccan negotiators are skeptical of the argument in light of the generous support given to farmers by U.S. agricultural policy.

Within the framework of this agreement, it is clear that the United States will profit from the level of agricultural trade on account of the privileges given to European agricultural products, without bearing a corresponding financial cost for the development of the Moroccan economy as the E.U. did through the Middle East and Developing Africa Fund.

The FTA between Morocco and the United States was signed in June 2004 and came into force in January 2006. In contrast to the gradual pace of implementation of the EMP agreement (over 1995–2012), the pace of implementation of the Morocco-U.S. FTA is quite rapid. Another contrast is that the E.U. agreement provides for financial assistance to help upgrade the Moroccan economy and legislation to take advantage of the new export opportunities, while the U.S. agreement does not provide for financial support.

Poverty

Based on the 1998/99 household survey of Morocco, poverty remains largely a rural phenomenon. Almost 1 Moroccan in 4 is poor in rural areas compared to 1 in 10 in urban areas. Although the rural population represents 46 percent of the total population, 66 percent of the poor live in rural areas. However, the percentage of the poor who live in urban areas has increased from 27 to 34 percent. In both rural and urban areas, the poor generally lack education and live in large households with many children and few working members. The incidence of poverty is much higher among children than it is among adults; 44 percent of children under age 15 are poor versus 16 percent of adults. Among the poor, 64 percent are illiterate (compared to 53 percent among the nonpoor). Poverty is heavily concentrated in the central and northwestern regions (World Bank 2001).

At the national level, the distribution of the poor by sector of activity of the head of household shows that most of the poor work in the agricultural sector (57 percent), followed by services (26 percent) and construction (13 percent). In urban areas, among 58 percent of the poor the breadwinner is working in services, while in rural areas, agriculture is the dominant source of income among 75 percent of the poor.

Because of the dynamics of urbanization in Morocco, the structural causes of urban and rural poverty are closely related. Poor rural households engaged in productive activities typically have access to agricultural land, but their landholdings are small, rarely irrigated, and less productive. Moreover, due to a lack of land titles and registration, they cannot obtain formal credit and invest in their property. They often have nonagricultural sources of income, working in the informal sector and moving back and forth throughout the year between rural and urban areas. The urban poor face multiple deprivations such as lack of employment and inadequacy of access to land, housing, and basic services.

The Impact of Trade Liberalization on the Poor

In this section, we examine the impact of trade liberalization on the rural poor in Morocco. First we discuss the issues and describe the results of an earlier study that simulated the distributional impact of wheat import liberalization. Then we describe the methods and findings of a new analysis with a CGE model that has been used to study the impact of various types of trade liberalization on the Moroccan economy. Although the model does not simulate the impact on different types of households, it does simulate the impact on the returns to four types of labor, including unskilled agricultural labor. Because small-scale farmers earn most of their income from unskilled agricultural labor (including labor allocated to production on their own farms), this is a close approximation of the impact of trade liberalization on small-scale, low-income farmers in Morocco (this analysis is described in more detail in Thomas et al. 2008).

Background

In Morocco, as in most developing countries, policymakers and researchers are concerned about the possible impact of agricultural trade liberalization. First, there is the concern that trade liberalization will adversely affect the rural poor, particularly small-scale farmers. Simulation studies (as well as economic logic) suggest that multilateral trade liberalization will raise the price of agricultural commodities, including wheat. Morocco would lose, on net, from an increase in wheat prices, but how would poor farmers be affected? The answer partly depends on Moroccan wheat import policy, the liberalization of which could partly offset, nullify, or even reverse the effect of higher world prices on domestic prices. Second, there is concern about the closed markets of trading partners. For example, if Moroccan farmers switch out of wheat and into horticultural crops, will there be export opportunities for these products in the E.U. or the United States?

The impact of agricultural reform on households has been difficult to address because the tools used to examine the economywide impacts of reform in agriculture have traditionally been able to assess only the impacts on a relatively small number of household types (Abdelkhalek 2002). Accordingly, identifying the households that are net sellers (which would gain from higher prices) and those that are net buyers (which would gain from lower prices) has been difficult.

Grain producers in Morocco are protected by tariffs on imports as high as 100 percent. This policy encourages farmers to grow wheat even if the costs of production exceed the costs of importing wheat. The high cost of production is partially absorbed by the government, which implements a complicated system of subsidies to mills and consumers. The cost is also shared by the consumers, who pay a higher price for wheat products than they would if wheat could be imported without trade tariffs. A policy that eliminated the border tariffs for cereals without any reform in the agricultural sector in developed countries would result in significantly lower producer prices for wheat and somewhat lower consumer prices for wheat products. This policy would benefit consumers, who would pay less for their flour and bread, but hurt producers, who would have to compete with lower-cost imported wheat.

A study carried out by Ravallion and Lokshin (2004) is one of the few that has used household survey data to examine the distributional impact of trade liberalization in the MENA region. It focused on the impact of removing tariffs on imported grains. The study used a CGE model to simulate the effect of reducing and eliminating wheat import tariffs. The price changes associated with different liberalization scenarios were combined with data on the sources of income and the allocation of expenditures for 5,117 households in the 1998–99 Morocco Living Standard Survey. The impact of each policy simulation on each household was calculated using standard methods of short-term welfare analysis. The results were aggregated to calculate changes in the mean income and incidence of poverty. According to this study, the elimination of wheat import tariffs would result in a 24 percent reduction in the producer price of grains and a 27 percent reduction in the consumer price of grain products. Not surprisingly, urban households would gain from the elimination of protection on grains because they are net consumers of grains. Furthermore, the urban poor would gain more proportionately than the urban rich because food in general and grains in particular account for a larger share of their budgets. Overall, the urban poverty rate would decline from 12.2 to 11.8 percent. In rural areas, the impact would be more complex. Most of the rural poor (60 percent) are net buyers of grain products, so they would benefit from the lower import tariffs. However, the losses of the net sellers is greater, on a per household basis, than the gains of the net consumers. Thus, full liberalization of wheat would increase rural poverty from 28.3 to 34.2 percent. Overall, the incidence of poverty in Morocco would rise from 19.6 to 22.1 percent. The average loss for the poorest quintile would be about 10 percent of household income.

The authors note two limitations in the analysis. First, the CGE model upon which it was based assumes that wage rates are fixed. As farmers switch out of wheat and other grains and into other crops, it is likely that the demand for unskilled labor would increase because grains tend to be less labor intensive than alternative crops. Thus, this study did not take into account the effect of trade liberalization in raising rural wages, which would benefit the rural poor, offsetting the losses associated with price changes and possibly reversing the overall welfare impact. Second, the CGE did not capture the dynamic gains from trade liberalization, defined as the gains associated with a higher rate of economic growth due to a higher rate of technology adoption and/or investment.

Methods

In our analysis of the impact of trade liberalization on Morocco we used the MIRAGE CGE model of the global economy. The MIRAGE model is a multisector, multiregion CGE model developed for trade policy analysis by the Centre d'Etudes Prospectives et d'Informations Internationales (CEPII) in Paris and is being used at CEPII and the International Food Policy Research Institute.

The MIRAGE model uses the GTAP (Global Trade Analysis Project) 6.2 database for national accounts and international trade data and the MAcMap-HS6 database for bilateral data on applied rates of protection. The applied rates of protection combine AVEs of tariffs (ad valorem and specific), tariff quotas, prohibitions, and antidumping duties. They are computed at the bilateral level, accounting for the preferential trade agreements that have been implemented through 2004. The bilateral measures of protection are aggregated across regions and products using a weighting methodology based on reference groups of countries instead of import weights.[5] The GTAP database

[5] This methodology reduces the endogeneity bias in measuring protection when aggregating across products and regions (Bouët et al. 2004).

contains 57 sectors and 96 countries and regions. Because the GTAP database includes only two Maghreb countries, Morocco and Tunisia, it was augmented with social accounting matrixes for Algeria, Libya, and Mauritania.[6]

Two versions of MIRAGE were used in this analysis:

- The static version assumed perfect competition in all sectors, and the trade policy changes were assumed to occur instantaneously in one period. The results reflect changes generated from various trade integration scenarios relative to a benchmark representing the state of the world before the tariff changes. It was a long-run simulation in that it assumed all sectors had fully adjusted to the new trade policy and a new equilibrium had been reached. The loss in tariff revenue from import liberalization was offset by increases in lump-sum taxes.
- The dynamic version of the model has a sequential recursive set-up (with the results in each year feeding into the simulation for the next year), and capital supply was modified each year due to depreciation and investment. In this way, the dynamic version could capture the effects of trade liberalization on investment and economic growth. In addition, some of the sectors were modeled under imperfect competition: textiles, wearing apparel, petroleum and coal products, and all services with the exception of trade and transport. The dynamic MIRAGE model generated a baseline extending from 2001 to 2020 based on World Bank projections of GDP and population levels through 2020. In this application of the model, the timeline for the implementation of changes in tariffs spanned 2006–2016, and the simulation results reflected deviations from the baseline at the end of the period, 2020.[7]

Although MIRAGE did not simulate the effect of policy simulations on different types of households (there was only one representative agent whose propensity to save was constant), it traced these effects across labor categories. The model assumed full employment of factors and wage flexibility. Skilled labor was the only factor that was perfectly mobile, while unskilled labor was imperfectly mobile between agricultural and nonagricultural sectors according to the ratio of remunerations between the two sectors.

The static version of the model was used to simulate the impact on Morocco of various options of trade integration: (1) liberalization within the AMU; (2) in addition to (1), bilateral liberalization between each Maghreb country and the E.U.; (3) In addition to (1), bilateral liberalization between

---

[6] The input-output data for the three missing Maghreb countries were constructed from input-output data for GTAP countries with a similar economic structure (Thomas et al. 2008).
[7] See Decreux and Valin (2007) for a more detailed description of the MIRAGE model.

each Maghreb country and the United States; (4) multilateral liberalization among the Maghreb countries, the E.U., and the United States; and (5) global trade liberalization. The dynamic model was used to consider the impact of multilateral liberalization among the Maghreb countries, the E.U., and the United States (Simulation 4), with and without three additional measures: liberalization of services, trade facilitation, and increased domestic investment. More information on the methods used in this analysis is available from Thomas et al. (2008).

Results

The results of the trade liberalization simulation using the static version of the MIRAGE model are shown in Table 7.1. The first simulation shows the impact of an AMU, which would eliminate tariff restrictions among Algeria, Libya, Mauritania, Morocco, and Tunisia. This "south-south" trade liberalization would have only a very modest impact on Morocco, increasing exports by 0.5 percent, but would have a negligible effect on the terms of trade, national income, and returns to labor. The explanation is that the North African economies have a relatively similar structure, so there would be few gains from liberalizing trade among them.

On the other hand, bilateral FTAs between each of the Maghreb countries and the E.U. would have a significant impact on Moroccan exports, boosting them by 37.5 percent. Moroccan exports would gain from this type of trade liberalization because the E.U. currently maintains high tariffs on fruits, vegetables, oilseeds, and vegetable oils (particularly olive oil). Although exports

Table 7.1 Estimated impact of trade liberalization in Morocco using the static MIRAGE model (percent change)

Trade scenario	Total exports	Terms of trade	National income	Returns to unskilled labor in agriculture	Returns to unskilled labor in other sectors	Returns to skilled labor
Arab Maghreb Union	0.5	0.0	0.0	-0.0	0.1	0.1
EU25-Maghreb bilateral FTAs	37.5	-5.9	-0.3	-1.1	-0.2	0.0
U.S.-Maghreb bilateral FTAs	4.8	-0.6	-0.3	-6.4	-0.2	2.3
U.S.-EU25-Maghreb FTA	39.8	-6.1	-0.1	-6.6	0.1	2.5
Full trade liberalization	47.8	-8.1	0.8	-8.3	0.5	5.7

Source: Thomas et al. (2008).

Notes: EU25, European Union (25 members as of 2004); FTA, Free Trade Agreement; U.S., United States.

would increase, the terms-of-trade effect would be negative, meaning that the prices of Moroccan exports would decline and/or the prices of its imports increase. The net effect would be a small decline in national income. The impact on the returns to unskilled labor would be negative but small (see Table 7.1).

Bilateral FTAs between the Maghreb countries and the United States would have a similar but more muted effect. Moroccan exports would expand, but only by 4.8 percent, partly because U.S. agricultural tariffs are initially lower and partly because there is less trade between Morocco and the United States. Again, there would be a small decline in national income, but the distributional effects would be stronger: the returns to unskilled agricultural labor would decline by 6.4 percent, while returns to skilled labor would rise by 2.3 percent. The adverse impact on unskilled labor would presumably be due to the fact that an FTA with the United States implies that there would be wheat imports and lower wheat prices (see Table 7.1).

Regional FTAs between the Maghreb countries and the E.U. and the United States would result in an almost 40 percent increase in exports for Morocco but a 6.1 percent decline in the terms of trade. Competing countries would now have better access to U.S. and particularly E.U. markets, thus depressing the price of Moroccan exports. Overall, national income in Morocco would decline by 0.1 percent, less than in the previous scenarios. Like the U.S. FTA, the regional FTA would result in a significant decline in the returns to unskilled agricultural labor and a small increase in the returns to skilled labor.

Full trade liberalization would generate the largest benefits for Morocco. Exports would grow by 47.8 percent thanks to more open borders in countries that import Moroccan goods. Although the terms of trade would decline by 8.1 percent, national income would grow by 0.8 percent. In this case, the expansion of exports would more than offset the disadvantage of the shift in prices in generating net gains for Morocco. These gains would be unequally distributed, however: returns to unskilled agricultural labor would fall by 8.3 percent, while returns to skilled labor would rise by 5.7 percent (see Thomas et al. 2008).

Under the dynamic framework of MIRAGE, Scenario 4 from the static version was simulated to examine the effect of (1) trade liberalization in services, (2) trade facilitation, and (3) increased domestic investment (see Table 7.2).

Restrictions on trade in services are an important barrier to trade, but they are difficult to measure because they result from a complex set of laws, regulations, and local standards rather than from a simple tariff rate. However, CEPII has estimated effective rates of protection in services by using a gravity model and assuming that differences between actual trade in services and what would be expected based on proximity represent implicit

Table 7.2 Trade liberalization scenarios under the dynamic version of MIRAGE

Trade scenario	EU25 and U.S. (2009-13)	Maghreb countries (2009-18)
Base: The U.S.-EU25-Maghreb FTA	2009-13: Eliminate all tariffs on imports on goods	2009-18: Eliminate all tariffs on imports on goods
Liberalization of services	2009-13: Reduce by 50% the export tax on services	2009-18: Reduce by 50% the export tax on services
Trade facilitation	No change	Reduce trade costs by 50%
Increased domestic investment in Maghreb countries	No change	Increase the saving rate by 5%

Source: Constructed from Thomas et al. (2008).
Notes: EU25, European Union (25 members as of 2004); FTA, Free Trade Agreement; U.S., United States.

import protection. According to these estimates, Morocco has implicit rates of protection of over 80 percent in construction and around 50 percent in business services and in trade and transportation. Although the restrictions on services are imposed by importing countries, they do not generate tariff revenue. They act as export taxes on services in the exporting countries, where they reduce the number of firms. Reducing or eliminating these export taxes is expected to have pro-competitive effects on exporting firms, increasing their numbers, decreasing their profits, and decreasing the price of imported services (Thomas et al. 2008). The liberalization of trade in services was simulated by assuming that the rates of protection (export tax in exporting countries) would be cut by 50 percent. As shown in Table 7.3, the liberalization of services would further increase the expansion in exports associated with the U.S.-E.U.-Maghreb regional FTA. The terms of trade would remain somewhat negative with or without liberalization in services, but the change in national income would switch from -0.2 with the regional FTA to +0.2 with the regional FTA and liberalization in services. These gains would be associated with increased efficiency as the high rates of protection on services were brought down. However, the effect on the returns to unskilled agricultural labor would remain negative. Presumably, small-scale farmers are not major consumers of the types of services that are heavily protected in Morocco and thus would not benefit from their liberalization.

Trade facilitation refers to measures that increase the speed and efficiency of the administrative procedures associated with moving goods into and out of the country, particularly processing goods through customs. Previous studies suggest that trade facilitation costs in developing countries are 5 percent of the value of trade in industrial goods and 7.5 percent of the value of trade in agro-food products (see Thomas et al. 2008). The simulation assumed that measures to improve trade facilitation could cut these costs by

Table 7.3 Estimated impact of trade liberalization in Morocco using the dynamic MIRAGE model (percent change)

Trade scenario	Total exports	Terms of trade	National income	Returns to unskilled labor in agriculture	Returns to unskilled labor in other sectors	Returns to skilled labor
U.S.-EU25-Maghreb FTA	37.8	-2.5	-0.2	-7.5	-0.2	3.4
+ liberalization of services	42.6	-2.6	0.2	-7.7	0.3	4.9
+ trade facilitation	47.9	-2.1	1.2	-7.2	1.4	6.8
+ increased investment	50.5	-2.2	1.6	-5.3	3.9	10.8

Source: Thomas et al. (2008).
Notes: EU25, European Union (25 members as of 2004); FTA, Free Trade Agreement; U.S., United States.

50 percent. As shown in Table 7.3, adding trade facilitation to the regional FTA would further boost exports and contribute to a higher national income compared to the regional FTA without trade facilitation. Trade facilitation would also have a modest effect in partially offsetting the negative effect of the regional FTA on the returns to unskilled agricultural labor, reducing it from -7.5 percent to -7.2 percent.

Finally, FTAs are expected to improve the environment for private-sector productive investment by increasing the size of the market, facilitating the inflow of new technology, and reassuring investors regarding the stability of the policy environment. This was simulated by assuming a 5 percent increase in the propensity to save in the Maghreb countries. The higher savings would result in greater domestic investment, which in turn would increase the productive capacity of the economy in future years. As shown in Table 7.1, adding increased investment to the effect of the regional FTA would have modest effects on exports and the terms of trade but would increase national income from -0.2 to +1.6 percent. In addition, it would have the strongest effect of the three complementary measures in offsetting the negative impact of the FTA on returns to unskilled agricultural labor.

Summary

The Kingdom of Morocco is a lower-middle-income country with a population of about 30 million, more than half of which lives in urban areas. The agricultural sector accounts for about 16 percent of GDP. Like most other countries in the region, Morocco is a net agricultural importer whose main agricultural import is wheat. The agricultural exports of Morocco are the second-largest among MENA countries. Fruits and vegetables, which typically account for 20–30 percent of agricultural exports in MENA countries, represent almost three-quarters of the agricultural exports of Morocco.

Since the mid-1980s, Morocco has carried out a series of economic reforms to allow the market to play a larger role in production and consumption decisions, including price liberalization, a reduced role for state enterprises, and the promotion of private investment. Morocco has signed an EMP agreement with the E.U. whereby tariffs on manufactured goods will be reduced over time. Morocco has also signed an FTA with the United States that entails gradual reduction in both industrial and agricultural protection. Nonetheless, the level of agricultural protection remains relatively high.

A study by Ravallion and Lokshin (2004) suggests that although many rural households are net buyers of grains, lower grain prices tend to adversely affect rural poverty. These results, however, do not take into account the effect of global trade liberalization, which would be expected to increase the world price of wheat and other grains.

Our analysis used two versions of the MIRAGE CGE model, a static version and a dynamic version. The static version of the model was used to simulate the impact of alternative types of trade liberalization. It appears that an FTA with the other Maghreb countries in the context of the AMU would have little impact on the Moroccan economy because of the similarities in the economies in the region. A bilateral FTA with the E.U. would stimulate exports significantly but would have a small negative effect on national income and returns to unskilled agricultural labor. Global trade liberalization would combine a strong positive effect on exports and a small positive effect on national income but would have a large negative effect on unskilled agricultural labor.

Simulations with the dynamic version of the MIRAGE model show that liberalization in services, trade facilitation, and increased investment would have a positive effect on exports and income, but they would not fully offset the negative effect of trade liberalization on the returns to unskilled agricultural labor.

CHAPTER 8

Summary and Policy Implications

Summary

Although trade liberalization has reduced barriers to trade in numerous sectors, the agricultural sector remains highly protected in many countries. Most countries use a variety of measures, including tariffs, tariff rate quotas, and nontechnical barriers, to protect their farmers from import competition. Some countries (particularly high-income countries) provide direct support to farmers in the form of subsidized inputs and price supports. As a result, agriculture is one of the most distorted sectors in the world economy. Economic theory and most empirical studies suggest that the benefits of trade liberalization exceed the costs, at least on balance. However, policymakers are reluctant to reduce trade protection for their own industries and farmers unless they are assured that other countries will reciprocate.

These issues are of interest to most developing countries because of the dependence of the rural poor on agricultural income and because of the importance of food prices to the well-being of the urban poor. This concern is even greater in the MENA region because most of the countries in this region are dependent on food imports to meet consumption requirements. Furthermore, the high level of protection for farmers in the MENA region implies that full trade liberalization would have a larger impact in this region than elsewhere.

The objectives of this report are

- to examine current agricultural trade policies in the MENA region;
- to evaluate the degree of agricultural liberalization likely to occur as part of various trade agreements;
- to analyze the impact of further trade liberalization on the poor, particularly the rural poor; and
- to explore policy options for mitigating the negative effects of agricultural trade liberalization on the poor, particularly the rural poor.

As defined by the World Bank, the MENA region comprises 21 countries. In this study we focus on the eight countries that are neither major oil exporters nor high-income countries: Djibouti, Egypt, Jordan, Lebanon, Morocco, Syria, Tunisia, and the West Bank and Gaza.

Basic Characteristics

In addition to their cultural, religious, and linguistic similarities, the MENA countries under consideration have other climatic and demographic similarities, as follows:

- Most of the MENA countries are semiarid and have limited water and arable land per capita, making agricultural production highly dependent on rainfall. The exceptions are Egypt and Djibouti, where virtually all crop production is irrigated.
- The overall population density of the region is low compared to other developing areas, though the West Bank and Gaza and the Nile River Basin in Egypt are quite densely populated.
- The region is also more urbanized than the average for developing countries. The share of urban population ranges from 43 to 87 percent.

In terms of the economies of the countries in the region, we can identify the following patterns:

- Seven of the eight countries under consideration are classified as lower-middle-income countries according to the World Bank. The exception is Lebanon, which is an upper-middle-income country.
- The economic performance of many of the MENA countries has been relatively weak; real per capita GDP growth was 2.0 percent per year during the 1990s. Per capita growth was negative over the decade in Djibouti. Performance was only slightly better (2.2 percent) during 2000-06, but this was a period in which the global economy was emerging from a recession.
- The region has been adversely affected by various conflicts, including the Arab-Israeli conflict, the insurgency in Algeria (until recently), and the Iraq war, which has affected the economies of Jordan and Syria.
- The slow economic growth means there has been little expansion in formal-sector employment, resulting in persistent problems of unemployment, particularly among youth.

Nonetheless, strong economic performance in Lebanon and Tunisia suggests that these problems are not insurmountable.

Agricultural and Trade Patterns

The eight MENA countries also exhibit some common features with regard to agricultural trade patterns:

- Agricultural exports represent a relatively small share of their total exports, exceeding 10 percent only in Syria.
- Wheat is a staple food and a major import for many of the MENA countries. It represents more than 15 percent of agricultural imports in Egypt, Morocco, and Tunisia.
- Most of the MENA countries are net food importers.
- Some countries in the region have relatively high levels of protection for farmers: Egypt, Morocco, and Tunisia are among the 15 most protected economies, according to Bouët (2006).
- The commodities that are the most protected in the region are wheat, sugar, dairy, and livestock products.
- The E.U. is the most important trading partner for most of the countries in the region.

The MENA countries have signed a series of multilateral, regional, and bilateral trade agreements. The URAA imposes some commitments on member countries; some of the more important commitments are

- to convert quantitative restrictions into tariffs or tariff rate quotas,
- to bind tariff rates by setting a maximum rate for each tariff line,
- to reduce bound tariff rates by an average of 36 percent and a minimum of 15 percent for each item, and
- to reduce trade-distorting measures of support for agriculture by 20 percent, on average.

Developing countries have been given more modest targets for tariff rate reductions and more time to comply, while the LDCs are effectively exempted from meeting most commitments under the URAA. The direct impact of these commitments on the MENA countries has been modest. Syria and West Bank and Gaza are not WTO members. Djibouti, as an LDC, is exempt from most URAA commitments. For the remaining five countries, the bound rates are often far above the applied tariff rates, particularly for agricultural products. Thus, commitments to reduce the bound rate have had little effect on the actual level of agricultural protection.

As part of the Euro-Mediterranean Partnership, the E.U. has EMAAs with four of the MENA countries under consideration (Egypt, Jordan, Morocco, and Tunisia) and interim agreements with two others (Lebanon and the West Bank and Gaza). These EMAAs commit the parties to phasing out almost all tariffs on manufactured goods, though the MENA countries have a longer period in which to comply. Although there are plans to incorporate agriculture at a later date, there are no firm targets or schedules for agricultural liberalization.

In 2001 the E.U. launched the Everything But Arms Initiative, under which the LDCs have duty-free access to E.U. markets for almost all goods. Among the eight countries under consideration, only Djibouti can take advantage of the initiative's provisions. Bananas, rice, and sugar were temporarily exempted.

Under the U.S.-Middle East Free Trade Initiative, the United States has signed bilateral FTAs with Jordan and Morocco and intermediate agreements with other MENA countries. The effect of the U.S.-Jordan FTA will be small because Jordan's level of protection is already low and because the volume of U.S.-Jordan trade is small. The effect of the U.S.-Morocco FTA will be larger because Moroccan trade barriers are higher. Of particular importance, Morocco's wheat tariffs will be phased out over 10 years.

The U.S. African Growth and Opportunity Act allows duty-free access to U.S. markets for Sub-Saharan African countries that meet certain criteria in human rights, reducing corruption, and fighting terrorism. Djibouti qualifies, but its exports to the United States are negligible. The other Sub-Saharan African countries in the MENA region (Somalia, the Sudan, and Yemen) do not qualify.

A number of bilateral and regional agreements within the MENA region have been signed, including that establishing GAFTA and the Agadir Agreement. Nonetheless, a number of MENA countries, most notably Egypt and Tunisia, have reduced tariff barriers unilaterally in recent years. In other words, trade liberalization does occur outside the context of global, regional, and bilateral trade agreements.

The Impact of Trade Liberalization

The evidence suggests that global trade liberalization will increase world agricultural prices by reducing agricultural support policies in OECD countries and by reducing protection. Wheat production is subsidized by the E.U. and the United States, and numerous countries (including those in the MENA region) impose high tariffs. Studies indicate that trade liberalization would increase world wheat prices by 5–12 percent. Rice is also subsidized by the E.U. and the United States, while Japan, the Republic of Korea, and other countries severely limit imports. Global models suggest that trade liberalization would raise the world price by 3–35 percent. Sugar producers are subsidized and protected from imports in many countries, making sugar one of the most distorted agricultural markets. Partial equilibrium models of trade liberalization suggest that sugar prices would rise by as much as 48 percent, while general equilibrium models show increases of less than 5 percent. Likewise, removing distortions in world cotton markets would increase the world price by 2–13 percent. Dairy production in the E.U., Japan, the United States, and many developing countries is protected through a complex system of support prices, import barriers, and market controls. One study has estimated that global trade liberalization would increase the price of nonfat dry milk by 13 percent.

Almost all the MENA countries are net agricultural importers, so there is clearly some basis for concern that these countries will lose as a result of global trade liberalization. Our analysis confirms that the terms-of-trade effect of a 15 percent increase in all world agricultural prices on the eight MENA countries would be approximately US$922 million, or 0.4 percent of regional GDP. The actual impact of trade liberalization, however, is likely to be more positive for three reasons:

- First, the previous analysis overstates the cost of higher world agricultural prices because it assumes no response on the part of producers and consumers in the region. A net importer that is almost self-sufficient could actually benefit if the higher prices induced it to become an exporter of one or more commodities (Anderson 2003).
- Second, it assumes that the price increase would be the same for all commodities. A net importer could gain if the increases in agricultural prices were not proportional across commodities. For example, Egypt could gain from global liberalization if the price of cotton (which it exports) were to increase more than the price of wheat (which it imports).
- Finally, the analysis estimates the terms-of-trade effect of trade liberalization, but it does not include the efficiency gains associated with reducing distortions in domestic agricultural markets. Most studies of trade liberalization suggest that the efficiency effects would be larger than the terms-of-trade effect.

Several dozen studies have been undertaken to examine the macroeconomic impact of various types of trade liberalization in the MENA region. Most of these studies use CGE models to simulate the effect of alternative trade policies. The results of these studies may be summarized as follows:

- Multilateral trade liberalization generally results in net gains to countries in the region, with real GDP expansion of 1–3 percent.
- The benefits of trade liberalization to a country depend largely on the degree of domestic liberalization carried out by the country. Most of the gains from agricultural trade liberalization are associated with domestic reform rather than with changes in trade policy in other countries. This confirms this well-known concept in studies of trade liberalization: what you do determines what you get.
- The benefits of multilateral trade liberalization are generally greater than the benefits of bilateral trade liberalization with the E.U. or the United States.

- The benefits of multilateral trade liberalization are generally greater than the benefits of regional trade agreements within MENA.
- Trade liberalization usually results in lower production and more imports of wheat but in higher production and more exports of fruits and vegetables.

In contrast, only a few studies have examined the distributional impact of trade liberalization, such as the effect on farmers or other poor groups in the MENA countries. One of the most thorough studies suggests that the lower agricultural prices associated with removing agricultural protection in Morocco could exacerbate poverty (Ravallion and Lokshin 2004). In the following sections we summarize the results of our analysis of the distributional impact of trade liberalization in Egypt, Tunisia, Syria, and Morocco.

Agriculture, Trade, and Poverty in Egypt

Until 1987, agricultural policy in Egypt was characterized by various forms of state intervention in production, marketing, and trade. The policy of import substitution industrialization meant that the agricultural sector was heavily taxed through low official prices and compulsory sales. At the same time, some commodities were protected by import restrictions. During the late 1980s and the 1990s, Egypt gradually liberalized its agricultural markets and reduced the level of import protection. Wheat markets remained distorted by a combination of import controls, fixed producer prices, consumer subsidies on certain types of bread, and government control over the channels leading to the subsidized bread. In 2004 a series of significant tariff reductions was implemented, leading the World Bank to declare that Egypt had made more progress in trade liberalization than almost any other country. Even so, the degree of protection is higher in Egypt than in 40 percent of the countries of the world.

Full global trade liberalization would increase the prices of agricultural commodities by 5–15 percent. This would probably negatively affect the economy because Egypt is a net agricultural importer, though the exact effect would depend on the price changes for each commodity. Given proportional increases for all agricultural commodities, Egypt would gain from higher rice and cotton prices but lose from higher wheat and maize prices. Domestic trade reform would reduce the domestic prices of imported commodities such as wheat, thus partly offsetting the effect of global trade liberalization, as well as providing efficiency gains.

We analyze the data from the 1998 Egypt Integrated Household Survey to examine the distributional effect of changes in agricultural prices. Changes in income for each household in the sample are estimated using hypothetical increases in agricultural prices and the composition of the income and expenditures of the household. In the short to medium run, net sellers would gain and net buyers lose from higher prices.

According to this analysis, higher wheat prices would reduce poverty among wheat producers because two-thirds of these producers are net sellers of wheat. For example, a 40 percent increase in wheat prices would result in a 3 percentage point decline in the poverty rate among wheat farmers. However, even a 40 percent increase in wheat prices would reduce the overall poverty rate by just 1 percentage point. This is because significant gains by the small number of wheat farmers would be largely offset by the small losses by the rest of the population.

A 40 percent increase in the price of rice or horticultural products would reduce poverty among growers but erode the purchasing power of urban households. The net effect would be to increase the national poverty rate by about 1 percentage point. This is because, compared to the case of wheat, the proportion of rural households that grow these crops is smaller and the share of households that are net buyers is larger.

For cotton and sugar, a 40 percent increase in price would reduce poverty among growers but have a negligible effect (less than 0.5 percent) on national poverty. This is because these two crops are not widely grown and because consumption of the final product associated with these crops is not a significant part of the spending patterns of urban households.

Overall, the results show that price increases have positive effects on growers of the relevant crops, but the overall effect of price increases on national poverty is generally small or negligible because only a small share of the population grows each crop. Even a 40 percent increase in all five crop categories has a small effect, raising rural and urban poverty rates by 1-2 percentage points. One implication of this analysis is that agricultural trade policy is a relatively ineffective policy instrument for assisting poor rural households.

Agriculture, Trade, and Poverty in Tunisia

Like Egypt, Tunisia adopted a structural adjustment program in the 1980s that reduced the intervention of the state in markets, including agricultural markets. Unlike Egypt, Tunisia maintains high tariffs on many products, including agricultural commodities. At the same time, Tunisia has a relatively good investment climate, which contributed to significant inflows of foreign direct investment and a healthy growth rate through the 1990s.

Tunisia's main exports are olives and dates, while its principal imports are wheat and maize. Like many MENA countries, Tunisia is a net agricultural importer. Multilateral liberalization is expected to raise agricultural prices. If all agricultural commodity prices were to rise proportionately, Tunisia would lose in terms of trade because it is a net importer. On the other hand, it would gain from domestic liberalization due to efficiency gains. The combined effect is likely to be positive for Tunisia as a whole because most estimates show that efficiency gains are larger than terms-of-trade effects. The net effect on agricultural prices and, hence, on farmers is ambiguous because domestic trade liberalization would reduce domestic agricultural prices relative to world prices, while multilateral trade liberalization would increase world prices. The effect of trade liberalization on labor markets and the returns to unskilled labor in particular would also influence the poverty impact.

In order to study the distributional impact of trade liberalization in Tunisia, we used a CGE model linked to data on 397 representative households from a household expenditure survey. The CGE simulated the effect of various policies on prices, wages, and returns to other factors, while the household survey data were used to simulate the effects of these changes on poverty and income distribution. Four simulations were examined: the removal of tariffs on industrial imports from the E.U., the removal of all tariffs on imports from the E.U., the removal of all tariffs on imports from any country, and the removal of all Tunisian tariffs combined with global trade liberalization, which it is assumed would raise agricultural prices by 15 percent.

According to these simulations, the removal of industrial tariffs on imports from the E.U. (which approximates Tunisian import liberalization under the EMP agreement) would cause both imports and exports to expand significantly, although almost all the change would be in nonagricultural trade. Real GDP would increase slightly (0.2 percent) because of the efficiency gains associated with the removal of distortions. Poverty would decline from 8.1 to 7.7 percent. Significant gains in rural poverty reduction would more than offset the small increase in urban poverty.

Eliminating *all* tariffs on imports from the E.U. (approximating the Tunisian side of an extended EMP agreement) would cause large increases in imports of meat, beverages and tobacco, fruit, dairy products, and vegetable oil as import barriers on these goods were lifted. The effect on GDP and poverty would be similar to that in the first simulation.

Removing tariffs on imports from *all* countries would increase the imports of almost all agricultural commodities, as well as stimulate agricultural exports to maintain the trade balance. The reduction in poverty would be slightly greater than in the first two simulations: poverty would decline from 8.1 percent in the base scenario to 7.6 percent. The rural poor would again be the main beneficiaries of these changes in trade policy.

Finally, the elimination of all Tunisian tariffs plus global trade liberalization (represented by a 15 percent increase in world agricultural prices) would not do much for the overall economy. This is partly because, as a net agricultural importer, Tunisia would lose out from higher world agricultural prices, but the agricultural sector would gain from the higher prices. Exports of fruit (mainly olives) would expand significantly, as would exports of a number of other agricultural commodities. As a result, poverty would decline to the lowest level among the four scenarios. Compared to the base scenario, rural poverty would be cut in half (from 15.8 to 7.9 percent) according to this simulation.

Thus, it seems that trade liberalization would have only minor effects on the level of GDP but would have a substantial effect in reducing poverty. Furthermore, the combined effect of global and domestic liberalization would be more pro-poor than the effect of domestic liberalization alone.

Agriculture, Trade, and Poverty in Syria

The agricultural sector in Syria is one of the most highly regulated in the MENA region. The government uses a variety of policy instruments to control production and marketing, including administered prices, state marketing boards, state monopolies in the marketing of strategic crops, state monopolies in the distribution of fertilizers, subsidies, and high tariff and nontariff barriers on food and agricultural products. Reforms in recent years have only begun to dismantle some of these restrictions.

Although Syria has been successful in achieving wheat self-sufficiency and promoting cotton exports, these accomplishments have come at a high cost in terms of inefficiency and an unsustainable fiscal burden. The likely depletion of oil reserves over the coming 10–15 years is forcing the government to reduce costs and find new sources of revenue.

The domestic liberalization of the agricultural sector would result in substitution away from wheat, sugar beets, and cotton and toward barley, lentils, and chickpeas. The completion of the EMP agreement with the E.U. would expand exports of fruits, vegetables, and olive oil if Syrian producers could meet the high quality and food safety requirements.

About two-thirds of agricultural subsidies are devoted to maintaining a high producer price for wheat and low consumer prices for bread and other wheat products. By banning the private importation of wheat and by limiting imports through the state marketing board, government policy keeps the domestic price of wheat 66 percent higher than the import parity price. Wheat is the most important staple food, as well as an important source of income for farmers, so the government is particularly sensitive to the impact of reducing or removing import protection and the subsidies for wheat.

In this report we use a CGE model to simulate the effect of trade policy options on households in 10 income categories. In particular, we focus on the effects of liberalizing wheat markets. The macroeconomic effects would be relatively modest, although government savings would increase by almost

3 percent of GDP. Complete liberalization would reduce the producer price of wheat by about 17 percent and production by about 2 percent. The effects of subsidy removal on the welfare of Syrian households would be regressive: high-income households would gain, while lower-income households would lose. The size of the effects would be quite small, however: less than 1 percent of the base income of all but the richest income group.

These results need to be interpreted with three factors in mind. First, the impact on farmers (particularly wheat farmers) will be larger than the impact on the poorer deciles. This is because each decile includes both farmers and nonfarmers, thus diluting the adverse impact of the reforms on wheat farmers. Second, the distributional impact will vary among farmers; it will be the most adverse among farmers for whom wheat sales are a large share of household income. The impact of lower wheat prices will be positive on urban households (particularly the poor) and rural households that are net buyers of wheat. More information on the share of income from wheat and other crops would be needed to explore the distributional impact among farmers. Third, the impact of liberalization on the poor will depend partly on complementary policies. For example, a recent study suggests that if the wheat market reform were implemented through a reduction in energy subsidies, the combined effect would be more pro-poor than wheat subsidy removal alone.

Agriculture, Trade, and Poverty in Morocco

The Kingdom of Morocco is a lower-middle-income country with a population of about 30 million, more than half of which lives in urban areas. The agricultural sector accounts for about 16 percent of GDP. Like most other countries in the region, Morocco is a net agricultural importer, and its main agricultural import is wheat. After Turkey's, Morocco's agricultural exports are the largest among the exports of MENA countries. Fruits and vegetables, which typically account for 20–30 percent of the agricultural exports of MENA countries, represent almost three-quarters of the agricultural exports of Morocco.

Since the mid-1980s, Morocco has carried out a series of economic reforms to allow the market to play a larger role in production and consumption decisions, including price liberalization, a reduced role for state enterprises, and the promotion of private investment. Morocco has signed an EMP agreement with the E.U. whereby tariffs on manufactured goods will be reduced over time. Morocco also signed an FTA with the United States that entails gradual reduction in both industrial and agricultural protection. Nonetheless, the level of agricultural protection remains relatively high.

Our analysis uses two versions of a global CGE model called MIRAGE, a static version and a dynamic version. The static version of the model is used to simulate the impact of alternative types of trade liberalization. It appears that an FTA with the other Maghreb countries in the context of the AMU would have little impact on the Moroccan economy because of the similarities in the economies in the region. A bilateral FTA with the E.U. would stimulate export significantly but have a small negative effect on national income and returns to unskilled agricultural labor. Global trade liberalization would combine a strong positive effect on exports and a small positive effect on national income but a large negative effect on the returns to unskilled agricultural labor.

Simulations with the dynamic version of the MIRAGE model show that liberalization in services, trade facilitation, and increased investment would have a positive effect on exports and income but would not fully offset the negative effect of trade liberalization on the returns to unskilled agricultural labor.

Policy Implications

In this section we examine the implications of these findings on policies and programs in the MENA countries. How can policymakers in these countries maximize the benefits of trade liberalization and minimize the costs, particularly with regard to the poor, particularly the rural poor? We divide the discussion into four topics: global trade liberalization, regional and bilateral trade liberalization, domestic liberalization, and complementary policies.

Policy on Global Trade Liberalization

As discussed earlier, global trade liberalization will likely increase world agricultural prices by 3–20 percent, imposing a terms-of-trade loss on all eight of the countries under consideration (though the loss would be small in Syria and Tunisia). The net food-importing countries have used the likely terms-of-trade loss associated with global trade liberalization to request special concessions in the form of reduced commitments to open their own borders. This position reflects the mercantilist perspective of trade negotiation, according to which import liberalization is a sacrifice that must be incurred to open up markets in other countries.

However, it is difficult to understand this position in terms of economic welfare. The mercantilist perspective is incomplete in that it takes into account only the gains and losses of producers, ignoring the effects of trade policy on consumers. As discussed earlier, economic studies on trade liberalization suggest that most of the benefits to a country deriving from trade liberalization would result from reforms within the country. Empirical studies of protection consistently demonstrate that the cost (in terms of higher prices to consumers) of saving each job in a protected sector is several times larger than the income earned through the job. Thus, the net food-importing countries appear to be demanding the right to forgo the efficiency gains associated with domestic trade liberalization as compensation for the terms-of-trade losses associated with reforms in other countries.

However, this analysis takes into account only the impact of trade liberalization on aggregate income or GDP. Policymakers in the MENA countries are also interested in equity considerations, such as the impact on poverty and unemployment. The effect of agricultural trade liberalization on poverty would vary widely across countries, in part because the effect of liberalization on agricultural prices is ambiguous. Global agricultural trade reform is likely to increase world agricultural prices, but domestic trade liberalization will reduce domestic agricultural prices relative to world prices. The net effect of liberalization on domestic agricultural prices will depend largely on the initial level of protection. If the level of domestic protection is high (as in Morocco, Syria, and Tunisia), full trade liberalization is likely to reduce domestic agricultural prices. If, on the other hand, domestic protection is modest (as in Egypt, Jordan, and Lebanon), full trade liberalization may have no effect or only slightly increase domestic agricultural prices.

Furthermore, the estimated impact of changes in agricultural prices on poverty is ambiguous. Higher agricultural prices would benefit farmers who can produce a marketed surplus but would hurt the urban poor and rural net buyers. The net effect would depend on the income sources and spending patterns of the poor. If the sales of tradable agricultural commodities are an important source of income and tradable food items are a small share of their expenditure, higher agricultural prices will reduce poverty. Alternatively, if the sale of tradable commodities is not important and tradable food accounts for a large share of their spending, higher agricultural prices will increase poverty.

Based on the analysis presented in this report, higher cereal prices would tend to reduce overall poverty, but the effect would range from small to negligible. In Egypt, higher wheat prices would reduce poverty (though this would not be true for other commodities). In Tunisia, global trade liberalization, which implies higher agricultural prices, would result in the greatest poverty reduction among the four simulations. In Syria, reducing subsidies on wheat production, which lowers producer prices, would have an adverse (though very small) effect on the poorest decile. And in Morocco, import trade liberalization, which lowers domestic agricultural prices, would tend to reduce the returns to unskilled agricultural labor.

Thus, the link between trade liberalization and agricultural price changes is ambiguous, and the effect of agricultural price changes on poverty is weak. This suggests that trade policy is a poor instrument for addressing overall poverty in the MENA region. Nonetheless, the impact of trade liberalization on certain agricultural producers may be substantial. Below we discuss targeted programs that may assist vulnerable households more effectively and more economically.

Thus far, we have assumed that adjustment to a new trade regime is costless. In fact, there are transition costs associated with any policy change that affects relative prices. As resources are reallocated within the economy, there will be a period during which factors of production will be underutilized. For example, as labor moves from formerly protected sectors to newly profitable ones, costs will be associated with unemployment and retraining. These transition costs are real and constitute an argument for phasing in the trade reform and for providing training and credit to assist those sectors that are adversely affected. Because the transition costs will be temporary, while the efficiency gains will be permanent, it is unlikely that transition costs represent a valid argument against implementing the trade reforms. The fact that the costs occur in the short term while the benefits accrue over time does, however, help explain the political resistance to trade liberalization.

Of course, the MENA countries should push aggressively for market access for the agricultural commodities that they export. Egypt, Jordan, and Morocco have a strong interest in opening up the E.U. market for fruits and vegetables. This would include taking steps to ensure that sanitary and phytosanitary regulations regarding fruit and vegetable imports into the E.U. are based on scientific evidence and are not a reflection of protectionist sentiment. Likewise, Tunisia would benefit from a reduction in E.U. tariffs on olive and olive oil imports, while Egypt would gain from reduced domestic support by the United States and (to a lesser extent) the E.U. for their cotton growers.

In contrast, none of the MENA countries would gain from global trade liberalization (including reductions in domestic support) in the wheat market. Such reforms would increase the world price of wheat by 4–20 percent, thus adversely affecting the terms of trade of importers in the region. The effects of these higher prices on consumers could be offset in many countries by reducing import tariffs to retain the original domestic price.

Policy on Regional Trade Liberalization

The benefits of regional integration within the MENA region have been limited to date. There are three explanations for this, two of which may be corrected and one of which cannot. One reason for the limited benefits of regional trade agreements such as GAFTA is that these agreements tend to be fairly flexible, allowing numerous exceptions for sensitive goods, permitting protection to vary by season, and granting countries the right to suspend tariff reductions under certain circumstances. Because the costs of protection rise more than proportionately with the level of protection, allowing a relatively small number of exceptions can largely negate the gains from trade liberalization. To generate significant gains for member countries, GAFTA and other regional agreements will have to insist on a greater level of discipline on tariffs and NTBs. One approach might be to gradually reduce the maximum level of tariff protection, thus constraining the highest tariffs first.

The second reason for the modest benefits associated with these trade agreements is that regional trade is hampered by a variety of factors in addition to trade policy. The infrastructure linking the MENA countries is generally poor. Transportation services in the region are characterized by a lack of competition and high costs, and many of the countries suffer from cumbersome customs procedures that raise the cost of trade. One study estimates that the delays and uncertainties associated with customs clearance alone are equivalent to 10 percent of the cost of the goods being traded (Dennis 2006a). Unfortunately, multiple and overlapping regional trade agreements may actually contribute to these costs because tariff rates differ depending on the country of origin. These different rates give traders an incentive to misrepresent the origin of imports, thus forcing customs officials to require additional documentation and further slowing the process. Thus, measures to streamline customs procedures and introduce greater competition in regional transportation services would enhance the benefits of regional trade agreements.

The third reason for the modest gains associated with regional trade agreements is the similarity in the economic structures of member countries. If all member countries import wheat and maize, export fruits and vegetables, and have similar wage rates, the gains from trade are likely to be limited. There will still be some gains from trade even if two countries have identical factor endowments (labor, land, capital, and other factors of production) because each country can specialize in different products so that both countries will gain from economies of scale. However, the basic point is that the gains will be less than they would be for trade between countries with different wage rates, different agroclimatic conditions, and different types of skills. Trade models tend to confirm that there would be benefits from economic integration among MENA countries, but the benefits would be substantially smaller than the benefits associated with multilateral trade liberalization or liberalization with developed countries.

Position with Regard to Bilateral Liberalization

The E.U. has signed EMAAs with four of the eight MENA countries under consideration and is preparing agreements with three more.[1] Although the E.U.

[1] The four countries with EMAAs are Egypt (2004), Jordan (2002), Morocco (2000), and Tunisia (1998). Lebanon and the West Bank and Gaza have interim association agreements, while Syria is a candidate for an AA.

is the largest trading partner for all of these countries, studies suggest that the impact of the agreements on welfare in the MENA countries is positive but rather small, typically less than 1 percent. The main reason for this is that the agricultural sector is largely excluded from the agreements. Simulation studies confirm the economic intuition that the gains from the agreements would be much larger if the agreements included liberalization in the agricultural sector. Because the broader Barcelona process envisages agricultural liberalization at some later date, the four countries with EMAAs should begin to explore the feasibility of a second round of negotiations that would include agriculture. While recognizing the political sensitivity of agricultural prices, leaders in the MENA countries should keep in mind that most of the benefits of an expanded AA will be related to the degree of domestic liberalization within their own countries. At the same time, the benefits will be larger if domestic liberalization is combined with a reduction in the trade barriers to agricultural imports in the E.U., which is the rationale for insisting on reciprocity. Liberalization in E.U. tariff and nontariff barriers on fruits, vegetables, olive oil, and sugar would be particularly beneficial to the MENA countries. If the MENA countries are not able to persuade the E.U. to explore agricultural liberalization, they would be advised to pursue the same objectives in the context of WTO multilateral trade negotiations.

The United States has signed FTAs with Jordan and Morocco and has interim trade and investment framework agreements with Egypt and Tunisia. The United States is a relatively minor trading partner with all of these countries, so the MENA countries should not expect large effects, positive or negative, as a result of increased trade with the United States. On the other hand, these agreements may facilitate foreign direct investment in the MENA countries in two ways. First, the agreements typically include measures to create a more favorable climate for private investment, including the streamlining of bureaucratic procedures and greater transparency in regulations. Second, the agreements constitute a signal that the government is committed to greater integration in the global economy, which is in itself an encouraging sign for prospective investors.

Position with Regard to Unilateral Liberalization

Economic analysis suggests that, in general, unilaterally reducing import protection and domestic support for agriculture will increase aggregate output. Under fairly plausible assumptions, it is easy to demonstrate that the static benefits of lower domestic prices to consumers are greater than the static losses to producers. Yet policymakers, trade negotiators, and many noneconomists see reducing domestic protection as the price a country must pay to gain access to markets in other countries. Is economic analysis flawed, perhaps based on simplifying assumptions that do not hold in the real world? Or is the conventional wisdom incorrect, biased by political pressures that give greater weight to the interests of producers over consumers?

A common argument for protectionism in general is the infant industry argument, whereby industries learn to be competitive while growing under the protection of trade barriers. Although there is a large body of literature on this topic, it is not relevant in this context because the infant industry argument is rarely invoked to defend agricultural protection.

In the case of agricultural protectionism, a more common argument is that, in developing countries in general and in the MENA region in particular, poor farmers cannot compete with large-scale technologically advanced farmers in developed countries, particularly if the latter receive production subsidies. Certainly commercial farmers in developing countries are hurt by the subsidies given to farmers in the E.U., the United States, and other countries, as well as the high barriers to agricultural imports in many countries. But in spite of these subsidies, Egypt is a competitive exporter of cotton and rice, Morocco exports tomatoes to Europe, and Tunisia is a major exporter of olive oil. This suggests that the MENA countries can compete in markets where they have comparative advantages. Small farmers in the MENA region can compete in some commodities because their costs for labor and land are lower and because they enjoy a climate that is more suitable for the production of some agricultural commodities, particularly during the European winter. However, they face challenges in meeting the quality and food safety standards for export.

Another argument revolves around the concept that import barriers on agricultural products reduce poverty among poor agricultural producers. However, the analysis presented in this report suggests that higher agricultural prices have small and mixed effects on the poor; for example:

- in Egypt, simulations reveal that higher wheat prices reduce poverty while higher rice and horticultural prices lower poverty, but the effects are quite small;
- in Syria, the removal of wheat subsidies (lowering the producer price but raising the consumer price) adversely affects poor households, but again the effect is very small;
- in Tunisia, global trade liberalization, which implies higher agricultural prices, tends to reduce poverty, particularly in rural areas; and
- in Morocco, removing agricultural protection lowers prices and reduces the returns to unskilled agricultural labor.

There are several reasons for these small and mixed effects, as follows:

- Higher agricultural prices benefit some poor households (farmers with net sales), but they hurt other poor households (the urban poor and net buyers in rural areas).

- The percentage of households that are net sellers of agricultural goods is relatively small because in most MENA countries, less than half the population is in farming and a significant share of farmers are net buyers.
- Farmers who are net sellers tend to be richer than the average farmer, so higher farm incomes do not always translate into lower poverty.
- Even those farmers who are both poor and net sellers rely on nonagricultural activities for a significant share of their incomes.

In other words, agricultural protection is a costly and imprecise tool with which to address the problem of rural poverty. In the sections that follow we discuss alternative policies that address rural poverty more directly.

Another argument for agricultural protection is that it serves as a useful bargaining chip in international negotiations, giving developing countries something to offer in exchange for greater access to markets in high-income countries. Although there is some merit in this argument, it is not clear that developing countries see agricultural protection merely as a means to extract reciprocal liberalization among trade partners. The fact that the LDCs have been able to avoid almost all of the disciplines built into the URAA suggests that they view agricultural protection as an end rather than a means.

Although political considerations may limit the ability of governments to implement unilateral trade liberalization, policymakers and trade negotiators should at least be aware that in many situations the aggregate benefits exceed the costs. The example of Egypt's trade reforms of 2004 indicates that there is some scope for trade reform outside the context of reciprocal trade agreements.

Complementary Policies to Facilitate Adjustment

Several studies have indicated that the size of the gains from trade liberalization depends on the existence of complementary policies and programs. The gains are smallest (or the losses largest) when consumers and producers are limited in their ability to respond to new opportunities and new prices. Studies of trade liberalization in Morocco and Tunisia show that if factor markets are flexible, the benefits of trade liberalization are three to five times greater than when factor markets are rigid (see Dennis 2006b). Flexible factor markets allow factors of production (such as land, labor, and capital) to be reallocated from formerly protected sectors to newly profitable sectors. Examples of rigidities in MENA factor markets include:

- regulations limiting the use of temporary workers and expatriates,
- the complicated bureaucratic procedures involved in dismissing workers,
- large severance allowances,
- delays in the application for and issuance of land and construction permits,

- significant capital requirements in starting a new business, and
- difficulties in closing a business.

Although these bureaucratic problems are common in many countries, business climate surveys suggest that they are more severe in the MENA countries than in most developing countries. As described in Chapter 2, in a ranking of countries based on the ease of doing business, only three MENA countries are in the top half (Jordan, Tunisia, and Lebanon are ranked in the 45th to 49th percentiles), and several are in the bottom 15 percent (Egypt and Djibouti) (IFC 2009).

Of course these regulations apply mainly to the formal sector. In agriculture, flexibility is more likely to be enhanced by effective agricultural services such as extension and market information systems that provide farmers with useful information about the agronomic and economic aspects of shifting into new commodities. It is sometimes claimed that farmers are not able to shift into new crops because of agroclimatic limitations. This view is contradicted by numerous studies showing that farmers respond to incentives in the form of input and output prices, as well as new technology.

Another type of complementary policy that enhances the economic effect of trade liberalization is trade facilitation. This category includes measures to reduce the transaction costs related to international trade, including excessive documentation requirements, authorizations from multiple agencies, unclear or subjective criteria for the application of duties, and delays and uncertainties related to customs clearance.

Complementary Policies to Support Agriculture

As discussed earlier, global trade liberalization will raise world agricultural prices, but domestic trade reform will partially or completely offset this effect. For MENA countries with a high level of agricultural protection, such as Morocco, Syria, and Tunisia, the combined effect would probably be a reduction in agricultural prices. Furthermore, the analysis presented in this report suggests that lower agricultural prices tend to raise the incidence of poverty, although the net effect is small because some poor households (such as urban consumers and net buyers in rural areas) gain. Policymakers may be interested in providing additional assistance to farmers both in the interest of alleviating poverty and as compensation to ensure political support for trade reform. This assistance may take the form of support for agricultural production or direct assistance to farm (or rural) households.

Under WTO rules, support for agricultural production is classified as amber box, blue box, or green box support. Amber box support includes various types of agricultural support prices and input subsidies. Some of the MENA countries are exempt, either because they are LDCs or because they are not WTO members; others are WTO members and are subject to restrictions on amber box expenditures.[2] In the WTO, developing countries are allowed *de minimis* amber box support for a commodity equivalent to up to 10 percent of the value of output. However, as discussed earlier, these policies are costly ways to help farmers and are not efficient in providing assistance to poor households.

Blue box support refers to agricultural support prices that are combined with policies to limit production through quotas or land set-asides. These are exempt from WTO restrictions based on the idea that the production limits prevent the support prices from distorting agricultural trade. Although these are legal under the URAA, it is not advisable to implement blue box policies in the MENA region for three reasons. First, it is difficult to justify the direct and administrative costs of such programs in terms of their benefits to the overall economy, nor are the programs particularly effective as anti-poverty measures. Second, these programs are difficult to administer and monitor. The producer subsidy creates a strong incentive to evade production limits, creating a need for monitoring and enforcement as well as the potential for corruption. Third, it is likely that blue box programs will be limited under the Doha Round. Both the E.U. and the United States have proposed limiting blue box expenditures to 2-5 percent of the value of production. De Gorter, Ingco, and Ignacio (2004) propose eliminating blue box support and counting these programs as amber box support.

Green box support for agriculture is exempt from WTO restrictions. It includes programs for the following:

- agricultural research and extension,
- pest and disease control,
- inspection services,
- marketing and promotion services,
- marketing infrastructure,
- public stockholding for food security,
- natural disaster relief,
- income insurance and safety net programs,
- environmental protection, and
- regional assistance.

[2] Among the eight MENA countries under consideration, Syria and the West Bank and Gaza are not WTO members, and Djibouti is considered an LDC. Lebanon is a WTO observer, which means that it intends to apply for membership within five years and will eventually be subject to WTO rules. Jordan, Morocco, and Tunisia have declared amber box expenditures and were obliged to cut them by 13.3 percent over 1995-2005 (de Gorter, Ingco, and Ignacio 2004).

Although most of these may be considered to support agriculture, they are allowed under WTO rules because, supposedly, they provide "no, or at most minimal trade distorting effects or effects on production" (WTO 1994, 59). In fact, some of these services may significantly facilitate agricultural production and exports. They are presumably exempted because they provide necessary services for the agricultural sector. In economic terms, they provide public goods that, because of externalities or difficulty in charging users for the services, are undersupplied by the private sector. One implication is that it is possible for well-designed government services in these areas to generate benefits for the public that exceed the costs of the program in value.

As discussed elsewhere, domestic trade liberalization in the MENA countries is likely to stimulate diversification from grain production into alternative crops such as oilseeds and fruits and vegetables. As the process of diversification proceeds, the importance of these services will inevitably rise. As farmers diversify into new crops, they will require more information about production methods and marketing opportunities. As they switch to perishable crops, disease and pest control will become more important. As they attempt to supply increasingly quality-sensitive consumers in urban areas and in foreign markets, grading and inspection services will become critical. Policymakers may facilitate this process by promoting agricultural institutions that provide public services, particularly for small and vulnerable farmers. Farmer associations are one strategy to reduce the cost of delivering inputs and technical assistance and facilitate the marketing of agricultural products. Funding is necessary because agricultural research and extension services cannot be effective if they are forced to recover costs by selling seeds and fertilizer. But greater funding is not sufficient: the institutions must be designed to provide incentives so that the services are demand driven, allowing them the flexibility to respond to changing demands.

Complementary Policies to Support Farmers

One type of green box program does not involve the provision of public goods: decoupled payments to farmers. Payments are decoupled when they are not based on current production but rather on some fixed criterion such as production or area planted in a base year. Over the past 15 years, economists and policymakers have become increasingly interested in agricultural reform that shifts from producer subsidies and import protection toward decoupled payments to farmers. The appeal of such reform is that decoupled payments may provide equivalent support to farmers at a lower fiscal and economic cost. The fiscal cost is lower for a given level of farm income support because the decoupled payments are direct income support rather than indirect support through agricultural prices. The economic cost is lower because decoupled payments do not distort agricultural production and trade and therefore do not influence farm decisions.

Decoupled payments to farmers have been tried in the E.U., Mexico, and the United States, among other countries (see Baffes and de Gorter 2004). We summarize these three experiences as follows:

- In the 1985 U.S. farm bill, the basis for payments was shifted from current production to current area and historical yield. The 1996 farm bill, known as the Federal Agriculture Improvement and Reform Act, replaced traditional agricultural programs with decoupled payments under production flexibility contracts that were to be phased out over six years. The act was undermined by the U.S. Congress, which provided supplemental farm aid in the form of emergency relief and loan deficiency payments almost every year.
- The E.U. has also moved toward decoupled payments to farmers. In 1992 the E.U. reformed the common agricultural policy to reduce price supports and switch from current planted area to area planted in a base year. Over the 1990s, decoupled payments rose so that they accounted for more than 20 percent of total producer support, while import protection was reduced. In 2003 the E.U. decided to increase decoupled payments to account for three-quarters of the support for crop production.
- Mexico introduced a decoupled payment program in 1994 in preparation for the North American Free Trade Agreement. The Procampo program shifted Mexican agricultural policy from support prices and input subsidies to a system of fixed payments based on historical area, thus compensating farmers for the reduction in import protection associated with the new agreement. The program was made more progressive by setting a minimum 1 hectare even for farms below this size and by capping the maximum payment allowed. As in the United States, the program was partially undermined in 2002 by the reintroduction of price supports.

Perhaps most relevant to the MENA countries is the case of Turkey. In 2000 Turkey was providing US$6.4 billion in support for agriculture, of which US$1.4 billion was price support and input subsidies and US$5 billion was in the form of import protection. In 2001 Turkey launched its Agricultural Reform Implementation Program with support from the World Bank. The objectives of the program were to (1) introduce direct income support payments, decoupled from production decisions; (2) phase out agricultural price supports and input subsidies; and (3) implement a system of direct income payments, decoupled from production levels. The program began with a pilot project to experiment with alternative methods of establishing a registry of farms. Then a massive farm registration program was launched that eventually registered 2.8 million farms. The direct income support payments were approximately US$90 per hectare per year up to 50 hectares. Over 2001-04, the payments increased while price supports and input subsidies were phased out, so that by 2004 the payments accounted for over 70 percent of the total (Cakmak 2004; Olhan 2006).

The impact of the program has been mixed, though the interpretation of trends has been complicated by an economic crisis in 2001 during which real GDP fell by 7.5 percent. Between 1999 and 2003, the total area cultivated declined by 4 percent. The production of wheat, barley, and maize increased by 5-6 percent, while cotton output expanded by 21 percent. The area under olive groves and orchards increased by 5 percent and 7 percent, respectively. On the other hand, the production of sugar beets and tobacco fell by one-fourth and one-half, respectively, in response to the elimination of price supports (Olhan 2006). Overall, the agricultural value added per worker in agriculture rose 10 percent between 1998-99 and 2003 (Cakmak 2004).

In summary, decoupled payments to farmers represent a promising approach to reducing the economic distortions associated with agricultural price supports, import protection, and input subsidies while compensating farmers and minimizing any adverse impact on poverty. At the same time, it should be recognized that most MENA countries use import protection to support farm prices rather than as direct subsidies. In this situation, switching from import protection to a program of decoupled payments implies both a loss in tariff revenue and significant new expenditure.

Complementary Policies to Assist the Rural Poor

Decoupled payments are a political solution to the problems of phasing out costly programs involving support prices, input subsidies, and import protection and of compensating farmers for their loss. Although the incidence of poverty is generally higher among farmers than among the general population, such programs cannot be considered safety net programs because they do not target poor households. Decoupled payments to farmers exclude poor nonfarmers, including agricultural wage laborers, owners of microenterprises, and the urban poor. Furthermore, among farmers, benefits are generally proportional to farm size, so the benefits are likely to be greater for richer farmers than for poor farmers.

If the objective is to assist poor and vulnerable households regardless of their occupation, a different type of program should be considered. A wide variety of safety net programs have been established in developing countries with the explicit objective of reducing poverty or at least some of the negative effects of poverty. Although a thorough review of alternative safety net programs is beyond the scope of this report, it is useful to briefly describe the main types of programs.

Universal food subsidies reduce the cost of selected foods (usually basic staples) for the benefit of all consumers. The advantages include relatively simple administration (no targeting) and the fact that the relative benefits are greater for poor households because food (particularly basic staples) is a larger share of the budgets of poor households. In the 1980s, Egypt, Jordan, Syria, and Tunisia offered universal food subsidies for goods such as bread, wheat flour, cooking oil, and sugar. These programs have become less popular in the past 15 years for several reasons: their high fiscal cost, the leakage of benefits to nonpoor households, and the low coverage among some groups of poor households, particularly in rural areas. One review of 15 food subsidy schemes has found that in only three of them were the per capita benefits greater among the poor than among the nonpoor (Coady, Grosh, and Hodinott 2002).

Targeted food subsidies make subsidized food available to selected households geographically through low-price shops located in poor neighborhoods or through some form of ration cards that entitle bearers to purchase food at subsidized prices. Egypt, Jordan, and Tunisia have attempted to introduce targeting into their food subsidy programs (Coady 2004). In Egypt, however, corruption and political pressure led to a situation in which large numbers of nonpoor households held ration cards. Efforts to narrow eligibility faced strong political opposition (Kherallah et al. 2000).

Labor-intensive public works programs usually combine infrastructure development (such as road building) with hiring policies to maximize their pro-poor impact. If designed well, they may improve community infrastructure and provide assistance to the poorest households with able-bodied members. If the wage rate is set appropriately (somewhat below the prevailing wage rate), the program is self-targeting in that the better-off members of the community will not find it worthwhile to participate, while the poor will. One drawback of these programs is the high cost of supervising the work relative to that in cash transfer programs. In addition, these programs cannot assist those unable to work because of age or disability. Finally, there is a trade-off between the goal of providing quality public infrastructure, which often requires semiskilled labor, and the goal of serving the poorest members of the community, who do not have these skills. One example of this is the Second Rural Employment Program in Algeria. This US$95 million program, funded by the World Bank, focuses on northwest and north central Algeria and emphasizes public works to maintain natural resources and reduce soil erosion (World Bank 2003b).

Conditional cash transfer programs have generated considerable interest among researchers and policymakers in the past 10-15 years. These programs provide cash grants to households that comply with certain requirements, usually keeping children in school, attending health clinics, or receiving pre- and postnatal care. Like food-for-work programs, conditional cash transfers serve a dual purpose: providing assistance to poor households and encouraging investments in human capital that reduce the chance that poverty will be transmitted to the next generation. The Progresa Program was launched in Mexico in 1997 and phased in over three years, eventually reaching 2.6 million rural families. Eligibility is determined in two stages by first selecting poor villages and then selecting poor families within these villages. Progresa is one of the more widely studied conditional cash transfer programs, in part because the gradual expansion of the program has been randomized by village, allowing quasi-experimental tests of the impact of the program. Studies show that it has been successful in increasing school attendance, reducing the incidence of child labor, and improving child health (Gertler 2004; Skoufias 2005). Conditional cash transfer programs have also been implemented in Bangladesh, Nicaragua, and Turkey, among other countries.

Although this section provides only a brief glimpse of alternative safety net programs, it demonstrates that there are a number of interesting and effective programs for providing assistance to poor rural families in developing countries. These programs may be used in conjunction with trade liberalization programs to alleviate some of the adverse effects of liberalization and facilitate transition to a more market-oriented agricultural sector.

References

Abdelkhalek, T. 2002. The impact of the liberalisation of the Moroccan grain market based on a rural household model. Cahier de recherche, Micro Impacts of Macroeconomic and Adjustment Policies / Institut National de Statistique et d'Économie Appliquée, Rabat. September.

Adams, R., Jr. 2001. *Non-farm income, inequality and poverty in rural Egypt and Jordan*. World Bank Policy Research Working Paper 2572. Washington, D.C.: World Bank.

Akesbi, N. 2002. *Développement et politiques agroalimentaires dans la région méditerranéenne*. National Report Morocco. Paris: Centre International des Hautes Études Agronomiques Méditerranéennes.

Anderson, K. 2003. *Trade liberalization, agriculture, and poverty in low-income countries*. WIDER Discussion Paper 2003/25. United Nations University, Helsinki: World Institute for Development Economics Research.

Anderson, K., W. Martin, and D. Van der Mensbrugghe. 2005. Market and welfare implications of Doha reform scenarios. In *Trade reform and the Doha Agenda*, ed. K. Anderson and W. Martin. Washington, D.C.: World Bank.

Augier, P., and M. Gasiorek. 2001. *Trade liberalization between the southern Mediterranean and the EU: The sectoral impact*. Discussion Paper 79 (December). Brighton, England: University of Sussex at Brighton.

Baffes, J., and H. de Gorter. 2004. Experience with decoupling agricultural support. In *Global agricultural trade and developing countries*, ed. M. A. Aksoy and J. C. Beghin. Washington, D.C.: World Bank.

Bailey, K. 2005. Implications of European policy reforms on the U.S. dairy industry. Pennsylvania State University Staff Paper 375. Pennsylvania State University, State College, PA., U.S.A. <http://dairyoutlook.aers.psu.edu/reports/Pub2005/staffpaper375.pdf>.

Bakour, Y. 2004. Reforming and developing the agricultural sector and the needs from trade and economic liberalization. Paper presented at the conference organized by the Syrian Association of Economic Sciences, Damascus, September 22-23.

Bayar, A. H., ed. 2001. Fiscal challenges of the Euro-Mediterranean Agreements. Forum Euro-Méditerranéen des Instituts Economiques, Marseille, and Economic Research Forum, Cairo. <http://www.femise.org/PDF/bayar_a_fisc_0105.pdf>.

Bayar, A. H., with contributions from G. Ben-Ahmed, W. Coscia, and J. Dupierreux. 2000. The impacts of a new round of multilateral trade liberalization on the MENA region. Paper presented at the Economic Research Forum's Seventh Annual Conference, Amman, October 26-29.

Beghin, J. C., and D. Van der Mensbrugghe. 2003. Global agriculture reform: What is at stake? In *Global agricultural trade and developing countries*, ed. M. A. Aksoy and J. C. Beghin. Washington, D.C: World Bank.

Benson, T., N. Minot, J. Pender, M. Robles, and J. von Braun. 2008. *Global food crises: Monitoring and assessing impact to inform policy responses.* Food Policy Report 9. Washington, D.C.: International Food Policy Research Institute.

Beuchelt, T. 2005. *The Euro-Mediterranean Partnership and agricultural trade liberalization.* Washington, D.C.: Market Trade and Institutions Division, International Food Policy Research Institute.

Blayney, D. P., and M. Gehlhar. 2005. U.S. dairy at a new crossroads in a global setting. *Amber Waves,* November. Washington, D.C.: Economic Research Service, U.S. Department of Agriculture. <http://www.ers.usda.gov/AmberWaves/November05/Features/USDairy.htm>.

Bouët, A. 2006. Defining a trade strategy for South Mediterranean countries. Draft working paper. International Food Policy Research Institute, Washington, D.C.

———. 2008. *The expected benefits of trade liberalization for world income and development: Opening the "black box" of global trade modeling.* Food Policy Review 8. Washington, D.C.: International Food Policy Research Institute.

Bouët, A., L. Fontagné, and S. Jean. 2006. Is erosion of tariff preferences a serious concern? In *Agricultural trade reform and the Doha development agenda,* ed. K. Anderson and W. Martin. Washington, D.C.: World Bank.

Bouët, A., S. Mevel, and D. Orden. 2006. More or less ambition in the Doha Round? Winners and losers from trade liberalization with a development perspective. Paper presented at the conference of the Food and Agriculture Organization of the United Nations, Rome, February 2–3.

Bouët, A., Y. Decreux, L. Fontagne, S. Jean, and D. Laborde. 2004. A consistent ad valorem equivalent measure of applied protection across the world: The MAc-Map-HS6 database. CEPII Working Paper 2004-22. Centre d'Etudes Prospectives et d'Informations Internationales, Paris.

Boumellassa, H., D. Laborde, and C. Mitaritonna. 2009. *A picture of tariff protection across the world in 2004: MAcMap-HS6, Version 2.* IFPRI Discussion Paper 00903. Washington, D.C.: International Food Policy Research Institute.

Bourguignon, F., A. S. Robilliard, and S. Robinson. 2002. *Representative versus real households in the macroeconomic modeling of inequality.* Working Paper. Washington, D.C.: World Bank.

Brunel, C. 2008. Maghreb regional integration. In *Maghreb regional and global integration: A dream to be fulfilled,* ed. G. C. Hufbauer and C. Brunel. Washington, D.C.: Peterson Institute for International Economics.

Bunte, F. 2005. Liberalising EU imports for fruits and vegetables. Paper prepared for presentation at the 99th seminar of the EAAE (European Association of Agricultural Economists), The Future of Rural Europe in the Global Agri-Food System, Copenhagen, August 23–27.

Burniaux, J.-M., G. Nicoletti, and J. Oliveira-Martins. 1992. GREEN: A global model for quantifying the costs of policies to curb CO_2 emissions. *OECD Economic Studies* 19 (Winter): 21–32.

Cakmak, E. H. 2004. *Structural change and market opening in agriculture: Turkey towards EU accession.* ERC Working Papers in Economics 04/10. Ankara: Middle East Technical University.

Central Bank of Tunisia. 2005. *Annual Report 2004.* Tunis.

CEPII (Centre d'Etudes Prospectives et d'Informations Internationales). 2008. MAcMap. Paris. <http://www.cepii.fr/francgraph/bdd/macmap.htm>.

Chaherli, N. 2002. Agricultural trade liberalization: Main issues for the MENA region. <http://lnweb18.worldbank.org/mna/mena.nsf/Attachments/Chaherli/$File/Chaherli.pdf>. Accessed December 2005.

Chemingui, M. A. 2007. Poverty effects from reforming agricultural policies in rich countries in a spatially small heterogeneous agricultural economy. Report prepared under the Global Development Network's Research Project on the Impact of Policy Reforms in Rich Countries on the Developing World. New Delhi: Global Development Network.

Chemingui, M. A., and S. Dessus. 1999. *La libéralisation de l'agriculture Tunisienne et l'Union Européenne: Une vue prospective.* OECD Development Centre Working Paper 144. Paris: Development Centre, Organisation for Economic Co-operation and Development.

——. 2001. The liberalization of Tunisian agriculture and the European Union: A prospective view. In *Towards Arab and Euro-Med regional integration,* ed. S. Dessus, J. Devlin, and R. Safadi. Paris: Development Centre, Organisation for Economic Co-operation and Development.

——. 2004. *Assessing non-tariff barriers in Syria.* Working paper. Washington, D.C.: World Bank.

Chemingui, M. A., and H. Fetini. 2006. Considerations for reforming energy price subsidies in Syria: A policy note. World Bank, Washington, D.C.

Chemingui, M. A., and M. H. Lahouel. 2006. Trade policy. In *Tunisian profile.* Paris: Forum Euro-Méditerranéen des Instituts Economiques and the European Commission.

Chemingui, M. A., and C. Thabet. 2009. Agricultural trade liberalization and poverty in rural areas in Tunisia: Micro-simulation in a general equilibrium framework. *Swiss Review of International Economic Relations* (1): 71-90.

CIA (Central Intelligence Agency of the United States). 2009. *World Factbook.* <http://www.cia.gov/cia/publications/factbook/index.html>. Accessed March 2009.

CIE (Centre for International Economics). 2001. Trade distortions and cotton markets: Implications for Australian cotton producers. Report prepared for the Cotton Research and Development Corporation, Canberra.

Cline, W. R. 2004. *Trade policy and global poverty.* Washington, D.C.: Institute for International Economics.

Coady, D. 2004. *Designing and evaluating social safety nets: Theory, evidence and policy conclusions.* Food Consumption and Nutrition Division Discussion Paper 172. Washington, D.C.: International Food Policy Research Institute.

Coady, D., M. Grosh, and J. Hodinott. 2002. *Targeting outcomes redux.* Food Consumption and Nutrition Division Discussion Paper 144. Washington, D.C.: International Food Policy Research Institute.

Cockburn, J., B. Decaluwé, and B. Costi. 1998. Les leçons du mariage entre modèles d'équilibre général calculable et la nouvelle théorie du commerce international: Application à la Tunisie. Centre de Recherche en Economie et Finance Appliquée, Université Laval, Quebec.

Cogneau, D., and A. S. Robilliard. 2000. *Income distribution, poverty and growth in Madagascar: Microsimulations in a general equilibrium framework.* IFPRI Working Paper 61/2000. Washington, D.C.: International Food Policy Research Institute.

Collier, P. 1999. On the economic consequences of civil war. *Oxford Economic Papers* 51 (1): 168–183.

Datt, G., D. Jolliffe, and M. Sharma. 1998. *A profile of poverty in Egypt: 1997.* Food Consumption and Nutrition Division Discussion Paper 49. Washington, D.C.: International Food Policy Research Institute.

Decaluwé, B., A. Patry, L. Savard, and E. Thorbecke. 1999. *Poverty analysis within a general equilibrium framework.* Cahiers de recherche 9909. Université Laval, Quebec: Département d'Économique.

Decreux, Y., and H. Valin. 2007. *MIRAGE: Updated version of the model for trade policy analysis: Focus on agriculture and dynamics.* CEPII Working Paper 2007-15. Paris: Centre d'Études Prospectives et d'Informations Internationales.

de Gorter, H., M. Ingco, and L. Ignacio. 2004. Domestic support: Economics and policy instruments. In *Agriculture and the WTO: Creating a trading system for development,* ed. M. Ingco and J. Nash. Washington, D.C.: World Bank.

Dennis, A. 2006a. *The impact of regional trade agreements and trade facilitation in the Middle East and North Africa Region.* Policy Research Working Paper 3837. Washington, D.C.: World Bank.

——. 2006b. *Trade liberalization, factor market flexibility, and growth: The case of Morocco and Tunisia.* Policy Research Working Paper 3857. Washington, D.C.: World Bank.

Dessus, S., K. Fukasaku, and R. Safadi. 1999. *La liberalisation multilatérale des droits de douane et les pays en développement.* Cahier de Politique Economique 18. Paris: Centre de Développement de de l'Organisation de Cooperation et de Developpement Economique.

Devarajan, S., and S. Robinson. 2002. *The influence of computable general equilibrium models on policy.* Trade and Macroeconomic Division Discussion Paper 98. Washington, D.C.: International Food Policy Research Institute.

Devarajan, S., D. Go, and H. Li. 1999. Quantifying the fiscal effects of trade reform: A general equilibrium model estimated for 60 countries. World Bank, Washington, D.C. Mimeo.

Diao, X., A. Somwaru, and T. Roe. 2001. *A global analysis of agricultural trade reform in WTO member countries.* Economic Development Center 01-1. Bulletin 12984. Minneapolis: University of Minnesota.

Diaz-Bonilla, E., M. Thomas, S. Robinson, and A. Cattaneo. 2000. *Food security and trade negotiations in the World Trade Organization: A cluster analysis of country groups.* Trade and Macroeconomics Division Discussion Paper 59. Washington, D.C.: International Food Policy Research Institute.

Elbehri, A., J. Umstaetter, and D. Kelch. 2008. *The EU sugar policy regime and implications of reform.* Report 59. Washington, D.C.: United States Department of Agriculture (USDA) Economic Research Service (ERS). July. <http://www.ers.usda.gov/Publications/ERR59/err59_reportsummary.pdf>.

El-Laithy, H., M. Lokshin, and A. Banerji. 2003. *Poverty and economic growth in Egypt,*

1995-2000. World Bank Policy Research Working Paper 3068. Washington, D.C.: World Bank.

El-Obeid, A., and J. C. Beghin. 2005. Multilateral trade and agricultural policy reforms in sugar markets. CARD Working Paper 04-WP 356. Food and Agricultural Policy Research Institute, Iowa State University, Ames. <http://www.card.iastate.edu/publications/DBS/PDFFiles/04wp356.pdf>.

Ender, Gary. 2000. *Accomplishments in agricultural policy reform in Egypt, 1997-2001*. Cambridge, Mass.: Abt Associates.

Europa. 2006. Towards a reform of the internal aspects of the common organization of the market in bananas. Consultation document. Impact Analysis Steering Group, Brussels. April 3.

European Commission. 2006. Proceedings of the workshop on Euro-Med Association Agreements: Agricultural trade—Regional impacts in the EU, Brussels, February 14. Annex 1. <http://eumed-agpol.iamm.fr/html/publications/on_subject/WP6-proceedings.pdf>.

——. 2009. European neighborhood policies. Brussels. <http://ec.europa.eu/world/enp/documents_en.htm#1>. Accessed April 2009.

FAO (Food and Agriculture Organization of the United Nations). 2003. Trade, market access and food safety in the Near East Region. Rome. <http://www.fao.org/docrep/meeting/007/ad388e/ad388e00.htm>. Accessed December 2005.

——. 2004. Agricultural development policies in the Near East: Situation, issues, institutional requirements and approaches. TCAS Working Document 57. Proceedings of the Joint FAO/NAPC Regional Workshop on Institution Building for Agricultural Policies in the Near East, Damascus, December 6-7, 2003.

——. 2009a. FAOSTAT agricultural database. Rome. <http://apps.fao.org/>.

——. 2009b. FAO country profiles and mapping information system. Rome. <http://www.fao.org/countryprofiles/index.asp?lang=en&iso3=LBN&subj=3>. Accessed March 2009.

FAPRI (Food and Agricultural Policy Research Institute). 2002. The Doha round of the World Trade Organization: Appraising further liberalization of agricultural markets. CARD Working Paper 02-WP 317 (November). Food and Agricultural Policy Research Institute, Iowa State University, Ames.

Feraboli, O., and T. Trimborn. 2008. Trade liberalization and income distribution: A CGE model for Jordan. <http://www.fiw.ac.at/fileadmin/Documents/FOKO_II/Feraboli_Trimborn.pdf>. Accessed April 7, 2010.

Foster, J., J. Greer, and E. Thorbecke. 1984. A class of decomposable poverty measures. *Econometrica* 52: 761-765.

Gallaway, M. P., C. A. McDaniel, and S. A. Rivera. 2000. *Long-run industry-level estimates of U.S. Armington elasticities*. Working Paper 2000-09a. Washington, D.C.: U.S. International Trade Commission.

Garcia-Alvarez-Coque, J. M. 2002. Agricultural trade and the Barcelona process: Is full liberalization possible? *European Review of Agricultural Economics* 29 (3): 399-422.

GCC (Gulf Cooperation Council). 2001. The economic agreement between the GCC States. Riyadh. <http://library.gcc-sg.org/English/Books/econagree2004.htm>.

Gertler, P. 2004. Do conditional cash transfers improve child health? Evidence from Progresa's control randomized experiment. *American Economic Review* 94 (2): 336–341.

Golan, A., G. Judge, and D. Miller. 1996. *Maximum entropy econometrics: Robust estimation with limited data.* Chichester, England: John Wiley and Sons.

Golan, A., G. Judge, and S. Robinson. 1994. Recovering information from incomplete or partial multisectoral economic data. *Review of Economics and Statistics* 76: 541–549.

Hanrahan, C., and R. Schnepf. 2005. WTO Doha Round: Agricultural negotiating proposals. CRS Report for Congress. Congressional Research Service, Washington, D.C. November 9.

Hoekman, B., and D. E. Konan. 1998. *Deep integration, regionalism and nondiscrimination.* Working Paper 199804. Manoa: Department of Economics, University of Hawaii at Manoa.

——. 2005. Deepening Egypt-US trade integration: Economic implication of alternative options. Paper presented at the Middle East Economic Association session of the Allied Social Sciences Association Annual Meeting, Philadelphia, January 18.

Hoekman, B., A. Mattoo, and P. English, eds. 2002. *Development, trade, and the WTO: A handbook.* Washington, D.C.: World Bank.

Hosoe, N. 2001. A general equilibrium analysis of Jordan's trade liberalization. *Journal of Policy Modeling* 23 (6): 595–600.

ICAC (International Cotton Advisory Committee). 2002. Production and trade policies affecting the cotton industry. Washington, D.C.

——. 2006. Production and trade policies affecting the cotton industry. <http://www.icac.org/govt_measures/documents/govt_measures06.pdf>. Accessed April 7, 2010.

IFAD (International Fund for Agricultural Development). 2003. *Assessment of rural poverty: Middle East and North Africa.* Rome.

IFAD/IFPRI (International Fund for Agricultural Development/International Food Policy Research Institute). 2007. *Impact of trade liberalization on agriculture in the Near East and North Africa.* Rome: IFAD.

IFC (International Finance Corporation). 2009. *Doing business 2009.* Washington, D.C. <http://www.doingbusiness.org/documents/fullreport/2009/DB09_Full_Report.pdf>.

Ingco, M., and J. D. Nash, eds. 2004. *Agriculture and the WTO: Creating a trading system for development.* Washington, D.C.: World Bank.

INS (Institut National de la Statistique). 1998. *1997 national labor survey.* Tunis.

——. 2002. *Résultats de l'enquête sur le budget des ménages*, Vol A, *Enquête nationale sur le budget, la consommation et le niveau de vie des ménages, 2000.* Tunis.

——. 2005. *National accounts, 1990–2002.* Tunis.

Institute of Quantitative Studies. 2003. Protection effective des activités économiques. In *Evolution et perspectives (2003–2008).* Tunis.

ITC (International Trade Center). 2008. Trade competitiveness map. ITC, Washington, D.C. <http://www.intracen.org/marketanalysis/TradeCompetitivenessMap.aspx>. Accessed April 17, 2009.

Kee, H. L., A. Nicita, and M. Olarreaga. 2006. *Estimating trade restrictiveness indices.* Policy Research Working Paper 3840. Washington, D.C.: World Bank.

Khasawneh, N. A. 2000. The Arab free trade zone: The Arab world's best kept secret. GlobalComment.com. <http://www.globalcomment.com>.

Kherallah, M., H. Lofgren, P. Gruhn, and M. Reeder. 2000. *Wheat policy reform in Egypt: Adjustment of local markets and options for future reforms.* Research Report 115. Washington, D.C.: International Food Policy Research Institute.

Konan, D. E., and K. E. Maskus. 1997. A computable general equilibrium analysis of Egyptian trade liberalisation scenarios. In *Regional partners in global markets: Limits and possibilities of the Euro-Med agreements,* ed. A. Galal and B. Hoekman. London: Centre for Economic Policy Research; Cairo: Egyptian Centre for Economic Studies.

——. 2000. Bilateral trade patterns and welfare: An Egypt-EU preferential trade agreement. Working Paper 00-01. Department of Economics, University of Hawaii at Manoa. <http://www.economics.hawaii.edu/research/workingpapers/001.pdf>. Accessed February 28, 2006.

Kuiper, M. 2004. *Fifty ways to leave your protection: Comparing applied models of the Euro-Mediterranean Association Agreements.* ENARPRI Working Paper 6. Brussels: European Network of Agricultural and Rural Policy Research Institute.

Laithy, H., K. Abu-Ismail, and K. Hamdan. 2008. *Poverty, growth and income distribution in Lebanon.* International Poverty Centre (IPC) Country Study 13. Brasilia: IPC.

Langley, S., A. Somwaru, and M. A. Normile. 2006. Trade liberalization in international dairy markets: Estimated impacts. Electronic report. Economic Research Service, U.S. Department of Agriculture, Washington, D.C. <http://www.ers.usda.gov/publications/ERR16/ERR16.pdf>.

Lebanon (Republic of). 2009. Ministry of Economics and Trade. Beirut. <http://www.economy.gov.lb/MOET/English/Panel/Trade/InternationalTradeAgreements/ArabCountries/GAFTA.htm>. Accessed April 2009.

Lofgren, H. 1999. *Trade reform and the poor in Morocco: A rural-urban general equilibrium analysis of reduced protection.* Trade and Macroeconomics Division Discussion Paper 38. Washington, D.C.: International Food Policy Research Institute.

Lofgren, H., M. El-Said, and S. Robinson. 1999. *Trade liberalization and complementary domestic policies: A rural-urban general equilibrium analysis of Morocco.* Trade and Macroeconomics Division Discussion Paper 41. Washington, D.C.: International Food Policy Research Institute.

Lofgren, H., R. L. Harris, and S. Robinson. 2002. *A standard computable general equilibrium (CGE) model in GAMS.* Microcomputers in Policy Research 5. Washington, D.C.: International Food Policy Research Institute.

Lorca, C. A., and J. Vicens. 2000. The impact of the Euro-Mediterranean liberalization of trade on agricultural trade. Forum Euro-Méditerranéen des Instituts Economiques Research Program, Universidad Autonoma de Madrid. September.

Madcour, M., and A. M. Abou Zeid. 1996. Egypt: Country report to the FAO. Paper presented at the International Technical Conference on Plant Genetic Resources, Leipzig, June 17–23.

MARH (Ministry of Agriculture, Environment and Water Resources). 2006. Enquête sur les structures des exploitations agricoles 2004-2005. Direction Générale des Études et du Développement Agricole, Ministry of Agriculture, Environment and Water Resources, Tunis.

McQueen, M. 2002. The EU's free trade agreements with developing countries: A case of wishful thinking? *World Economy* 25 (9): 1369-1385.

Ministry of Agriculture and Land Reclamation, Arab Republic of Egypt. Website. <http://www.agri.gov.eg/>.

Minot, N., and L. Daniels. 2005. Impact of global cotton markets on rural poverty in Benin. *Agricultural Economics* 33, Supplement: 453-466.

Mitchell, D. O., and M. Mielke. 2004. Wheat: The global market, policies and priorities. In *Global agricultural trade and developing countries*, ed. M. A. Aksoy and J. C. Beghin. Washington, D.C.: World Bank.

Muaz, S. 2004. *The impact of Euro-Mediterranean partnership on the agricultural sectors of Jordan, Palestine, Syria, Lebanon and Egypt: The case of horticultural exports to EU Markets*. FEM21-03. Paris: Forum Euro-Méditerranéen des Instituts Économiques Research.

Nashashibi, K. 2002. *Fiscal revenues in South Mediterranean Arab Countries: Vulnerabilities and growth potential*. Working Paper 02/67. Washington, D.C.: International Monetary Fund.

Obara, K., J. Dyck, and J. Stout. 2005. Dairy policies in Japan. Electronic Outlook Report (August). Economic Research Service, U.S. Department of Agriculture, Washington, D.C. <http://www.ers.usda.gov/publications/LDP/Aug05/ldpm13401/ldpm13401.pdf>.

OECD (Organisation for Economic Co-operation and Development). 2007. Agricultural policies in OECD countries: Monitoring and evaluation 2007. <http://www.oecd.org/dataoecd/61/3/39524780.pdf>. Accessed April 2009.

Olhan, E. 2006. The impact of the reforms: Impoverished Turkish agriculture. Paper presented at the 96th European Association of Agricultural Economists Seminar Causes and Impacts of Agricultural Structures, Tänikon, Switzerland, January 10-11.

Oliva, M. 2000. *Estimation of trade protection in Middle East and North African Countries*. IMF Working Paper WP/00/27. Washington, D.C.: International Monetary Fund.

Pal, P., and S. Prakash. 2005. The Dalian mini ministerial and the road to Hong Kong: Uncertain future for WTO. International Development Economics Associates. <http://www.ideaswebsite.org/news/aug2005/WTO_Dalian_HK.pdf>.

Radwan, S., and J.-L. Reiffers. 2003. The impact of agricultural liberalization in the context of the Euro-Mediterranean partnership. Report. Forum Euro-Méditerranéen des Instituts Economiques. Alexandria. <http://www.femise.org/PDF/femise-agri-gb.pdf>.

Ravallion, M., and M. Lokshin. 2004. Gainers and losers from trade reform in Morocco. Policy Research Working Paper 3368. World Bank, Washington, D.C. <http://www-wds.worldbank.org/servlet/WDSContentServer/WDSP/IB/2004/08/25/000009486_20040825085439/Rendered/PDF/377040wps3368.pdf>.

Reefat, A. 1999. *New trends in Egypt's trade policy and future challenges*. Discussion Paper 36. Cairo: Egyptian Centre for Economic Studies.

Robinson, S., A. Cattañeo, and M. El-Said. 2001. Updating and estimating a social accounting matrix using cross entropy methods. *Economic Systems Research* 13 (1): 47-64.

Robinson, S., and M. El-Said. 2000. *GAMS code for estimating a social accounting matrix (SAM) using cross entropy (CE) methods.* Trade and Macroeconomics Division Discussion Paper 64. Washington, D.C.: International Food Policy Research Institute.

Roe, T., A. Dinar, Y. Tsur, and X. Diao. 2005. *Feedback links between economy-wide and farm-level policies: Application to irrigation water management in Morocco.* Policy Research Working Paper 3550. Washington, D.C.: World Bank.

Rutherford, T. F., E. E. Rutström, and D. G. Tarr. 1997. Morocco's free trade agreement with the EU: A quantitative assessment. *Economic Modeling* 14 (2): 237-269.

Schiff, M., and A. Valdes. 1992. *The plundering of agriculture in developing countries.* Washington, D.C.: World Bank.

Siam, G. M. 2002. GATT and Egyptian agriculture: Implication and effects. Egyptian Association of Agricultural Economics and Centre for Agricultural Economic Studies, Faculty of Agriculture, Cairo University, Cairo. September.

——. 2005. Impact of agricultural trade liberalization between the EU and Mediterranean countries. Project Report. Centre for Agricultural Economic Studies, Faculty of Agriculture, Cairo University, Cairo.

Skoufias, E. 2005. *PROGRESA and its impacts on the welfare of rural households in Mexico.* Research Report 139. Washington, D.C.: International Food Policy Research Institute.

Stanbury, W. T. 2002. The politics of milk in Canada. Fraser Institute Digital Publication (August). Fraser Institute, Vancouver. <http://www.fraserinstitute.ca/admin/books/files/Milk.pdf>.

Thomas, M., M. H. Bchir, A. Bouët, and B. Dimaranan. 2008. Evaluation of trade integration using the MIRAGE model. In *Maghreb regional and global integration: A dream to be fulfilled,* ed. G. C. Hufbauer and C. Brunel. Washington, D.C.: Peterson Institute for International Economics.

Tokarick, S. 2005. Who bears the cost of agricultural support in OECD Countries? *World Economy* 28 (4): 573-593.

Turner, P. 2005. America's role in the emerging global dairy markets. Power Point presentation. International Food and Agricultural Trade Policy Council, Washington, D.C. <http://www.agritrade.org/Plenary/DC/Presentations/Turner.ppt#259, 1,Slide 1>.

UNDP (United Nations Development Programme). 2005a. Egypt human development report 2005: Choosing our future; Towards a new social contract. UNDP and Institute for National Planning, Egypt.

——. 2005b. Poverty in Syria: 1996-2004: Diagnostics and pro-poor policy considerations. Geneva.

USDA (U.S. Department of Agriculture). 1999. *Product specific import regulations Syria.* GAIN Report SY9004. Washington, D.C.: USDA.

——. 2001. *The road ahead: Agricultural policy reform in the WTO.* Summary Report. AER 797. Washington, D.C.: Market and Trade Economics Division, Economic Research Service, USDA.

——. 2009. Production, supply and distribution online. Foreign Agricultural Service, USDA, Washington, D.C. <http://www.fas.usda.gov/psdonline/>. Accessed March 2009.

USTR (U.S. Trade Representative). 2006. U.S.-Middle East free trade efforts. USTR, Washington, D.C. <http://www.ustr.gov/Trade_Agreements/Regional/MEFTA/US_Middle_East_Free_Trade_Efforts.html>. Accessed February 28, 2006.

Vocke, G., E. W. Allen, and M. Ali. 2005. Wheat backgrounder. Electronic Outlook Report. Economic Research Service, U.S. Department of Agriculture, Washington, D.C. <http://www.ers.usda.gov/publications/whs/dec05/whs05K01/whs05K01.pdf>.

Von Braun, J. 2008. *Food and financial crises: Implications for agriculture and the poor.* Food Policy Report. Washington, D.C.: International Food Policy Research Institute.

Wailes, E. 2004. Rice: Global trade, protectionist policies and the impact of trade liberalization. In *Global agricultural trade and developing countries*, ed. M. A. Aksoy and J. C. Beghin. Washington, D.C.: World Bank.

Westlake, M. 2003. The economics of strategic crops. In *Syrian Agriculture at the Crossroads*, ed. C. Fiorillo and J. Vercuil. FAO Agricultural Policy and Economic Development Series 8. Rome: Food and Agriculture Organization of the United Nations.

Winters, L. A., N. McCulloch, and A. McKay. 2004. Trade liberalization and poverty: The evidence so far. *Journal of Economic Literature* 42 (March): 72–115.

Wippel, S. 2005. The Agadir agreement and open regionalism: The new forum for integration on the southern shore of the Mediterranean in the context of multiple regional orientations. *EuroMeSCopaper* 45 (September). <http://www.euromesco.net/media/euromesco_paper_45.pdf>.

World Bank. 2001. *Kingdom of Morocco poverty update*, vol. 1: *Main Report.* Report 21506-MOR. Washington, D.C.

——. 2002a. *Arab Republic of Egypt, poverty reduction in Egypt: Diagnosis and strategy.* Report 24234-EG. Washington, D.C.

——. 2002b. *Global economic prospects: The developing countries: Making world trade work for the world's poor.* Washington, D.C.

——. 2003a. *Tunisia poverty update.* 2 vols. Washington, D.C.

——. 2003b. World Bank loan to fight poverty in rural Algeria with job creation. Press Release 2003/314/MNA. Washington, D.C.

——. 2004. *Global economic prospects: Realizing the development promise of the Doha Agenda.* Washington, D.C.

——. 2005. *Economic development and prospects: Oil booms and revenue management.* Washington, D.C.

——. 2007. World development report 2007: Development and the next generation; Regional highlights—Middle East and North Africa. Washington, D.C. <http://siteresources.worldbank.org/INTWDR2007/Resources/1489782-1158076403546/WDR2007RegionalHighlights_MENA_Aug29_draft6.pdf>.

——. 2008a. Prospects for developing countries. In *Global economic prospects 2008: Technology diffusion in the developing world.* Washington, D.C.

——. 2008b. *World development indicators*. CD-ROM. Washington, D.C.

——. 2009. *2008 MENA economic developments and prospects: Regional integration for global competitiveness*. Washington, D.C.

WTO (World Trade Organization). 1994. Annex 2: Domestic support; The basis for exemption from the reduction commitments. *Agreement on Agriculture*. Geneva.

——. 2001a. Proposal by Morocco. Document G/AG/NG/W/105. Geneva.

——. 2001b. Comprehensive proposal by the Arab Republic of Egypt to the WTO negotiations on agriculture. Document G/AG/NG/W/107. Geneva.

——. 2002. Overview of development in the international trading environment. Geneva. <http://www.wto.org/english/res_e/booksp_e/anrep_e/anrep02_chp3_e.pdf>.

——. 2003. Trade policy review Morocco. Report by the Secretariat. Document WT/TPR/S/116. Geneva.

——. 2005a. Trade policy review: Egypt. Report by the Secretariat. Document WT/TPR/S/150. Geneva.

——. 2005b. Trade policy review: Tunisia. Report by the Secretariat. Geneva.

——. 2005c. Understanding the WTO: Developing countries. Geneva. <http://www.wto.org/english/thewto_e/whatis_e/tif_e/understanding_e.pdf>.

——. 2006. Uruguay round agreement: Decision on measures concerning the possible negative effects of the reform program on least-developed and net food-importing developing countries. Geneva. <http://www.wto.org/english/docs_e/legal_e/35-dag.pdf>. Accessed March 2006.

——. 2008. Trade profiles 2007. Various countries. Geneva. <http://stat.wto.org/CountryProfile/WSDBCountryPFHome.aspx?Language=E>. Accessed March 2009.

Zarrouk, J. 2003. A survey of barriers to trade and investment in Arab countries. In *Arab economic integration: Between hope and reality*, ed. A. Galal and B. Hoekman. Washington, D.C.: Brookings Institution.

Zarrouk, J. E. 1998. Arab free trade area: Potentialities and effects. Paper presented at the workshop Benefiting from Globalization: Mediterranean Development Forum, Marrakech, September 3-6.

Zarrouk, J. E., and F. Zallio. 2000. Integrating free trade agreements. World Bank, Washington, D.C. <http://www.worldbank.org/mdf/mdf3/papers/global/Zarrouk.pdf>.

About the Authors

Nicholas Minot is a senior research fellow in IFPRI's Markets, Trade, and Institutions Division.

Mohamed Abdelbasset Chemingui is a first economic affairs officer in the macroeconomics section of the Economic Development and NEPAD Division, United Nations Economic Commission for Africa.

Marcelle Thomas is a research analyst in IFPRI's Markets, Trade, and Institutions Division.

Reno Dewina is a research analyst in IFPRI's Markets, Trade, and Institutions Division.

David Orden is a senior research fellow in IFPRI's Markets, Trade, and Institutions Division and professor and director of the Global Issues Initiative, Institute for Society, Culture, and Environment, Virginia Polytechnic Institute and State University.

Index

Page numbers for entries occurring in figures by *f*, those for entries occurring in notes by *n*, and those for entries in tables by *t*.

Made in the USA
Monee, IL
04 November 2026

67381376R00138